Lecture Notes in Economics and Mathematical Systems

Managing Editors: M. Beckmann and W. Krelle

Economic Theory

211

Paul van den Heuvel

The Stability of a Macroeconomic System with Quantity Constraints

Springer-Verlag
Berlin Heidelberg New York 1983

Author

Paul van den Heuvel
Economic Institute Tilburg
P.O. Box 90153, 5000 LE Tilburg, The Netherlands

ISBN 3-540-11992-2 Springer-Verlag Berlin Heidelberg New York
ISBN 0-387-11992-2 Springer-Verlag New York Heidelberg Berlin

Printing and binding: Beltz Offsetdruck, Hemsbach/Bergstr.
2142/3140-543210

Acknowledgement

I am very grateful to Professor Claus Weddepohl for his advice, suggestions and constant support. I am also indebted to Professors Malo Hautus, Chiel Paardekooper and Pieter Ruys. I thank Dr. Jan de Jong and Dr. Bob Kaper for their valuable remarks. Furthermore, I benefited from the comments of an anonymous referee. Finally, my thanks to Mrs. Elsina Baselmans for her excellent typewriting.

CONTENTS

1. INTRODUCTION

1.1. Scope

A central concept in (neo-)classical economics is a general equilibrium known as a "*Walras Equilibrium*". This equilibrium is characterized by the equality of demand and supply for all goods. Such an equality may be reached, if the prices are fully *flexible*.
On the other hand, Keynes and the "(neo-)keynesian" economists have introduced models, in which *rigid* prices cause an inequality between demand and supply. Following a recent interpretation, some agents perceive *quantity constraints*. An equilibrium of these models is often called a "*Non-Walrasian Equilibrium*".

One of these neokeynesian models is the Barro and Grossman/Malinvaud model (cf. Barro and Grossman, 1971, Malinvaud, 1977), where economic agents are aggregated into two sectors, the consumption sector and the production sector. There are three commodities: labour, a consumption good and money. The consumption sector supplies labour and buys consumption goods and the production sector uses labour as an input to produce the consumption good. We allow the production sector to hold a stock of the consumption good.
We will study this model in a somewhat longer run, in which the quantity constraints, caused by the rigid prices on the short term, give rise to price adjustments. Furthermore, the stock adjusts. The adjustments can be described by a system of differential equations.
It is our purpose to study the stability properties of equilibria of this system. The fact that this system is piecewise differentiable raises mathematical problems. Stability properties of piecewise differentiable systems have hardly been studied in mathematical literature.
In the present chapter some results from mathematical economics are given that are relevant for our subject.

Section 1.2 is a brief survey of some economic concepts that are frequently used in the rest of this thesis.
In Sections 1.3 and 1.4, respectively, Walrasian and Non-Walrasian properties such as existence and uniqueness are given.
In Section 1.5 some results are mentioned with respect to dynamics and stability of Walrasian and Non-Walrasian Equilibria.

1.2. Relevant economic notions

Before going into some relevant results of mathematical economics, we give a brief explanation of some concepts. For a more extensive discussion, the reader is referred to Debreu (1959), Arrow and Hahn (1971), Takayama (1974), a.o.
Two types of economic *agents* are considered: *consumers* and *producers*. These agents are concerned with (private) *commodities* or *goods*. Services (including labour) and money may be reckoned among the goods. A commodity bundle is a vector in the commodity space, in which the j-th component represents a quantity of the j-th good.
A *price* is related to each commodity. Sometimes one of the goods is given the unit price. Such a good is called the numéraire. This role is often played by money, which also holds for our model. The price vector is the vector in which the j-th component is the price of commodity j.
A *market* is a device of exchange of a commodity with other commodities where also the price of the commodity is determined. In a monetary economy the good is exchanged against money and the price is fixed relative to the (unity) price of money.
A *consumption set* is the set of possible commodity bundles for a certain consumer.
The *budget set* is a subset of the consumption set, bounded by the *budget equality* or *budget constraint*. This budget equality depends on income and wealth of a consumer and on the prices.
The *production set* is the analogue of the consumption set for a certain producer. It represents the technologically feasible input-output combinations of the producer.
The *constrained budget set* is a subset of the budget set, which is restricted by additional quantity constraints. Analogously, we will speak of a *constrained production set*.

The commodity bundles of each agent are ordered by preference relations. *Objective functions* are possible representations of the preferences of the agents. A consumers objective function is called a *utility function*. This function may associate a real number to any commodity bundle from the consumption set. The consumer is assumed to maximize his utility function for commodity bundles in his (constrained) budget set. Similarly, a producer maximizes his objective function on his (constrained) production set. This objective function depends on the profits corresponding with a commodity bundle.
If the maximization problem of an agent depends on the commodity bundles of other agents, we have "external effects".
An *allocation* is an array consisting of commodity bundles of all the agents. An allocation is called *feasible*, if for each good the total demand equals the total supply.

In a *macro-economic* model the agents are aggregated into a few sectors and the commodities in some groups. In a *micro-economic* model, on the other hand, the preferences and the production activities of each of the agents are given separately. The model studied by us is macro-economic.

1.3. Walras Equilibria

1.3.1. Definitions and background

The concept of "Walras Equilibrium" is based on the work of Walras in the nineteenth century. Walras was the first who constructed a general equilibrium model of an economy, i.e., a model in which all markets are considered simultaneously and all the equilibrium relations are specified.
In this model there is a great (finite) number of agents. These agents cannot affect the prices individually. Their behaviour is "price taking" or "competitive". Though the agents have no individual influence on the prices, the latter are considered to be the result of total demand and supply.
In an economy with only private goods and no external effects (see Section 1.2), the following formulation can be given.

A *Walras Equilibrium* is an array consisting of a *price vector* and an *allocation* such that

(i) the allocation is feasible;

(ii) the allocation consists of commodity bundles that maximize the objective functions

- of the consumers in their budget sets,
- of the producers in their production sets.

The price component of a Walras Equilibrium is called a *Walras Equilibrium Price Vector*. The budget sets and the producers' objective functions (mostly determined by profits) depend on the prices. A Walras Equilibrium Price Vector represents a price constellation, such that there exists a feasible allocation corresponding with the solutions of the maximization problems of the agents. The agents do not perceive any additional quantity constraints so that the constrained budget (production) set of each consumer (producer) is equal to his budget (production) set.

The decisions of the agents may also concern future goods and a Walras Equilibrium may also consist of contracts for future goods.
Another possibility to link the present and the future is a stock of, for instance, money. If money can be carried over to later periods, the money stock embodies a potential resource to buy goods in the future. The savings behaviour depends on preferences and expectations with respect to prices. A Walras Equilibrium with respect to only present goods is called a *Temporary Walras Equilibrium*. Walras Equilibria in the Barro and Grossman/Malinvaud model are of this type.

1.3.2. Existence and uniqueness

The existence of a Walras Equilibrium has already been studied by Walras. However, the techniques were then insufficient. In the 1950's the existence problem was solved with the help of Kakutani's fixed point theorem (McKenzie, 1954, Arrow and Debreu, 1954, Debreu, 1959). The question is, whether it is possible to carry out a number of maximization problems simultaneously, such that the solutions form a "feasible allocation". Under some conditions with respect to consumption sets, production sets and objective functions, the answer is positive.

With an additional (very strong) assumption the uniqueness of a Walras Equilibrium Price Vector (up to a positive scalar multiple) can be obtained, see Nikaido (1968).

1.4. Non-Walrasian Equilibria

1.4.1. Definitions

For a given price vector the demands and supplies are not necessarily compatible. If the prevailing prices are rigid a Walras Equilibrium may not be realized. By introducing additional *quantity constraints* a feasible allocation can be obtained: extra upper and lower bounds for quantities may enforce the solutions of the maximization problems forming a feasible allocation.
Imposing quantity constraints on demand and supply is called *rationing*. the "rationing schemes" may be exogenous as well as endogenous in the model.
A more extensive concept of an equilibrium in an economy is necessary.

A *Non-Walrasian Equilibrium* is an array consisting of a *price vector*, an *allocation* and *quantity constraints*, such that

(i) the allocation is feasible;
(ii) the allocation consists of commodity bundles, that maximize the objective functions
  - of the consumers in their constrained budget sets,
  - of the producers in their constrained production sets;
(iii) only the maximum of demand and supply (the "long" side) can be restricted by a quantity constraint;
(iv) a demander can neither be forced to sell nor to purchase more than his demand; a supplier can neither be forced to purchase nor to sell more than his supply.

It can be observed that a Walras Equilibrium is a special case of a Non-Walrasian Equilibrium. It is a Non-Walrasian Equilibrium without additional constraints.
Conditions (i) and (ii), feasibility and *optimality* are also valid for a Walras Equilibrium.

The third condition is called "*rationing on the long side only*" or "*frictionless market*". It requires that demanders and suppliers of a certain good are not constrained at the same time. This condition restricts the number of rationing schemes.
Condition (iv) states that the trade must be "*voluntary*". The agents cannot be forced to go downhill by trading. They always have the possibility of refusing a trade which is worse than the "no trade".

Some Non-Walrasian Equilibrium concepts will be mentioned. The term "*disequilibrium*" is sometimes used as an equivalent of a Non-Walrasian Equilibrium. A "*Fix-price Equilibrium*" is a Non-Walrasian Equilibrium with fixed prices.
A "*Temporary Non-Walrasian Equilibrium*" is the Non-Walrasian counterpart of a "Temporary Walras Equilibrium" (see Section 1.3). In the former, expectations concerning constraints will play a role, as well as price expectations. This kind of equilibrium will be very important in our model.

In order to make conditions (iii) and (iv) more precise, it is desirable to have suitable definitions for "demand" and "supply". How should demand (and supply) be defined in case of rationing?
We follow the sign convention to consider supply a negative demand. Let us start with an unconstrained agent, i.e. an agent who perceives no quantity constraints besides his budget or production restriction. The demand can now be defined to be the component of the commodity bundle which maximizes the agents objective function in his budget/production set. This demand is called *notional* or *Walrasian* demand. If there are quantity constraints, a similar formulation with the addition of the word "constrained" to "budget/production set", yields the *constrained* demand.
Finally, the *effective* demand for a commodity is the component of the commodity bundle which maximizes the objective function in the constrained budget/production set, in which the constraint on the commodity itself is neglected. Effective demand plays an important role in Keynesian literature. The demand in the definition of the Non-Walrasian Equilibrium is often considered to be effective demand.

1.4.2. Background and some literature.

In the thirties of this century the Walrasian Equilibrium model seemed to be not realistic anymore. Demand and supply (for instance of labour) were not in equilibrium. To explain this, Keynes presented in his "General Theory" (1936) a model in which rigid prices give rise to a "disequilibrium".

Keynes noticed that too low wages cause a low consumption demand, which leads to a small production, accompanied by unemployment. This conclusion contradicts the one of the classical economists. The latter contended that lowering the wage rate would induce an increase of labour demand and a decrease of labour supply. This would result in a smaller unemployment.

Keynes' theory had an important influence on government policies. Hicks (1946) was an important precursor of the neokeynesian economists. Hicks studied fixed prices. Together with Patinkin (1956), Clower (1965) and Leyonhufvud (1968), he gave a new impulse to Keynesian theory. These "Neokeynesians" emphasized, just like Keynes had done, the impact of the interaction of several markets. After them, micro- and macro-economic studies emerged. Micro-economic disequilibrium models were given by Drèze (1975), Benassy (1975), a.o. Barro and Grossman (1971), Malinvaud (1977), a.o. developed macro-economic models with Non-Walrasian Equilibria.

The basic ideas of Non-Walrasian economics come out in the terms "dual decision hypothesis" and "spillover".

From Clower (1965) is the concept of "dual decision hypothesis". In the classical theory purchasing plans and financing plans are tacitly assumed to be made simultaneously. According to Clower, Keynes made a distinction between these plans. The decision process takes two steps. First, the purchasing plans are made. Then transactions take place. Final demands are based on the income, which is a result of the transaction. Thus the final demands that are expressed on the markets are the "effective" demands, as defined in the preceding subsection.

The term "spillover" is used by Patinkin (1956). A spillover is the extent to which the demand for a commodity is influenced by the constraints on other markets. Hence, the difference between effective and notional demand represents the magnitude of a spillover.

In Patinkin's work the producers make production plans based on expectations of the output they can sell. The resulting labour demand restricts the labour supply and therefore the wage income of the consumers (workers).
Barro and Grossman (1971) and Malinvaud (1977) made fix-price models in which the works of Patinkin and Clower were combined. These models will be the basis for our study.

We also mention some micro-economic literature.
In Drèze (1975) a Non-Walrasian Equilibrium is introduced with an exogenous rationing scheme. Drèze proves the existence of such an equilibrium: There exist a price vector, an allocation and vectors of lower bounds (related with supplies) and upper bounds (related with demands) that form a Non-Walrasian Equilibrium. Drèze's model gives rise to the problem of the specification of the rationing scheme. Drèze introduces a uniform rationing scheme, i.e., the constraints are equal for all agents.
The work of Benassy (1975) is based on the Barro and Grossman model. Benassy puts forward a rationing scheme, which associates to all effective demands such a feasible allocation that price vector, allocation and constraints form a Non-Walrasian Equilibrium. The quantity constraints that are perceived now, give rise to new effective demands. Benassy shows the existence of an equilibrium in which these new effective demands are equal to the old ones.
Extensive qualitative descriptions of sets of Fix-price Equilibria can be found in Laroque (1978, 1981a) and Laroque and Polemarchakis (1978).

1.4.3. The logic of Non-Walrasian Equilibria

A theory of how Non-Walrasian Equilibria can occur, involves an investigation of the synchronicity of the process of realization of a transaction (cf. Grandmont, 1977b and Drazen, 1980). If this process is followed step by step, it can be seen at which phase, which information is available to the agents. Price and quantity signals influence the decision processes.

Let us consider an economy in several subsequent periods. During a period the prices are fixed. Within a period the agents maximize their objective functions which concern both the present and the next period.

Commodities are traded against money, successively on the markets. If these exchanges were synchronized, then possibly a "better" allocation could be obtained. However, as long as recontracting is impossible, there is no such allocation.
The nonsimultaneous (market-by-market) trade is made easier by money as a medium of exchange. Nevertheless, as Drazen points out, money as a medium of exchange is not essential to "break" the synchronicity of the exchange process. It is a widespread misunderstanding that quantity constraints are possible only in a monetary economy (see Drazen, 1980, p.299).

The agents can hold a stock of an asset, for instance money. This asset transfers values to the next period. The stock is adjusted according to the preferences and expectation with respect to the future period. The market-by-market trade will generally not lead to the notional solutions of the agents. It might be said that assets enable the agents to accept quantity constraints. If an agent is forced to purchase less of a commodity than his notional demand, his stock of the asset, ceteris paribus, is larger than the originally planned stock. If the sales are less than the notional supply, the reversal holds. Thus, an asset is an indispensable element of a (Temporary) Non-Walrasian Equilibrium.

1.4.4. Existence and uniqueness

Drèze (1975), Benassy (1975) and Grandmont and Laroque (1976) prove the existence of the equilibria they introduce in the articles concerned. (Local) uniqueness of Non-Walrasian Equilibria is studied by Laroque (1981a). A proof of the (existence and) uniqueness of a Fixprice Equilibrium (for given prices) in a macromodel à la Barro and Grossman can be found in Böhm (1978). This uniqueness will be important in Chapter 3, see Subsection 3.5.2.

1.5. *Dynamics and Stability*

1.5.1. Walras Equilibria

In the Walrasian model prices are supposed to adjust rapidly enough to equalize demand and supply. The question can be raised, how a Walras Equilibrium is established. Which behaviour of the agents leads to a stable Walras Equilibrium? Does a process exist, leading to a Walras Equilibrium Price Vector and can anything be said about its stability properties?

Several processes of this kind have been proposed, known as the tâtonnement and the non-tâtonnement processes. In the "*tâtonnement process*" there is an auctioneer, who quotes the prices. The agents determine their demands and supplies at the quoted price levels and they inform the auctioneer of their exchange offers. The auctioneer compares demand and supply and adjusts the prices in such a way that they are raised in case of excess demand and lowered in case of excess supply. He quotes the new prices. The process is repeated until demand and supply are equal. Then a transaction takes place. There is no trade until the equality of demand and supply is established for all markets. Hence during the process endowments are constant. Two kinds of tâtonnement processes are possible. The adjustments can take place successively, market by market. They can be simultaneous as well. In both processes there is only trading after a Walras Equilibrium Price Vector has been reached.
Unfortunately, the existence of a price formation as above is unrealistic in most cases.
In "*non-tâtonnement processes*" intermediate transactions are allowed out of an equilibrium.
Since after a transaction the endowments are redistributed over the agents, the excess demands are influenced by the (disequilibrium) transaction. The process ends as soon as a Pareto Optimum has been established.

The very crucial assumption of tâtonnement and non-tâtonnement lies in the competitive nature of the markets. As a consequence of the competitive behaviour the prices follow the "*law of demand and supply*": prices increase in case of excess demand and decrease in case of excess supply. So the prices will be constant only in the case of equilibrium. We follow the sign convention to take (excess) demands as positive and (excess) supplies as negative, such that supply is considered to be negative demand.

The price increase is assumed to be a sign preserving, monotone, differentiable, real valued function of excess demand. Usually, this function is assumed to be linear. Both discrete and continuous time-adjustments have been studied in literature. Since in a Walras Equilibrium all excess demands are zero, it is an equilibrium of the resulting differential (difference) system (see Chapter 2).

The prices are the only information from the markets. There is no information on quantities, like possible quantity constraints, etc.

Stability of a Walras Equilibrium of an economy without production in the tâtonnement process is proved by Arrow, Block and Hurwicz (1959) under conditions that will be successively mentioned below. These conditions are of course additional to the above price adjustment assumptions.

The first condition is known as "gross substitutability": the excess demand of a commodity increases if the price of any other good increases. (The term "net substitutability" is used if the effect of the price change on the real income is properly compensated.)

The second assumption is "Walras' law": the price-weighted sum of all excess demands equals zero, whether the economy is in equilibrium or not.

Finally, "zero homogeneity" is assumed. This condition states that the price vector can be multiplied by a positive scalar without affecting the excess demands.

Zero homogeneity and gross substitutability together imply that the Walras Equilibrium Price Vector is unique up to a positive scalar multiple. It is proved by Arrow, Block and Hurwicz that such a vector, if normalized, is a globally stable equilibrium, i.e., any sequence of normalized price vectors, generated by a process with the above assumptions, converges to the normalized Walras Equilibrium Price Vector.

With respect to non-tâtonnement processes it is necessary to introduce variable stocks of commodities in the system, describing the process. Then the result of Arrow, Block and Hurwicz is not valid anymore.

Non-tâtonnement processes leading to a Pareto Optimum are described by Negishi (1961), Uzawa (1962) and Hahn and Negishi (1962).

1.5.2. Non-Walrasian Equilibria

Non-Walrasian Equilibria are supposed to prevail, if prices are rigid in the short run. Beside price adjustments, there are quantity adjustments, i.e., demands and supplies are made compatible not only via the prices, but also by means of direct adjustments on quantities (or via quantities only). It is assumed that these quantity adjustments are much faster than price adjustments. The former give rise to disequilibria. In the medium run the prices are adjusted.

We give a brief survey of these price adjustments in literature. Grandmont and Laroque (1976) present a comparison of "neoclassical" and "neokeynesian" price adjustments. In neoclassical price adjustments the price is a result of the "law of demand and supply". Hence the tâtonnement and non-tâtonnement processes can be reckoned among the neoclassical price adjustments. In these processes the demand and supply on which the "law of demand and supply" is based are the "notional" ones. In most models with quantity rationing the "effective" demand and supply are considered instead. Examples are the price adjustments in Varian (1977) and Veendorp (1975). It can be remarked that although these adjustments are called "neoclassical" the concepts "effective demand and supply" are Keynesian!
In neokeynesian price adjustments, the prices are determined by the sellers, in a monopolistic way. The approach of Benassy (1976) can be called neokeynesian. Prices depend on "perceived" demands, which is information the seller has with respect to the demand and several prices.
Picard (1979) analyzes both types of price adjustments. Honkapohja (1979) and Malinvaud (1980) give ad hoc assumptions for each of the market states separately.

The new prices (again rigid in the short term) give rise to new quantity adjustments and a new Non-Walrasian Equilibrium, etc.
As in the non-tâtonnement processes the adjustments of endowments must be incorporated in the system. The phenomenon of rationing, however, and the introduction of effective demand in the price adjustments make

Non-Walrasian Equilibria candidates for equilibria of the resulting dynamic systems. It should be noted that Walras' law (see Subsection 1.5.1) does not hold for effective demands.

Fisher (1978) incorporates quantity constraints and spillovers in the Hahn-Negishi non-tâtonnement process. He proves the convergence of the resulting system to some Walras Equilibrium.
Varian (1977) on the other hand, shows the existence of a Non-Walrasian Equilibrium in addition to a Walras Equilibrium. The first one is an inefficient "self-fulfilling expectations equilibrium". It is stable in contrast to the Walras Equilibrium.
Other papers on stability of Non-Walrasian Equilibria are Böhm (1978), Veendorp (1975), Laroque (1981b), Honkapohja (1979), Picard (1979) and Eckalbar (1980). These papers will be discussed in Chapters 2 and 5. Also the work of Malinvaud (1980) is worth mentioning.

1.6. Outline

Chapter 2 is an introduction to the mathematical problems, appearing in the subsequent chapters. The model to be analyzed is introduced in Chapter 3 in a static context, in which prices and stocks are constant. The possible types of Non-Walrasian Equilibria are described.
In Chapter 4 a somewhat longer run is studied. The price and stock adjustments that can occur are analyzed. A differential system, describing the behaviour of the model, is introduced. Stability properties of equilibria of this system are investigated in Chapter 5. Finally, some concluding remarks are made in Chapter 6.

2. *MATHEMATICAL RESULTS IN OPTIMIZATION AND STABILITY*

2.1. *Introduction and notation*

The purpose of this chapter is to provide the mathematical background for the rest of the thesis. We are especially interested in two fields of mathematics: optimization and the theory of differential systems. Section 2.2 contains, in addition to some necessary analytic concepts, a theorem on the differentiability of a solution of a maximization problem with regard to the parameters of the problem.
The major part of this chapter is devoted to autonomous differentiable systems and stability of these systems. In Section 2.3 some well-known results are mentioned for ordinary differential systems with differentiable right-hand sides.
The systems that are investigated in Section 2.4 have piecewise differentiable right-hand sides. These systems will be very important for the description of our dynamic model. Both systems with continuous and discontinuous right-hand sides are considered.

In this thesis the following symbols are used.

$\mathbb{R}^n$	n-dimensional real space
$\mathbb{R}^n_+$	nonnegative orthant of $\mathbb{R}^n$
$\mathbb{R}^n_{++}$	positive orthant of $\mathbb{R}^n$
$F: S_1 \to S_2$	function from S_1 into S_2
$F: S_1 \rightrightarrows S_2$	multifunction from S_1 into S_2
$C(S_1 \to S_2)$	set of continuous functions from S_1 into S_2
$C'(S_1 \to S_2)$	set of continuously differentiable functions from S_1 into S_2
$C^k(S_1 \to S_2)$	set of k times continuously differentiable functions from S_1 into S_2

If $S_2 = \mathbb{R}$ we will write $C(S_1)$, $C'(S_1)$, $C^k(S_1)$

$F_{x_i} := \frac{\partial}{\partial x_i} F$ partial derivative of the function F with respect to x_i

$F_{x_i x_j} := \frac{\partial^2}{\partial x_i \partial x_j} F$

$\nabla F := \left(\frac{\partial F}{\partial x_1}, \ldots, \frac{\partial F}{\partial x_n}\right)$ gradient of the function $F: \mathbb{R}^n \to \mathbb{R}$

$\nabla^2 F$ Hessian of the function F, i.e., the matrix $\left(\frac{\partial^2 F}{\partial x_i \partial x_j}\right)$

$DF(x)$ Jacobian matrix of the function $F: \mathbb{R}^n \to \mathbb{R}^m$ evaluated at x

$F|S$ restriction of the function F to the set S

$x \mapsto F(x)$ function which attaches the value $F(x)$ to the variable x

Let $x \in \mathbb{R}^n$ and $y \in \mathbb{R}^n$.

$x > y$ for any $i = 1,\ldots,n$: $x_i > y_i$
$x \geq y$ for any $i = 1,\ldots,n$: $x_i \geq y_i$
x' transpose of vector x
$\|x\| := [x'x]^{\frac{1}{2}}$ Euclidean norm of vector x

$M_{m \times n}$ set of real matrices with m rows and n columns

$|A|$ determinant of matrix A

tr A trace of matrix A

cl S closure of set S

int S interior of set S

$B(0;\rho) := \{x \mid \|x\| < \rho\}$

sgn α sign of the scalar α

2.2. *Some concepts in analysis and optimization*

In this section some mathematical tools are given concerning (asymptotic) analysis and optimization, that will be applied in the sequel. Landau's o-symbol (small o) is defined as follows (cf. De Bruijn, 1961).

DEFINITION 2.1. *Let* $f: S_1 \to S_2$, *where* $S_1 \in \mathbb{R}^n$ *and* $S_2 \in \mathbb{R}^m$ *and let* $a \in S_1$ *and* k *be a nonnegative integer. We write*

$$f(x) = o(\|x-a\|^k) \qquad (x \to a)$$

if

$$\lim_{x \to a} \frac{\|f(x)\|}{\|x-a\|^k} = 0 .$$

The "implicit function theorem" (see Rudin, 1976, p.224) will be applied several times. In the theorem below, $x \in \mathbb{R}^n$ and $y \in \mathbb{R}^m$. We write $(x,y) \in \mathbb{R}^{n+m}$. Furthermore, $D_x f(x_0,y_0)$ denotes the Jacobian matrix of f as a function of x for $y = y_0$, evaluated at x_0. The matrix $D_y f(x_0,y_0)$ is defined similarly.

THEOREM 2.2 (implicit function theorem). *Let* $\Omega \subset \mathbb{R}^{n+m}$, Ω *open and let* $f \in C'(\Omega \to \mathbb{R})$ *and for some* $(x_0,y_0) \in \Omega$: $f(x_0,y_0) = 0$ *and* $|D_x f(x_0,y_0)| \neq 0$.
Then there exist open sets $\Omega \subset \mathbb{R}^{n+m}$ *and* $\mathcal{Y} \subset \mathbb{R}^m$, *with* $(x_0,y_0) \subset \Omega$ *and* $y_0 \in \mathcal{Y}$, *having the following property:*
To every $y \in \mathcal{Y}$ *corresponds a unique* x *such that*

$$(x,y) \in \Omega \quad \textit{and} \quad f(x,y) = 0 .$$

If this x *is defined to be* $g(y)$, *then* $g \in C'(\mathcal{Y} \to \mathbb{R}^n)$, $g(y_0) = x_0$,

$$f[g(y),y] = 0 \qquad (y \in \mathcal{Y})$$

and

$$Dg(y_0) = -[D_x f(x_0,y_0)]^{-1} D_y f(x_0,y_0) .$$

Consider the maximization problem

$$(2.1) \qquad \max\{f(x) \mid g_i(x) \geq 0,\ i = 1,2,\ldots,n\} ,$$

where $x \in \mathbb{R}^k$, $f: \mathbb{R}^k \to \mathbb{R}$, f is strictly concave on $\mathbb{R}^k$ and $g_i: \mathbb{R}^k \to \mathbb{R}$, g_i is concave on $\mathbb{R}^k$ $(i = 1,2,\ldots,n)$.
The vector $x^* \in \mathbb{R}^k$, such that $g_i(x^*) \geq 0$, $i = 1,2,\ldots,n$, and

$$f(x^*) = \max\{f(x) \mid g_i(x) \geq 0,\ i = 1,2,\ldots,n\} ,$$

is called the *solution* of (2.1). If a solution of (2.1) exists, it is unique.

The inequalities $g_i(x) \geq 0$, $i = 1,2,\ldots,n$, are called the *constraints* of (2.1). We call the constraint $g_j(x) \geq 0$ *strictly active*, if the solution x^* of (2.1) is not the solution of the maximization problem

$$\max \{f(x) \mid g_i(x) \geq 0,\ i = 1,2,\ldots,n,\ i \neq j\} .$$

THEOREM 2.3. *Let* Y *be an open subset of* $\mathbb{R}^m$ *and* X *an open convex subset of* $\mathbb{R}^k$.

Let $f \in C^2(X \times Y)$, *the Hessian* $\nabla^2_{xx} f := \left(\frac{\partial^2 f}{\partial x_i \partial x_j}\right)$ *be negative definite for* $(x,y) \in X \times Y$. *If the solution of*

$$\max_x \{f(x,y) \mid x \in X\}$$

exists for all $y \in Y$ *and is denoted by* $\varphi(y)$, *then* $\varphi \in C'(Y \to X)$.

PROOF. Since the set X is convex and the function f is strictly concave, φ is a (single valued) function from Y into X.

The definition of φ implies

$$\nabla_x f(\varphi(y),y) = 0 , \tag{2.2}$$

where $\nabla_x f := \left(\frac{\partial f}{\partial x_1}, \ldots, \frac{\partial f}{\partial x_k}\right)$. Since $|\nabla^2_{xx} f(\varphi(y),y)| \neq 0$, the implicit function theorem (Theorem 2.2) applied on (2.2) yields the continuous differentiability of φ in y on Y. □

We will approximate sets by cones. To this extent some concepts are defined.

DEFINITION 2.4. *A set* $C \subset \mathbb{R}^n$ *is called a* <u>*cone*</u> *if for any* $x \in C$ *and* $\lambda \in \mathbb{R}_+$ *we have* $\lambda x \in C$. *If, in addition, the set* C *is closed,* C *will be called a* <u>*closed cone*</u>.

DEFINITION 2.5. *Let* $0 \in S \subset \mathbb{R}^n$. *A vector* $b \in \mathbb{R}^n$ *is called a* <u>*tangent vector*</u> *of* S *in* 0, *if there exists a function* $H \in C'([0,\varepsilon) \to S)$ *for some* $\varepsilon \in \mathbb{R}_{++}$ *such that*

$$H(\xi) = \xi b + o(\xi) \qquad (\xi \to 0) .$$

The closure of the set of tangent vectors of S in 0 is called the <u>*tangent cone*</u> *of S in 0 and is denoted by* Co(S). *The tangent cone of S in any nonzero element s of S can be defined similarly.*

The tangent cone (see Figure 2.1) can be considered as the linearization of the set S. It obviously has the following properties.

PROPOSITION 2.6.

(i) Co(S) *is a closed set.*

(ii) *If* $S_1 \subset S_2$ *and* $0 \in S_1$, *then* $Co(S_1) \subset Co(S_2)$.

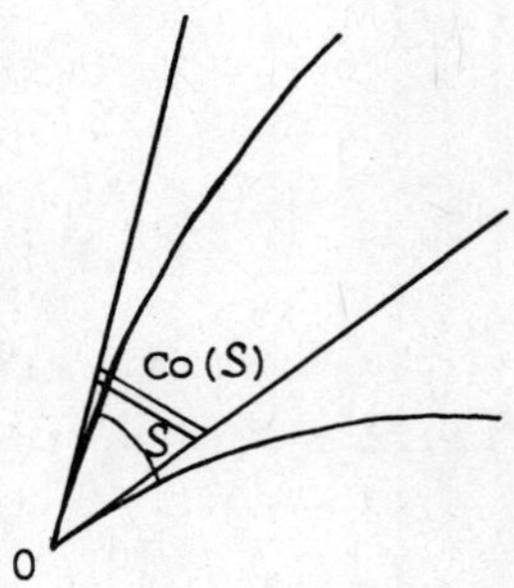

<u>Figure 2.1</u>.
tangent cone.

Continuous differentiability is usually defined on an open set, see Rudin (1976), p.219. The following definition is an extension for non-open domains:

DEFINITION 2.7. *Let* $S \subset \mathbb{R}^n$ *such that for every* $s \in S$ *the tangent cone of S in s has a nonempty interior. Let* $S \subset \mathbb{R}^n$ *and* $F: S \to \mathbb{R}^k$. *We write*

$$F \in C'(S \to \mathbb{R}^k)$$

if there exists an open set $\Omega \in \mathbb{R}^n$ *which contains S and a function* $\tilde{F} \in C'(\Omega \to \mathbb{R}^k)$ *such that* $\tilde{F}|S = F$.
The derivatives of F *at* $x \in S$ *are defined as the derivatives of* $\tilde{F}$ *at* x.
The condition that the tangent cone of S has a nonempty interior in all elements of S ensures uniqueness of the derivatives.

The following theorem shows an alternative expression for a tangent cone of a particular set.

THEOREM 2.8. *Let* $G \in C(\mathbb{R}^n \to \mathbb{R}^2)$ $(n \geq 2)$, *with* $G(x) = Bx + o(\|x\|)$ $(x \to 0)$, *where* $B \in M_{2\times n}$. *If* $S = \{x \in \mathbb{R}^n \mid G(x) > 0\}$ *and* $G \in C'(S \to \mathbb{R}^2)$ *and* B *is of rank* 2, *then*

$$\mathrm{Co}(S) = \{x \in \mathbb{R}^n \mid Bx \geq 0\} .$$

PROOF. Let the set C be defined by

$$C := \{x \in \mathbb{R}^n \mid Bx \geq 0\} .$$

Since rank $B = 2$, int $C \neq \emptyset$.
We will first prove $C \subset \mathrm{Co}(S)$. Let $b \in \mathrm{int}\, C$, or, equivalently, $Bb > 0$:

$$G(b\xi) = Bb\xi + o(\xi) \quad (\xi \to 0)$$
$$= \xi(Bb + o(1)) \quad (\xi \to 0) .$$

$G(b\xi)$ is positive for sufficiently small positive ξ. Hence $b\xi \in S$. Therefore, b is a tangent vector of S. Since $C = \mathrm{cl}(\mathrm{int}\, C)$, this implies $C \subset \mathrm{Co}(S)$.
Now we have to prove $\mathrm{Co}(S) \subset C$. Let $q \notin C$, equivalently, at least one of the components of the vector Bq is negative.
If $H \in C'([0,\varepsilon) \to \mathbb{R}^n)$ satisfies

$$H(\xi) = q\xi + o(\xi) \quad (\xi \downarrow 0) ,$$

then at least one of the components of the left-hand side of

$$G[H(\xi)] = Bq\xi + o(\xi) \quad (\xi \downarrow 0)$$

is negative for sufficiently small positive ξ. Hence $H(\xi) \notin S$, so that $q \notin \mathrm{Co}(S)$. Therefore, $\mathrm{Co}(S) \subset C$. □

2.3. *Definitions and properties concerning stability*

2.3.1. Differential systems

Since our main goal is to examine (asymptotic) stability of equilibria of systems, we will recall some well-known results with relation to systems of differential equations. For a more complete introduction the reader is referred to Bellman (1953), Coddington and Levinson (1955), Hille (1969), Hurewicz (1958), La Salle and Lefschetz (1961) and Wilson (1971). At the end of this section some special attention is given to systems in $\mathbb{R}^2$ and $\mathbb{R}^3$.

DEFINITION 2.9. *Let* T *be an interval in* $\mathbb{R}$ *and* $S \subset \mathbb{R}^k$, $t \in \mathbb{R}$, $x \in \mathbb{R}^k$, $f: S \times T \to \mathbb{R}^k$. *The system of equations*

$$\mathring{x}(t) = f[x(t),t]$$

where

$$\mathring{x}(t) := \left(\frac{dx_1(t)}{dt}, \ldots, \frac{dx_k(t)}{dt}\right)'$$

is a *differential system of first order.*
If the function f *is constant in* t *for each fixed* x*, the above system is called an* *autonomous* *system. If* $F: S \to \mathbb{R}^k$*, such a system can be denoted by*

$$\mathring{x} = F(x) \; . \tag{2.3}$$

System (2.3) *is called* *linear,* *if* F *is a linear function of* x.
In a similar way, *continuous* *and* *discontinuous* *systems can be defined.*

We will restrict ourselves to autonomous differential systems of first order.
In the rest of this section we confine ourselves to continuous systems. If the right-hand side of a system is continuous, then the question how to define a solution of the system can be answered in the least difficult way. Then the following definition can be given.

DEFINITION 2.10. *Let* $S \subset \mathbb{R}^k$ *be open and connected and let* $T \subset \mathbb{R}$ *be an interval and* $F \in C(S \to \mathbb{R}^k)$. *Then* $x \in C(T \to \mathbb{R}^k)$ *is a* *solution* *of the system* $\mathring{x} = F(x)$ *if*

(i) $x(t) \in S$ *for all* $t \in T$.

(ii) $\mathring{x}(t) = F(x(t))$ *for all* $t \in T$.

The initial value problem of finding a solution of the system $\mathring{x} = F(x)$ under the initial condition $x(t_0) = x_0$ will be denoted by $IVP(F,x_0,t_0)$. The solution of $IVP(F,x_0,t_0)$ is denoted by $x(t;x_0,t_0)$. The set $\{x(t;x_0,t_0) \mid t \in T\}$ is called a *trajectory*. These notations and this concept of trajectory will also be applied if the function F is discontinuous (see Subjection 2.4.3).

The concepts defined below are important with respect to existence and uniqueness of a solution of a continuous system.

DEFINITION 2.11. *Let* $S \subset \mathbb{R}^k$ *be open and connected and* $F \in C(S \to \mathbb{R}^k)$. *Then* F *is* *<u>Lipschitz continuous</u>* *on* S *if*

$$\exists \lambda \in \mathbb{R}_{++}\ \forall x_1, x_2 \in S:\ \|F(x_1) - F(x_2)\| \le \lambda \|x_1 - x_2\| .$$

The function F *is* *<u>locally Lipschitz continuous</u>* *on* S *if for every* $x_0 \in S$, *there is a neighbourhood* $\Omega(x_0)$, *such that the above condition is satisfied on* $\Omega(x_0)$ *instead of on* S.

Now the following existence and uniqueness theorem can be given (cf. Bellman, 1953, p.68, Hille, 1969, p.60 and Hurewicz, 1958, p.28).

THEOREM 2.12. *Let* $S \subset \mathbb{R}^k$ *be open and connected,* F *locally Lipschitz continuous on* S, $x_0 \in S$ *and* $t_0 \in \mathbb{R}$. *There exists an interval* $T \subset \mathbb{R}$ *such that* $t_0 \in \operatorname{int} T$ *and a function* $y \in C(T \to \mathbb{R}^k)$ *such that* $y(t;x_0,t_0)$ *is the unique solution of* $\mathrm{IVP}(F,x_0,t_0)$ *of system* $\overset{\circ}{x} = F(x)$ *on* T.

2.3.2. Stability properties of autonomous differential systems

In this subsection we consider (asymptotic) stability of equilibria of the autonomous differential system $\overset{\circ}{x} = F(x)$, where $F: \mathbb{R}^k \to \mathbb{R}^k$. First, definitions are given for "equilibrium" and (asymptotic) stability of the system $\overset{\circ}{x} = F(x)$. The Definitions 2.13 and 2.14 are valid for both continuous and discontinuous systems.

DEFINITION 2.13. *The vector* $\hat{x}$ *is an* *<u>equilibrium</u>* *of the system* $\overset{\circ}{x} = F(x)$ *if* $F(\hat{x}) = 0$.

DEFINITION 2.14. *Let the origin be an equilibrium of the system* $\overset{\circ}{x} = F(x)$. *It is a* *<u>stable</u>* *equilibrium of this system, if for any* $\varepsilon > 0$ *there is a* $\delta > 0$, *such that for any* $a \in \mathbb{R}^k$

$$\|a\| < \delta \Rightarrow \forall t \ge t_0:\ \|x(t;a,t_0)\| < \varepsilon .$$

If the origin is a stable equilibrium of the system $x = F(x)$ *and there is an* $\eta > 0$ *such that*

$$\|a\| < \eta \Rightarrow \lim_{t\to\infty} \|x(t;a,t_0)\| = 0 ,$$

then the origin is called an <u>*asymptotically stable*</u> *equilibrium of the system* $\overset{\circ}{x} = F(x)$.

In the rest of this section, A denotes a real k by k matrix. The following theorem gives a condition for the asymptotic stability of the linear autonomous system $\overset{\circ}{x} = Ax$ (see Wilson, 1971, p.311).

THEOREM 2.15. *The origin is an asymptotically stable equilibrium of the system* $\overset{\circ}{x} = Ax$, *if and only if each of the eigenvalues of the matrix* A *has a negative real part.*

For nonlinear systems, the following theorem can be formulated (cf. Wilson, 1971, p.317).

THEOREM 2.16 (Poincaré-Liapunov). *Let* $f \in C(\mathbb{R}^k \to \mathbb{R}^k)$ *and* $f(x) = o(\|x\|)$ $(x \to 0)$.
If the origin is an asymptotically stable equilibrium of the system $\overset{\circ}{x} = Ax$, *it is also an asymptotically stable equilibrium of the system*

$$\overset{\circ}{x} = Ax + f(x) .$$

Hence, if $F \in C'(\mathbb{R}^k \to \mathbb{R}^k)$ and $F(0) = 0$, then it follows from Theorem 2.16 that the origin is an asymptotically stable equilibrium of system $\overset{\circ}{x} = F(x)$, if the Jacobian matrix of the function F evaluated at $x = 0$ has only eigenvalues with negative real parts. In order to verify the condition of Theorem 2.16 the so-called "Routh-Hurwitz-criterion" can be applied (see Gantmacher, 1954, Ch. XV).

THEOREM 2.17 (Routh-Hurwitz). *Let*

$$\lambda^k + \alpha_1\lambda^{k-1} + \dots + \alpha_k = 0$$

be the characteristic equation of the matrix A *and let the real numbers* Δ_i, $i = 1,2,\dots,k$, *be defined by*

$$\Delta_1 = \alpha_1 , \quad \Delta_2 := \begin{vmatrix} \alpha_1 & \alpha_3 \\ 1 & \alpha_2 \end{vmatrix} , \quad \Delta_3 := \begin{vmatrix} \alpha_1 & \alpha_3 & \alpha_5 \\ 1 & \alpha_2 & \alpha_4 \\ 0 & \alpha_1 & \alpha_3 \end{vmatrix} , \quad \Delta_4 := \begin{vmatrix} \alpha_1 & \alpha_3 & \alpha_5 & \alpha_7 \\ 1 & \alpha_2 & \alpha_4 & \alpha_6 \\ 0 & \alpha_1 & \alpha_3 & \alpha_5 \\ 0 & 1 & \alpha_2 & \alpha_4 \end{vmatrix} ,$$

etc. The origin is an asymptotically stable equilibrium of the system $\mathring{x} = Ax$, *if and only if* $\Delta_i > 0$, $i = 1,2,\dots,k$.

For two- and three- dimensional spaces the Routh-Hurwitz criterion can be formulated in a simple way.

COROLLARY 2.18. *For* $k = 2$, *the origin is an asymptotically stable equilibrium of system* $\mathring{x} = Ax$, *if and only if*

$$\text{tr } A < 0$$

$$|A| > 0 .$$

COROLLARY 2.19. *For* $k = 3$, *the origin is an asymptotically stable equilibrium of system* $\mathring{x} = Ax$, *if and only if*

$$\text{tr } A < 0$$

$$|A| < 0$$

$$|A| - (\text{tr } A) \sum_{i=1}^{3} A_{ii} > 0 ,$$

where A_{ii} *is the* i'*th principal minor of* A.

Corollaries 2.18 and 2.19 yield the following property, which will be useful in the comparison of systems with two and three variables (see Chapter 5).

THEOREM 2.20. *Let the matrix* $A \in M_{3\times 3}$ *be defined as*

$$A := \begin{pmatrix} B & c \\ q' & \alpha \end{pmatrix}$$

where $q,c \in \mathbb{R}^2$, $\alpha \in -\mathbb{R}_+$ *and the matrix* $B \in M_{2\times 2}$ *has the properties*

$$\text{tr } B < 0 , \quad |B| > 0 .$$

Let $P \in M_{2\times 2}$ *be defined by*

$$P := \begin{pmatrix} 0 & 1 \\ -1 & 0 \end{pmatrix} .$$

The origin is an asymptotically stable equilibrium of system $\overset{\circ}{x} = Ax$, *if and only if*

$$\alpha|B| + q'PB'Pc < 0$$

$$(-\operatorname{tr} B)(\alpha^2 + \alpha \operatorname{tr} B + |B|) + q'(\alpha I + B)c > 0 .$$

PROOF. The proof of this theorem is a direct application of the Corollaries 2.18 and 2.19. The left-hand sides of the inequalities in Corollary 2.19 can be expressed in B, q, c and α:

$$\operatorname{tr} A = \alpha + \operatorname{tr} B ,$$

$$|A| = \alpha|B| + q'PB'Pc ,$$

$$|A| - (\operatorname{tr} A) \sum_{i=1}^{3} A_{ii} =$$

$$= \alpha|B| - q'P'BPc - (\alpha + \operatorname{tr} B)\{|B| + (\alpha b_{11} - c_1 q_1) + (\alpha b_{22} - c_2 q_2)\} =$$

$$= - q'P'BPc - (\operatorname{tr} B)|B| - (\alpha + \operatorname{tr} B)(\alpha \operatorname{tr} B - q'c) =$$

$$= (-\operatorname{tr} B)(\alpha^2 + \alpha \operatorname{tr} B + B) + q'(\alpha I + B)c .$$

It is obvious that tr A < 0. Hence, according to Corollary 2.19, the origin is an asymptotically stable equilibrium of the system $\overset{\circ}{x} = Ax$ if and only if $\alpha|B| + q'PB'Pc < 0$ and $(-\operatorname{tr} B)(\alpha^2 + \alpha \operatorname{tr} B + |B|) + q'(\alpha I + B)c > 0$. □

REMARK 2.21. If $\alpha \neq 0$, the following equality holds:

$$|A| = |\alpha B - cq'| .$$

2.3.3. Liapunov functions

In this subsection a special kind of function is introduced.

DEFINITION 2.22. *A function* $V: \mathbb{R}^k \to \mathbb{R}$ *is a* <u>*Liapunov function*</u> *of the system*

(2.4) $\quad \overset{\circ}{x} = F(x)$

with $F: \mathbb{R}^k \to \mathbb{R}^k$ *and* $F(0) = 0$, *if in some neighbourhood of the origin*

(i) $V(x)$ *is continuous;*

(ii) $V(0) = 0$, $V(x) > 0$ *for* $x \neq 0$;

(iii) $V(x)$ *is strictly decreasing on any solution path of system* (2.4).

Liapunov functions are very important for stability investigations. It should be noted that in most literature the Liapunov functions are defined as continuously differentiable functions (cf. La Salle and Lefschetz, 1961). The relevance of Liapunov functions follows from the following theorem, which can be found in La Salle and Lefschetz (1961), p.37.

THEOREM 2.23. *If there exists a Liapunov function of system* (2.4) $\mathring{x} = F(x)$, *then the origin is an asymptotically stable equilibrium of system* (2.4).

REMARK 2.24. The Definitions 2.14 and 2.22, the Theorems 2.15, 2.16, 2.20 and 2.23 and the Corollaries 2.18 and 2.19 can be formulated for any equilibrium $\hat{x}$. (It is possible to select a translation of the coordinate system, such that this equilibrium is the origin of the new basis.) The matrix A in Theorems 2.15, 2.16 and 2.20 and Corollaries 2.18 and 2.19 is the Jacobian matrix of the function F in the right-hand side of system $\mathring{x} = F(x)$, evaluated at $\hat{x}$.

2.4. Stability of piecewise differentiable systems

2.4.1. General results

Let $\mathcal{B}$ be a closed ball around the origin in $\mathbb{R}^k$ and let the sets $S_i \subset \mathbb{R}^k$, $i = 1,2,\ldots,n$, satisfy $S_i \cap S_j = \{0\}$ for $i \neq j$ and $\mathcal{B} = \bigcup_{i=1}^{n} S_i$. We are especially interested in stability properties of the following type:

$$\mathring{x} = F(x) \tag{2.5}$$

where the function $F\colon \mathcal{B} \to \mathbb{R}^k$ is defined as

$$F(x) := A_i x + f_i(x) \quad \text{for } x \in S_i\,,\ i \in \{1,\ldots,n\}\ ;$$

$A_i \in M_{k\times k}$, $f_i\colon \mathcal{B} \to \mathbb{R}^k$ for $i = 1,2,\ldots,n$.

The relevant systems will be classified according to the conditions below.

CONDITION I. *For* $i = 1,2,\ldots,n$*:*

(i) $f_i \in C'(S_i \to \mathbb{R}^k)$,

(ii) $f_i(x) = o(\|x\|) \quad (x \to 0)$.

CONDITION II. $F \in C(B \to \mathbb{R}^k)$.

DEFINITION 2.25. *Under Condition* I*, the function* F *in system* (2.5) *and system* (2.5) *itself are called* *piecewise continuously differentiable* *on* B *and the sets* S_i*,* int S_i *and* cl S_i*,* $i = 1,2,\ldots,n$*, are called the* *regimes* *of system* (2.5). *The systems* $\overset{\circ}{x} = A_i x + f_i(x)$*,* $i = 1,2,\ldots,n$*, are called the* *subsystems* *of* (2.5)

Under Condition II, the system (2.5) is continuous (see Definition 2.9).
Under Conditions I and II, $f_i \in C'(\text{cl } S_i \to \mathbb{R}^k)$ and the Jacobian matrix of F is bounded on the (compact) set B. As a consequence, the function F is Lipschitz continuous on B (see Definition 2.11), so that initial value problems of continuous, piecewise continuously differentiable systems have unique solutions (see Theorem 2.12).

In the literature mentioned below, system (2.5) is also called a system with "regime switching" or a "patched up system". Since there are not many physical applications of piecewise differentiable systems, mathematical literature on this subject is scarse. In economic literature, however, a number of papers have appeared, in which several adjustment "regimes" surround an equilibrium: a.o. Henry (1972), Veendorp (1975), Aoki (1976), Varian (1977), Laroque (1981b), Picard (1979), Ito (1980), Eckalbar (1980) and Honkapohja and Ito (1982). The papers of Veendorp (1975) and Laroque (1981b) will be discussed briefly in the next subsection.
In the proof of his Theorem 1 (p.217), Aoki applies the following property. On a trajectory of differential system $\overset{\circ}{x} = Ax$ there are only a finite number of crossings over a hyperplane through the origin, if the Jacobian matrix A has real eigenvalues. However, this is only known to be true, if the Jacobian matrix is the same on both sides of the hyperplane. Picard (1979) and Ito (1980) prove a theorem on the stability of a system in $\mathbb{R}^2$ with two regimes, divided by a

straight line on which the equilibrium is situated. Honkapohja and Ito (1982) use the complicated concept of a "Filippov solution".

In Subsection 2.4.2, system (2.5) will be investigated for $k = 2$ and for continuous functions F. Subsection 2.4.3 will be devoted to discontinuous systems.

2.4.2. Continuous systems

We will start with a theorem of Laroque (1981b) for continuous piecewise continuously differentiable, linear systems in $\mathbb{R}^2$; both subsystems and regimes in system (2.5) are linear. Next, it will be shown that the linearity restrictions on both subsystems and regimes can be relaxed (cf. Theorem 2.16, Poincaré-Liapunov).

THEOREM 2.26 (Laroque). *Let C_i, $i = 1,2,\ldots,n$, be closed cones in $\mathbb{R}^2$ with vertices in the origin, with disjoint interiors and such that*

$$\bigcup_{i=1}^{n} C_i = \mathbb{R}^2 .$$

Let the numbering of the cones around the origin be clockwise, with $C_0 := C_n$.
If

$$\operatorname{tr} A_i < 0 \quad \textit{and} \quad |A_i| > 0 \quad \textit{for } i = 1,\ldots,n$$

and if $G: \mathbb{R}^2 \to \mathbb{R}^2$ *defined by*

$$G(x) := A_i x \quad \textit{for } x \in C_i$$

is continuous, then the origin is an asymptotically stable solution of the system

$$\text{(2.6)} \qquad \overset{\circ}{x} = G(x) .$$

The proof of Laroque's result consists of two parts.
First he considers the case in which there exists a real eigenvector in one of the cones, let us say C_i. He shows that trajectories cannot pass this eigenvector, so each trajectory stays ultimately in some fixed cone C_j and converges to the origin.
The second part of the proof concerns the case, where there does not

exist such an eigenvector. Then the function $\mathcal{E}(x)$ defined by

$$\mathcal{E}(x) := |x, G(x)|$$

is nonzero for $x \neq 0$. On account of the continuity of $G(x)$ in system (2.6), $\mathcal{E}(x)$ is continuous and now it can be proved that

$$\mathring{\mathcal{E}}(x)\mathcal{E}(x) < 0$$

on a trajectory. Therefore, $[\mathcal{E}(x)]^2$ is a Liapunov function.

Theorem 2.26 can be applied to prove the asymptotic stability of the (Walras) equilibrium of a linearized version of the system in Veendorp (1975). Veendorp proved this asymptotic stability incorrectly (see Laroque, 1981b). The generalization of Theorem 2.26, which is proved below, can be used for the asymptotic stability of the (Walras) equilibrium in the original (nonlinearized) Veendorp model.
The rest of this subsection is devoted to the proof of this generalization. The system we start with is system (2.5). Only $\mathbb{R}^2$ is considered, hence the following restriction is made.

CONDITION III. $k = 2$.

Henceforth the following notations and assumptions will be used.
Let q_i, $i = 1,2,\dots,n$, be vectors in $\mathbb{R}^2$ with $\|q_i\| = 1$, no two of them equal. The numbering of these vectors is clockwise with regard to the origin and $q_0 := q_n$.
Let there be given n curves represented by

$$x = h_i(\xi) = q_i\xi + o(\xi) \quad (\xi \downarrow 0) \ , \quad i = 1,2,\dots,n \ .$$

It is assumed that the radius of the ball $\mathcal{B}$ is sufficiently small to let $\mathcal{B}$ be divided by the curves $x = h_i(\xi)$ into n subsets S_i, $i = 1,2,\dots,n$, that have only the origin in common and that are defined in the following condition.

CONDITION IV. *For* $i = 1,2,\dots,n$*:*

(i) $h_i \in C'(\mathbb{R}_+)$.

(ii) S_i *is defined as the closure of a subset of* $\mathcal{B}$*, which has the boundaries* $x = h_{i-1}(\xi)$ *and* $x = h_i(\xi)$ *(and part of the boundary of* $\mathcal{B}$*), but with the exception of the set*

$$\{x = h_{i-1}(\xi) \mid \xi > 0\} .$$

The impossibility of equal q_i's ensures that $Co(S)$ has a nonempty interior so that the derivatives in the origin are determined uniquely.

It will be shown (see Lemma 2.27) that the continuity of the right-hand side is preserved, if both the subsystems and the regimes are linearized. As a consequence of this property the same Liapunov function that plays a role in Laroque's proof can be applied. We will also have to show that linearization of the regimes gives rise to differences that are $o(x)$. This linearization is handled in Lemma 2.28.

With relation to the tangent cones (see Definition 2.5) the following lemma can be proved.

LEMMA 2.27. *Under Conditions* I-IV *the function* $G: \mathbb{R}^2 \to \mathbb{R}^2$ *defined by*

$$G(x) := A_i x \quad \text{for } x \in \{0\} \cup [Co(S_i) \setminus Co(S_{i-1})]$$

is continuous on $\mathbb{R}^2$.

PROOF. It suffices to prove that the function $G(x)$ is continuous on the common boundary of $Co(S_1)$ and $Co(S_2)$.
The common boundary of $Co(S_1)$ and $Co(S_2)$ is given by

$$x = \xi q_1 .$$

Since $F(x)$ is continuous on $x = h_1(\xi) = q_1\xi + o(\xi)$ $(\xi \downarrow 0)$, we have

$$(A_1 - A_2)q_1\xi = f_2[h_1(\xi)] + o(\xi) - f_1[h_1(\xi)] + o(\xi) \qquad (\xi \downarrow 0) .$$

Since the right-hand side is $o(\xi)$, it follows that

$$(A_1 - A_2)q_1 = o(1) \qquad (\xi \downarrow 0)$$

and this can only be true if

$$(A_1 - A_2)q_1 = 0 .$$

This equation implies that the function $G(x)$ is continuous on the boundary given by $x = \xi q_1$. (In a similar way it can be proved that this function is continuous on each of the boundaries.) □

It follows from the lemma that $G(x)$ is equal to

$$G(x) = A_i x \quad \text{for } x \in Co(S_i) .$$

LEMMA 2.28. *Let the function* $g_i(x)$ *be defined on* $\mathrm{Co}(S_i) \cap B$ *by*

$$g_i(x) := F(x) - A_i x \quad \text{for } x \in \mathrm{Co}(S_i) \cap B ,$$

where $F(x)$ *is defined in the same way as in system* (2.5).
Then under Conditions I-IV

$$g_i(x) = o(\|x\|) \quad (x \to 0) .$$

PROOF. The proof will be given for $i = 1$. Note that $g_1(x) - f_1(x)$ can only be nonzero if

$$x \in \mathrm{Co}(S_1) \cap \mathrm{int}\, S_2 \quad \text{or} \quad x \in \mathrm{Co}(S_1) \cap \mathrm{int}\, S_n .$$

Let ξ be defined by the property that ξq_1 is the orthogonal projection of x onto the ray generated by q_1. Then, if $x \to 0$ and $x \in \mathrm{Co}(S_1) \cap \mathrm{int}\, S_2$, it is easily seen that

$$\frac{\|x - \xi q_1\|}{\xi} \to 0 \quad (\xi \downarrow 0) .$$

Hence

$$x = \xi q_1 + o(\|x\|) \quad (x \to 0)$$

and

$$(A_1 - A_2)x = \xi(A_1 - A_2)q_1 + o(\|x\|) \quad (x \to 0) .$$

Application of Lemma 2.27 yields

$$(A_1 - A_2)x = o(\|x\|) \quad (x \to 0) .$$

Therefore, for $x \in \mathrm{Co}(S_1) \cap \mathrm{int}\, S_2$

$$g_1(x) = (A_2 - A_1)x + f_2(x) = o(\|x\|) \quad (x \to 0) . \qquad \square$$

It will be convenient to introduce the following definitions:

$$\gamma := x'x$$

denotes the square of the Euclidean norm of the vector x;

$$P := \begin{pmatrix} 0 & 1 \\ -1 & 0 \end{pmatrix} .$$

We will use a similar function as Laroque used for a construction of a Liapunov function.

Let $\mathcal{E}_i : \mathbb{R}^2 \to \mathbb{R}$ and $\mathcal{E}: \mathbb{R}^2 \to \mathbb{R}$ be defined by

$$\mathcal{E}_i(x) := |x, A_i x| \quad \text{for } 1,2,\ldots,n ,$$

$$\mathcal{E}(x) := \mathcal{E}_i(x) \quad \text{for } x \in \{0\} \cup [\mathrm{Co}(S_i) \setminus \mathrm{Co}(S_{i-1})]$$

$$(i = 1,2,\ldots,n) .$$

It can easily be seen that $\mathcal{E}(x)$ can be written as follows:

$$\mathcal{E}(x) = x' P A_i x \quad \text{for } x \in \mathrm{Co}(S_i) \quad (i = 1,2,\ldots,n) .$$

Furthermore, $\mathcal{E}(x)$ is continuous on $\mathbb{R}^2$.

LEMMA 2.29. *Under Conditions* I-IV

$$\mathring{\mathcal{E}}(x) = (\mathrm{tr}\, A_i)\mathcal{E}(x) + o(\gamma) \quad (\gamma \downarrow 0) \quad \textit{for } x \in \mathrm{Co}(S_i) .$$

PROOF. For $x \in \mathrm{Co}(S_i)$ we have, using the notation of Lemma 2.28,

$$\mathring{\mathcal{E}}(x) = (\mathring{x})' P A_i x + x' P A_i \mathring{x} =$$

$$= [A_i x + g_i(x)]' P A_i x + x' P A_i [A_i x + g_i(x)] =$$

$$= x' A_i P A_i x + x' P A_i^2 x + [g_i(x)]' P A_i x + x' P A_i g_i(x) .$$

The first term equals zero. To the second term the Cayley-Hamilton theorem

$$A_i^2 - (\mathrm{tr}\, A_i) A_i + |A_i| I = 0$$

can be applied. The third and fourth terms are $o(\|x\|^2)$ $(x \to 0)$ (cf. Lemma 2.30) and therefore they are $o(\gamma)$ $(\gamma \downarrow 0)$. Hence

$$\mathring{\mathcal{E}}(x) = (\mathrm{tr}\, A_i) x' P A_i x + |A_i| \cdot x' P x + o(\gamma) \qquad (\gamma \downarrow 0)$$

$$= (\mathrm{tr}\, A_i)\mathcal{E}(x) + o(\gamma) \quad (\gamma \downarrow 0) . \qquad \square$$

LEMMA 2.30. *Let Conditions* I-IV *hold. Let* $y_0 \in \mathrm{Co}(S_i)$ *with* $\|y_0\| = 1$ *be an eigenvector of* A_i *with real negative eigenvalue* λ_0.
For $x \in \mathrm{Co}(S_i)$

$$\overset{\circ}{\gamma} = 2x'A_i x + o(\gamma) \qquad (\gamma \downarrow 0) .$$

There is a positive ρ *and an open cone* K *such that* $y_0 \in K$ *and*

$$\overset{\circ}{\gamma} < 0 \qquad \textit{for } x \in K \cap B_\rho ,$$

where B_ρ *is a ball around the origin with radius* ρ.

PROOF. For $x \in Co(S_i)$ we have

$$\overset{\circ}{\gamma} = 2x'\overset{\circ}{x} =$$

$$= 2x'[A_i x + g_i(x)] .$$

Using Lemma 2.28

$$g_i(x) = o(\|x\|) \qquad (x \to 0) ,$$

$$2x'g_i(x) = o(\gamma) \qquad (\gamma \downarrow 0) .$$

Hence, for $x \in Co(S_i)$,

$$\overset{\circ}{\gamma} = 2x'Ax_i + o(\gamma) \qquad (\gamma \downarrow 0) .$$

Choose ε such that $\varepsilon \in (0,-\lambda_0)$. Then the set K defined by

$$(2.7) \qquad K := \{x \in \mathbb{R}^2 \mid x'G(x) < -\varepsilon x'x\}$$

contains y_0 and K is an open cone.
For sufficiently small ρ for any $x \in K \cap B_\rho$

$$\overset{\circ}{\gamma} < -\varepsilon\gamma < 0 . \qquad \square$$

The result of Lemma 2.30 is also valid if y_0 lies on the common boundary of $Co(S_i)$ and $Co(S_{i-1})$ $(i = 1,2,\ldots,n)$.

For the time being it is assumed that there is only one such eigenvector as in Lemma 2.30) (with eigenvalue λ_0).
We define

$$(2.8) \qquad \nu := \min \{[\mathcal{E}(x)]^2 \mid \|x\| = 1, x \notin K\}$$

where K is defined as in (2.7).
Since the set $\{x \mid \|x\| = 1, x \notin K\}$ is compact and the function $\mathcal{E}(x)$

is continuous, this minimum exists. For $x \notin K$ the inequality $[\mathcal{E}(x)]^2 > 0$ holds, hence

$$\nu > 0 .$$

Define the real numbers β and α by

$$\beta := \max_j \max \{\| A_j x\| \mid \|x\| = 1\} , \tag{2.9}$$

$$\alpha := -(\max_j \operatorname{tr} A_j)\nu / 3\beta , \tag{2.10}$$

where ν is defined as in (2.8).
Since $\nu > 0$ and $\beta > 0$, α is positive if for each j the inequality $\operatorname{tr} A_j < 0$ holds.
Now the following theorem can be proved.

THEOREM 2.31. *Let Conditions* I-IV *hold. If*

$$\operatorname{tr} A_i < 0 \quad \textit{and} \quad |A_i| > 0 \quad \textit{for } i = 1,2,\ldots,n$$

then the function $V\colon \mathcal{B} \to \mathbb{R}$ *defined by*

$$V(x) := [\mathcal{E}(x)]^2 + \alpha(x'x)^2$$

where α *is defined by* (2.10), *is a Liapunov function of system* (2.5).

PROOF. The function $V(x)$ is continuous. Furthermore, $V(0) = 0$ and

$$V(x) > 0 \quad \text{for } x \neq 0 .$$

Along a solution path the following equation holds:

$$\mathring{V}(x) = 2\mathcal{E}(x)\mathring{\mathcal{E}}(x) + 2\alpha\gamma\mathring{\gamma} .$$

The Lemmas 2.29 and 2.30 imply that for $x \in \operatorname{Co}(S_i) \cap \mathcal{B}$

$$\mathring{V}(x) = 2(\operatorname{tr} A_i)[\mathcal{E}(x)]^2 + 2\alpha\gamma x'A_i x + o(\gamma^2) \qquad (\gamma \downarrow 0) .$$

From Lemma 2.30 we know that, if ρ is sufficiently small, the inequality $\mathring{\gamma} < 0$ holds for $K \cap \mathcal{B}_\rho$.
Since also $\operatorname{tr} A_i < 0$, it follows that

$$\mathring{V}(x) < 0 \quad \text{for } x \in K \cap \mathcal{B}_\rho .$$

For $x \notin K$ we have, by Cauchy-Schwarz and the definitions of β (see (2.9)) and γ

$$|x'A_i x| \le \|x\|\cdot\|A_i x\| \le \beta\|x\|^2 = \beta\gamma \ .$$

Hence

$$2\alpha\gamma x'A_i x \le 2\alpha\gamma^2\beta < -(\max_j \ \mathrm{tr}\, A_j)\nu\gamma^2 \ .$$

By definition of ν and γ

$$\nu\gamma^2 \le [\varepsilon(x)]^2 \ .$$

Therefore, for $x \in \mathrm{Co}(S_i) \setminus K$

$$\mathring{V}(x) < (2\,\mathrm{tr}\, A_j - \max_j \mathrm{tr}\, A_j)\nu\gamma^2 + o(\gamma^2) \qquad (\gamma \downarrow 0)$$

and $\mathring{V}(x)$ is negative for sufficiently small γ.
It can be concluded that $V(x)$ is a Liapunov function of system (2.5).□

If there are several real eigenvectors such as in Lemma 2.30, Theorem 2.31 still holds, since each of these eigenvectors belongs to the cone K defined in (2.7).

Theorems 2.23 and 2.31 and Corollary 2.18 immediately imply:

THEOREM 2.32. *Let Conditions* I-IV *hold. If*

$$\mathrm{tr}\, A_i < 0 \quad \textit{and} \quad |A_i| > 0 \quad \textit{for } i = 1,2,\ldots,n$$

then the origin is an asymptotically stable equilibrium of system (2.5).

2.4.3. Discontinuous systems

For discontinuous systems a somewhat more general solution concept is necessary than the one of Definition 2.10. The definition below is first given by Caratheodory (1948), see also Hautus (1970), p.6.

DEFINITION 2.33. *Let S be an open set in $\mathbb{R}^n$ and T an open interval in $\mathbb{R}$. Let $x_0 \in S$ and $F: S \to \mathbb{R}^n$. We call $x: T \to S$ a* _solution_ *of the differential system with initial condition*

$$\mathring{x} = F(x) \ , \quad x(t_0) = x_0$$

on T, if $t_0 \in T$, the function $t \mapsto F(x(t))$ is locally integrable on T

and

$$x(t) = x_0 + \int_{t_0}^{t} F(x(s))ds \quad \textit{for } t \in T .$$

For continuous functions F the above definition is equivalent to Definition 2.10. In the rest of this section we take t_0 equal to 0.

If the function F in Definition 2.33 is discontinuous on S, it is not locally Lipschitz continuous on S (see Definition 2.11). Then Theorem 2.12 cannot be applied. However, local Lipschitz continuity is not a necessary condition for the existence of solutions. Theorem 2 on page 9 of Hautus (1970) can be formulated as follows.

THEOREM 2.34 (Hautus). *Let the set* $\mathcal{D} \subset \mathbb{R}^k$ *be open and connected,* $g \in C'(\mathcal{D} \to \mathbb{R})$ *and*

$$G_0 := \{x \in \mathcal{D} \mid g(x) = 0\} ,$$
$$G_1 := \{x \in \mathcal{D} \mid g(x) > 0\} ,$$
$$G_2 := \{x \in \mathcal{D} \mid g(x) < 0\} .$$

Let $F\colon \mathcal{D} \to \mathbb{R}^k$ *with*

$$F(x) = F_j(x) \quad \textit{for } x \in G_j \quad (j = 0,1,2) ,$$

where $F_j \in C'(\mathrm{cl}\ G_j \to \mathbb{R}^k)$, $j = 1,2$.
Define the functions $h_j\colon G_0 \to \mathbb{R}$ *by*

$$h_j(c) := (\nabla g(c))F_j(c) \quad (j = 0,1,2) .$$

If for every $c \in G_0$

$$(2.11) \qquad h_1(c)h_2(c) > 0$$

holds, then for every $x_0 \in \mathcal{D}$, *there is a* $t_1 \in \mathbb{R}_{++}$ *such that the initial value problem* IVP$(F,x_0,0)$ *of system* $\mathring{x} = F(x)$ *has a solution on the time interval* $[0,t_1)$.
If, in addition, for every $c \in G_0$

(2.12) $h_0(c) \neq 0$,

then this solution is unique.

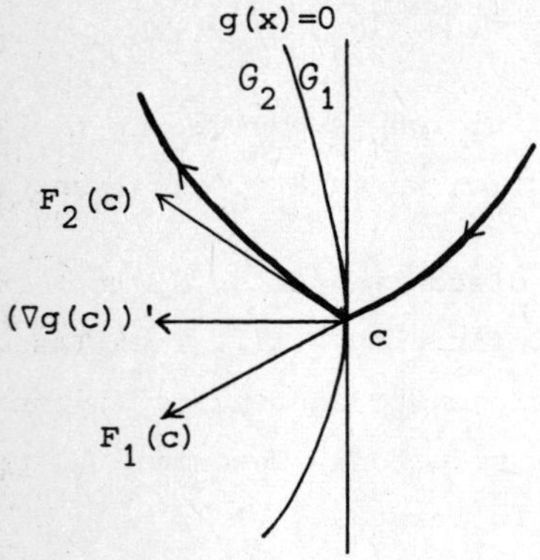

Figure 2.2.
A situation in which (2.11) is true.

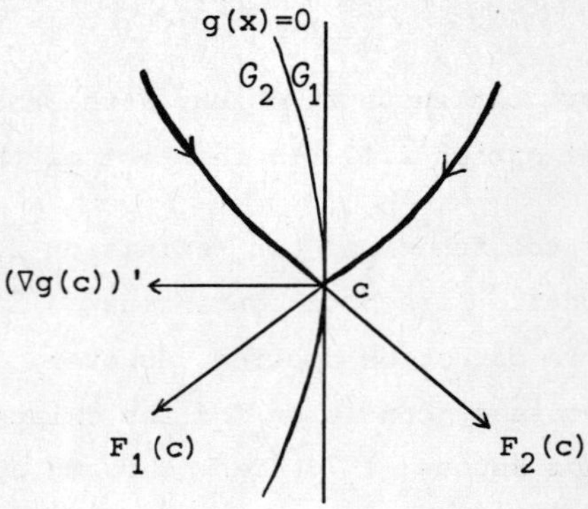

Figure 2.3.
A situation in which (2.11) is false.

Theorem 2.34 is illustrated in the plane, in Figures 2.2 and 2.3. An application of Theorem 2.34 in $\mathbb{R}^2$ yields Theorem 2.35 below.

THEOREM 2.35. *Let* $\mathcal{D}$, g, G_j, F *and* h *be defined as in Theorem* 2.34 *and* $k = 2$. *In addition, let the vector* q *be defined by*

$$q := P[\nabla g(0)]'$$

where P *is defined by* $P := \begin{pmatrix} 0 & 1 \\ -1 & 0 \end{pmatrix}$ *and suppose the following equalities hold:*

$$g(0) = 0 ,$$

$$F_j(c) = A_j c + o(\| c \|) \quad (c \to 0,\ c \in G_0) ,\ j = 0,1,2 .$$

If

$$\mathcal{E}_1(q)\mathcal{E}_2(q) > 0 ,$$

where $\mathcal{E}_i(x) = x' P A_i x$, $i = 0,1,2$, *then there exists a* $\rho \in \mathbb{R}_{++}$ *such that for every* $x_0 \in \mathcal{B}(0;\rho) \setminus \{0\}$, *there is a* $t_1 \in \mathbb{R}_+$ *such that the initial value problem* IVP$(F,x_0,0)$ *of system* $\mathring{x} = F(x)$ *has a solution on the interval* $[0,t_1)$. *If in addition* $\mathcal{E}_0(q) \neq 0$, *this solution is unique.*

PROOF. From the definition of q it follows that

$$\nabla g(c) = q'P + o(1) \qquad (c \to 0,\ c \in G_0)\ .$$

Hence, the following equality holds:

$$h_j(c) = q'PA_jc + o(\|c\|) \qquad (c \to 0,\ c \in G_0)\ .$$

The definitions of q and $g(0) = 0$ imply that, if $\rho \in \mathbb{R}_{++}$ is sufficiently small, there exists a unique $\alpha_c \in \mathbb{R} \setminus \{0\}$ for every $c \in G_0 \cap B(0;\rho) \setminus \{0\}$, such that

$$c = \alpha_c q + o(\alpha_c) \qquad (\alpha_c \to 0)\ .$$

Therefore we find

$$h_j(c) = \alpha_c q'PA_jq + o(\alpha_c) \qquad (\alpha_c \to 0,\ c \in G_0)\ .$$

Hence

$$h_1(c)h_2(c) = \alpha_c^2\, \mathcal{E}_1(q)\mathcal{E}_2(q) + o(\alpha_c^2) \qquad (\alpha_c \to 0,\ c \in G_0)\ ,$$

$$h_0(c) = \alpha_c\, \mathcal{E}_0(q) + o(\alpha_c) \qquad (\alpha_c \to 0,\ c \in G_0)\ ,$$

where $\mathcal{E}_i(q)$ is independent of α_c. Hence for sufficiently small α_c the inequality $\mathcal{E}_1(q)\mathcal{E}_2(q) > 0$ implies $h_1(c)h_2(c) > 0$ and the inequality $\mathcal{E}_0(q) \neq 0$ implies $h_0(c) \neq 0$. Application of Theorem 2.34 yields the assertions. □

The vector q in Theorem 2.35 generates the tangent to the curve determined by $g(x) = 0$ in the origin. This tangent is the common boundary of the tangent cones $\mathrm{Co}(G_1)$ and $\mathrm{Co}(G_2)$ of the sets G_1 and G_2. It can be observed that the functions $\mathcal{E}_i$ also play a role in the proof of Theorem 2.32. We can even formulate a generalization of Theorem 2.32 for discontinuous systems. For this, however, a generalization of the concept "Liapunov function" is necessary (cf. Moisseev, 1936).

DEFINITION 2.36. *A function* $V: \mathbb{R}^n \to \mathbb{R}$ *is a* ***generalized Liapunov function*** *of the system* (2.4) $\dot{x} = F(x)$, *with* $F: \mathbb{R}^k \to \mathbb{R}^k$ *and* $F(0)$, *if in some neighbourhood of the origin*

(i) $V(0) = 0$, $V(x)\quad 0$ *for* $x \neq 0$.

(ii) $V(x)$ *is strictly decreasing on any solution path of system* (2.4)

One can dispense with the continuity requirement in Definition 2.22 and prove an analogue of Theorem 2.23 (see Moisseev, 1936).

THEOREM 2.37. *If there exists a generalized Liapunov function of system* (2.4) $\mathring{x} = F(x)$, *then the origin is an asymptotically stable equilibrium of system* (2.4).

We return to system (2.5) from the beginning of this section and do not assume Condition II (continuity) to hold. Instead of Condition I we consider

CONDITION I'. *For* $i = 1,2,\dots,n$:

(i) $f_i \in C'(\mathrm{cl}\, S_i \to \mathbb{R}^k)$;

(ii) $f_i(x) = o(\|x\|) \quad (x \to 0)$.

It has been noticed already, that under Condition II, Condition I' is an immediate consequence of Condition I. Under Condition I', the function F_j defined by $F_j(x) := A_j x + f_j(x) \ (x \in \mathcal{B})$, satisfies $F_j \in C'(\mathrm{cl}\, S_j \to \mathbb{R}^k)$, $j = 1,2,\dots,n$, and Theorems 2.34 and 2.35 can be applied.

Now the "discontinuous version" of Theorem 2.32 can be formulated.

THEOREM 2.38. *Let Conditions* I', III *and* IV *hold, if*

1) $\mathrm{tr}\, A_i < 0$ *and* $|A_i| > 0$ *for* $i = 1,2,\dots,n$;

2) $\mathcal{E}_{i-1}(q_i)\mathcal{E}_i(q_i) > 0$ *for* $i = 1,2,\dots,n$;

3) $\forall x \neq 0: \mathcal{E}(x) \neq 0 \Rightarrow \forall i \in \{1,\dots,n\}: \mathcal{E}_{i-1}(q_i) \leq \mathcal{E}_i(q_i)$,

where $\mathcal{E}_i: \mathbb{R}^2 \to \mathbb{R}$ *and* $\mathcal{E}: \mathbb{R}^2 \to \mathbb{R}$ *are defined by* $\mathcal{E}_i(x) = x' P A_i x$, $i = 1,2,\dots,n$, *and* $\mathcal{E}(x) := \mathcal{E}_i(x)$ *for* $x \in \{0\} \cup [\mathrm{Co}(S_i) \setminus \mathrm{Co}(S_{i-1})]$ $(i = 1,2,\dots,n)$, *then the origin is an asymptotically stable equilibrium of system* (2.5).

PROOF. Condition 2) implies that there is a solution of the initial value problem $\mathrm{IVP}(F,x_0,0)$ of system (2.5) for x_0 in some neighbourhood of the origin (see Theorem 2.35).

Let the inequality $\mathcal{E}(x) > 0$ hold for all $x \neq 0$. It can be observed that $\mathcal{E}_i(x) > 0$ corresponds with anti-clockwise motions of trajectories. Hence the ray generated by q_i is crossed by a trajectory, coming from the tangent cone $Co(S_i)$ and going into $Co(S_{i-1})$.
Therefore, the function $\mathcal{E}$ is non-increasing on the common boundary of $Co(S_i)$ and $Co(S_{i-1})$. Furthermore, $\mathcal{E}(x)$ is positive for $x \neq 0$.
If, analogously, $\mathcal{E}(x) < 0$ for all $x \neq 0$, then trajectories have a clockwise motion. Therefore, trajectories go from $Co(S_{i-1})$ into $Co(S_i)$ and the function $-\mathcal{E}$ is non-increasing on the common boundary of $Co(S_i)$ and $Co(S_{i-1})$. Clearly, $-\mathcal{E}(x)$ is a Liapunov function of system (2.5). If there is an $i \in \{1,2,\dots,n\}$ and an $\tilde{x} \in \text{int } Co(S_i)$ such that $\mathcal{E}_i(\tilde{x}) = 0$, then $\tilde{x}$ is an element of $Co(S_i)$ and also an eigenvector of A_i (cf. the proof of Theorem 2.31). In this case a cone K can be defined like in the proof of Lemma 2.30.
The theorem can now be proved similar to Theorem 2.32, with the function V defined in Theorem 2.31. This function V is now a generalized Liapunov function. Due to Theorem 2.37, the existence of a generalized Liapunov function of system (2.5) is sufficient for asymptotic stability of the origin as an equilibrium of this system. □

In Chapter 5 we will meet three-dimensional systems of a special type. The following definition will be useful.

DEFINITION 2.39. *A* <u>*common line partition*</u> $(C_1,\dots,C_n)$ *of* $\mathbb{R}^3$ *is an n-tuple of closed cones (see Definition 2.5) with the following properties:*

(i) $\exists q \in \mathbb{R}^3$: $C_1 \cap \dots \cap C_n = \{\lambda q \mid \lambda \in \mathbb{R}\}$;

(ii) $C_1 \cup \dots \cup C_n = \mathbb{R}^3$;

(iii) $\forall i,j \in \{1,\dots,n\}$: $\text{int } C_1 \cap \text{int } C_j = \emptyset$.

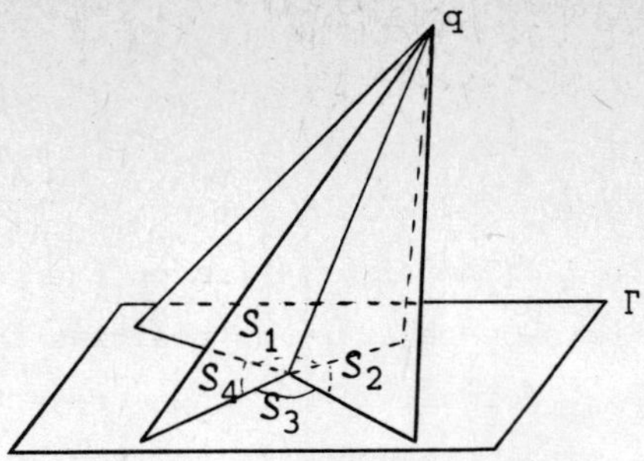

Figure 2.4.
Common line partition.

The intersections of the cones of a common line partition with a plane Γ, such that $q \notin \Gamma$, are closed cones again (in the plane). See Figure 2.4. Any vector is an element of the same cone as its projection along the vector q on the plane Γ is. The top angles of the planar closed cones are invariant with respect to parallel translations of the plane Γ. The sets of a common line partition can be numbered clockwise (cf. Theorem 2.26). In Chapter 5 systems play a role, in which the regimes form common line partitions.

3. STATIC MODEL

3.1. *Introduction*

In this chapter a short run macromodel is considered with three commodities. This model is similar to the ones of Barro and Grossman (1971, 1976), Malinvaud (1977), Böhm (1978, 1980), Muellbauer and Portes (1978) and Gepts (1977) (cf. Chapter 1). In the model there is a consumption sector and a production sector. The two sectors take into account the future. The preferences of the consumption sector are represented by a utility function. The preferences concerning the future are supposed to be worked up in the utility function via a money variable as one of the arguments. The utility for money reflects the preferences and expectations of the consumption sector with respect to future expenditure and income. Nevertheless, for sake of simplicity, the utility function is assumed to be independent of present prices and quantity constraints.
The objective function of the production sector is assumed to be the sum of the real cash flow and a "valuation function of stock". The latter function represents the preferences with respect to the quantity of consumption goods that are kept in stock. It depends on the expected future profits and quantity constraints. We shall, however, introduce a very simple "valuation function of stock", which is independent of present prices and constraints. The role of inventory in the objective function of the production sector is similar to the role of money in the utility function of the consumption sector.

There are two markets, where commodities are exchanged against money: the labour market and the consumption goods market. We understand by a "trade" a pair representing quantities of labour and consumption goods. Following Subsection 1.4.1, a Non-Walrasian Equilibrium is associated with the concepts "voluntary", "optimal" and "rationing on the long side only". A trade is "optimal" for a sector, if it maximizes the

objective function on the constrained budget c.q. production set. A trade is called "voluntary" for the consumption sector if this sector is neither forced to supply more labour nor to consume more goods than desired. A similar definition can be given for the production sector. The "long side" is the sector related with the maximum of demand and supply on a certain market. If demand and supply are unequal, the "long side" is rationed, but not the other sector.
We specify a Non-Walrasian Equilibrium (NWE-) state as a sequence of parameters, a trade and upper bounds, such that the trade is the solution of the maximization problems of both sectors, under the given parameters and upper bounds. Furthermore, the condition "rationing on the long side only" holds, i.e., it is not allowed that both sectors meet "strictly active" constraints (see Section 2.2) on a single market. The trade of an NWE-state is "optimal" and "voluntary". NWE-states are classified following Malinvaud (1977) and Muellbauer and Portes (1978).

The subdivision of this chapter is as follows.
Section 3.2 contains the basic model and assumptions on the objective functions of the two sectors. The maximization problems of the sectors are formulated. In the case of "rationing", these maximization problems have to be adjusted slightly. These new problems lead to the introduction of "voluntary trades" that are dealt with in Section 3.3. Furthermore, the "effective demand and supply functions" are introduced. Some properties of demand and supply are investigated in Section 3.4.
In Section 3.5 attention is given to the trade which takes place between the sectors as a result of the interaction. A Non-Walrasian Equilibrium state, as mentioned above, is defined.
In Section 3.6 it is investigated for which values of the parameters the different types of NWE-states occur. Some extensions are mentioned in Section 3.7.
All the proofs concerning utility function, voluntary trades and effective demand and supply functions can be found in an appendix.

3.2. *Description of the basic model*

We consider an economy with two sectors: a consumption sector and a production sector. There are three commodities: money, labour and a single consumption good.
The preferences of the consumption sector are represented by a *utility function*. The consumption sector maximizes this utility function given a budget constraint and, if it is rationed (see Subsection 1.4.1), given quantity constraints imposed by the markets.
The production sector uses labour, supplied by the consumption sector, to produce the consumption good. The production process is described by a *production function*.

Government is considered to be part of the production sector. An exogenous amount of the production goes to the government. This government demand is not rationed. The production function represents the relationship between the level of labour input and the maximum output of consumption goods, that remains after satisfying government demand. The production sector can hold an inventory of the consumption good. The value of this inventory is determined by a *valuation function of stock*. The production sector maximizes an *objective function*, which is assumed to be the sum of the real cash flow and the value of stocks. This sector may be rationed as well as the consumption sector.
The profits are not supposed to be distributed among the consumers. The exact destination of the profits will not be specified further.

In this section the short run will be studied. This means that the wage rate and the price of the consumption good are fixed. Capital is neglected.

The following notations will be used:

- ℓ : number of units of labour;
- r : number of units of the consumption good;
- z_n : amount of nominal money in the consumption sector after the exchange on the markets;
- m_n : initial amount of nominal money in the consumption sector;
- w_n : nominal wage rate, i.e., the price of one unit of labour;
- p : price of one unit of the consumption good;

y : initial inventory of consumption goods in the production sector;

q : inventory of consumption goods in the production sector after the exchange on the markets;

ℓ_{max} : maximum number of units of labour, that can be supplied by the consumption sector;

$\tilde{r}$: number of units of production of the consumption good;

z : real money in the consumption sector after the exchange on the markets;

m : initial real money stock in the consumption sector;

w : real wage rate;

x : triple $(m,w,y)'$.

With respect to the price p of goods, the nominal wage rate w_n, the initial nominal money stock m_n, the initial inventory y and the maximum labour supply ℓ_{max}, only positive values are considered. The exchange of labour, goods and money takes place simultaneously. A pair (ℓ,r), representing the amounts of labour and goods exchanged, is called a *trade*. The amount of money in the consumption sector, after the realization of the trade (ℓ,r) is defined by

(3.1) $$z_n := m_n + w_n\ell - pr$$

where $w_n\ell$ is income and pr is expenditure.
(3.1) will be called the *budget equation*.
Similarly, the inventory of the production sector after trade (ℓ,r) is defined by the *inventory equation*

(3.2) $$q := y + \tilde{r} - r \,.$$

The increase of the stock equals the difference of production $\tilde{r}$ and sales r. Stocks are the stores of value that can be carried over to the next period. They are not rationed.

Real values of final money stocks, initial money stocks and the wage rate are defined as follows $(p > 0)$

$$z := z_n/p \,,$$

$$m := m_n/p \,,$$

$$w := w_n/p \,.$$

Clearly, the budget equation (3.1) can be written as

$$(3.3) \qquad z = m + w\ell - r \ .$$

The *consumption set* $\Delta \subset \mathbb{R}^3_+$ (cf. Section 1.2) is the set of possible commodity bundles (ℓ,r,z) representing a quantity of labour, goods and real money holdings. The consumption sector as a whole is assumed to have a single *utility function* $U\colon \Delta \to \mathbb{R}_+$ (cf. Section 1.2). This sector could, for instance, consist of identical agents, rationed at the same levels.

ASSUMPTION As 1. *The consumption set* Δ *is given by*

$$\Delta = \{(\ell,r,z) \in \mathbb{R}^3_+ \mid \ell \le \ell_{max}\} \ .$$

In the next assumption, we shall make use of the "bordered Hessian". The bordered Hessian of the function U evaluated at $(\ell_0,r_0,z_0) \in \text{int}\,\Delta$ is the following matrix:

$$(3.4) \qquad \begin{bmatrix} 0 & U_\ell & U_r & U_z \\ U_\ell & U_{\ell\ell} & U_{\ell r} & U_{\ell z} \\ U_r & U_{r\ell} & U_{rr} & U_{rz} \\ U_z & U_{z\ell} & U_{zr} & U_{zz} \end{bmatrix}$$

where

$$U_\ell := \partial U/\partial \ell \ , \quad U_{\ell\ell} := \partial^2 U/\partial \ell^2 \ , \quad \text{etc.}$$

and each of the derivatives is evaluated at (ℓ_0,r_0,z_0).

It will be assumed that the utility function U has a negative definite bordered Hessian. (This implies that the function U is quasi-concave, see Arrow and Enthoven, 1961, Theorem 5.)

ASSUMPTION As 2. *The utility function of the consumption sector* $U\colon \Delta \to \mathbb{R}_+$ *satisfies*

1) $U \mid \text{int}\,\Delta \in C^2(\text{int}\,\Delta \to \mathbb{R}_+)$ *and* $U \in C(\Delta \to \mathbb{R}_+)$;
2) U *has a negative definite bordered Hessian for all* $(\ell,r,z) \in \text{int}\,\Delta$;
3) U *is monotonously increasing in* r *and* z *and decreasing in* ℓ.

The production sector can be considered as an aggregate of producers and of government. This sector as a whole has a single production function $F\colon \mathbb{R}_+ \to \mathbb{R}$, a valuation function of stock $Q\colon \mathbb{R}_+ \to \mathbb{R}_+$ and an objective function $V\colon \mathbb{R} \to \mathbb{R}_+$. For these three functions assumptions are given below.

ASSUMPTION As 3. *The production function of the production sector* $F\colon \mathbb{R}_+ \to \mathbb{R}$ *has the following properties:*

1) $F \in C(\mathbb{R}_+)$; $F \mid \mathbb{R}_{++} \in C^2(\mathbb{R}_{++})$;
2) $F(0) \leq 0$;
3) F *is strictly concave;*
4) F *is increasing;*
5) $\lim_{\ell\to\infty} F(\ell) = \infty$;
6) $\lim_{\ell\to\infty} F_\ell(\ell) = 0$.

For the production "decreasing returns" are assumed (properties 3) and 4)). Since government demand is subtracted from the production, the value of the production function at a zero level of input might be negative. The value $-F(0)$ can be considered to be the government demand. The properties 1) and 3) - 6) of the above assumption are compatible with assumptions in Böhm (1978) and Hildenbrand and Hildenbrand (1978). In Muellbauer and Portes (1978) the objective of the production sector is the expectation of present and future profits. We will "summarize" the future profits in a valuation function of stock. This function represents the subjective value for the production sector of a stock of goods, which can be hold.

ASSUMPTION As 4. *The valuation function of stock of the production sector* $Q\colon \mathbb{R}_+ \to \mathbb{R}_+$ *has the following properties:*

1) $Q \in C(\mathbb{R}_+ \to \mathbb{R}_+)$; $Q \mid \mathbb{R}_{++} \in C^2(\mathbb{R}_{++} \to \mathbb{R}_+)$;
2) $Q(0) = 0$;
3) Q *is strictly concave;*
4) Q *is increasing.*
5) $\lim_{q\to 0} Q_q(q) > 1$.

The function Q is independent of the price of goods p and the nominal wage rate w_n, which is a rather restrictive assumption. An increase of the inventory is considered to be favourable (4)) but every extra increase is appraised less (3)). The production sector tries to avoid a too large accumulation of stock. Assumption 5) is made to ensure that the optimal inventory is positive.
In the Barro and Grossman/Malinvaud models there is no inventory. This is equivalent with $Q(q) \equiv 0$ and $y \equiv 0$ in our model. Clearly these identities are contradictory to Assumption As 4, 3), 4) and 5). Therefore, when we deal with this case later (see Section 4.6), Assumption As 4 will be omitted.

For the objective function of the production sector we assume the following

ASSUMPTION As 5. *The objective function of the production sector* $V: \mathbb{R}^3_+ \times \mathbb{R}_{++} \to \mathbb{R}$ *satisfies the equality*

$$V(\ell,r,q;w) = -w\ell + r + Q(q) \qquad (\ell,r,q;w) \in \mathbb{R}^3_+ \times \mathbb{R}_{++} .$$

The value of the objective function is equal to the sum of cash flow $-w\ell + r$ and the valuation of stock $Q(q)$. Equivalently, the objective function could be assumed to have the following form

$$-w\ell + r - Q(y) + Q(q) ,$$

so that it represents the sum of real profits and the valuation of stock. Since $Q(y)$ is given, maximization of the latter function gives the same solution as maximization of the function V of Assumption As 5.
The feasible solutions for the production sector are elements of the production correspondence. Before an assumption is made concerning this map, a remark can be made with respect to the production constraint $\tilde{r} \leq F(\ell)$. Since extra goods are always favourable for the production sector (cf. Assumptions As 4 and As 5), this constraint is always active (efficient production). Therefore, the production variable $\tilde{r}$ can be replaced by $F(\ell)$. The inventory equation (3.2) can be written as

$$(3.5) \qquad q = y + F(\ell) - r .$$

Henceforth, the vector $(m,w,y)'$ will be denoted by x.

ASSUMPTION As 6. *The production correspondence* $D^P: \mathbb{R}^3_{++} \rightrightarrows \mathbb{R}^2_+$ *satisfies*

$$D^P(x) = \{(\ell,r) \in \mathbb{R}^2_+ \mid F(\ell) \geq 0,\ y+F(\ell)-r \geq 0\} .$$

The production correspondence is such that the production and the inventory after the trade are nonnegative. Note that it is independent of m and w.

Now the maximization problems of the sectors can be given:

$$\text{(3.6)} \qquad \max\ \{U(\ell,r,z) \mid (\ell,r,z) \in \Delta,\ z = m+w\ell-r\}$$

$$\text{(3.7)} \qquad \max\ \{V(\ell,r,q;w) \mid (\ell,r) \in D^P(x),\ q = y+F(\ell)-r\} .$$

(3.6) is the maximization problem of the consumption sector. Its solution is denoted by $(\ell^{C*}(x), r^{C*}(x), z^*(x))$, where $\ell^{C*}(x)$ is called the *notional labour supply* and $r^{C*}(x)$ is called the *notional demand of goods*. It can be observed that the solution of (3.6) is independent of the initial inventory y in the production sector.

(3.7) is the maximization problem of the production sector. The solution of (3.7) is denoted by $(\ell^{P*}(x), r^{P*}(x), q^*(x))$, in which $\ell^{P*}(x)$ and $r^{P*}(x)$ are called, respectively, the *notional labour demand* and the *notional supply of goods*. The notional labour demand is determined as follows:

$$\text{if } \lim_{\ell \downarrow 0} F_\ell(\ell) \leq w\,, \text{ then } \ell^{P*}(x) = 0\,,$$

$$\text{if } \lim_{\ell \downarrow 0} F_\ell(\ell) > w\,, \text{ then } F_\ell[\ell^{P*}(x)] = w\,.$$

The value of $\ell^{P*}(x)$ is finite as a consequence of Assumption As 3.6. It is easy to verify that the notional labour demand $\ell^{P*}(x)$ is independent of both inventory y and real money stock m of the consumption sector. The notional supply of goods $r^{P*}(x)$ is independent of m.

Since we are especially interested in the space of trades (ℓ,r), we will reformulate the maximization problems (3.6) and (3.7) by eliminating the stock variables z and q. For this reason a budget correspondence and adapted formulations of objective functions are introduced.

DEFINITION 3.1. *The* <u>*budget correspondence*</u> $D^C: \mathbb{R}^3_{++} \rightrightarrows \mathbb{R}^2_+$ *is defined by*

$$D^C(x) := \{(\ell,r) \in \mathbb{R}^2_+ \mid \ell \le \ell_{max},\ m + w\ell - r \ge 0\} .$$

Observe that a trade (ℓ,r) in the budget correspondence $D^C(x)$ corresponds with a triple $(\ell,r,z) \in \Delta$, which satisfies the budget equation. The z-component in the utility function can be eliminated by substitution of the budget equation (cf. Svensson, 1977).

DEFINITION 3.2. *The* <u>*restricted utility function*</u> $\tilde{U}: \mathbb{R}^2_+ \times \mathbb{R}^3_{++} \to \mathbb{R}$ *is defined by*

$$\begin{aligned} \tilde{U}(\ell,r;x) &:= U(\ell,r,m+w\ell-r) \quad \textit{if } (\ell,r) \in D^C(x) \\ &:= 0 \qquad \textit{elsewhere} \end{aligned}$$

where U *is the utility function of the consumption sector.*

Some possible contour curves of the function $\tilde{U}$ in (ℓ,r)-space are depicted in Figures 3.3 and 3.4 in the next section. From Assumption As 2 concerning the utility function, differentiability and concavity properties can be derived for the restricted utility function $\tilde{U}$.

THEOREM 3.3. *Under Assumptions* As 1 *and* As 2, *the function* $\tilde{U}$ *is twice continuously differentiable in* x *on* $\mathbb{R}^3_{++}$ *and in* (ℓ,r) *on* int $D^C(x)$ $(x \in \mathbb{R}^3_{++})$. *Furthermore, the Hessian of* $\tilde{U}$ *with respect to* (ℓ,r) *on* int $D^C(x)$ $(x \in \mathbb{R}^3_{++})$ *is negative definite.*

Similar to the function $\tilde{U}$, a "restricted objective function" of the production sector can be defined.

DEFINITION 3.4. *The* <u>*restricted objective function*</u> *of the production sector is the function* $\tilde{V}: \mathbb{R}^2_+ \times \mathbb{R}^3_{++} \to \mathbb{R}_+$ *defined by*

$$\begin{aligned} \tilde{V}(\ell,r;x) &:= V(\ell,r,y+F(\ell)-r;w) \quad \textit{if } (\ell,r) \in D^P(x) \\ &:= 0 \qquad \textit{elsewhere.} \end{aligned}$$

Obviously, the following equality holds:

$$\tilde{V}(\ell,r;x) = -w\ell + r + Q[y+F(\ell)-r] .$$

Contour curves of the function $\tilde{V}$ in the (ℓ,r)-plane can be depicted analogously to the Figures 3.3 and 3.4 (see Section 3.3).
The analogue of Theorem 3.3 is the following.

THEOREM 3.5. *Under Assumptions* As 3-6, *the function* $\tilde{V}$ *is twice continuously differentiable in* x *on* $\mathbb{R}^3_{++}$ *and in* (ℓ,r) *on* int $D^P(x)$ $(x \in \mathbb{R}^3_{++})$. *Furthermore, the Hessian of* $\tilde{V}$ *with respect to* (ℓ,r) *on* int $D^P(x)$ $(x \in \mathbb{R}^3_{++})$ *is negative definite.*

The maximization problems of the sectors can now be written as

$$\text{(3.8)} \qquad \max \{\tilde{U}(\ell,r;x) \mid (\ell,r) \in D^C(x)\} \qquad (x \in \mathbb{R}^3_{++}) ,$$

$$\text{(3.9)} \qquad \max \{\tilde{V}(\ell,r;x) \mid (\ell,r) \in D^P(x)\} \qquad (x \in \mathbb{R}^3_{++}) ,$$

where the solution of (3.8) equals the solution components $(\ell^{C*}(x),r^{C*}(x))$ of (3.6) and the solution of (3.9) equals the solution components $(\ell^{P*}(x),r^{P*}(x))$ of (3.7). For a given parameter vector $x \in \mathbb{R}^3_{++}$ the sectors choose a trade (ℓ,r) in a feasible set. These trades maximize the "restricted" objective functions, that are strictly concave (see Theorems 3.3 and 3.5).

REMARK 3.6. It has already been noticed that the notional labour demand $\ell^{P*}(x)$ is finite. The notional goods supply $r^{P*}(x)$ satisfies $r^{P*}(x) \leq y+F[\ell^{P*}(x)]$ and is also finite. Since the objective function $\tilde{U}$ in (3.8) is continuous and the feasible set $D^C(x)$ is compact, the solution $(\ell^{C*}(x),r^{C*}(x))$ exists as well.

3.3. *Voluntary trades*

If for given values of the parameters m, w and y, the optimal trades that are derived as the solutions of the maximization problems (3.8) and (3.9) do not coincide, one of the sectors, or both of them, have to be rationed. Then extra constraints must be imposed to make the solutions of (3.8) and (3.9) equal.

In Subsection 1.4.1 it is mentioned that one of the conditions of a Non-Walrasian Equilibrium is "voluntariness". A trade is "voluntary" for a buyer, if he is neither forced to buy more than he wants, nor forced to sell. For a seller a similar definition holds.
We shall impose the condition of "voluntariness" on the trades that are candidates to be realized. Extra constraints will be added to the maximization problems (3.8) and (3.9). Next, it can be investigated which of the solutions of the new maximization problems are "voluntary trades". A definition will be given which is of specific use for our model.

Let $(\bar{\ell},\bar{r}) \in \bar{\mathbb{R}}^2_+$. The bar on $\mathbb{R}^2_+$ indicates that infinite values of $\bar{\ell}$ and $\bar{r}$ are allowed. If the scalar $\bar{\ell}$ is an extra upper bound on labour supply and $\bar{r}$ is an extra upper bound on goods demand, the maximization problem of the consumption sector becomes

$$(3.10) \qquad \max \{\tilde{U}(\ell,r;x) \mid (\ell,r) \in D^C(x),\ \ell \le \bar{\ell},\ r \le \bar{r}\} \qquad (x \in \mathbb{R}^3_{++}) .$$

Similarly, the maximization problem of the production sector becomes

$$(3.11) \qquad \max \{\tilde{V}(\ell,r;x) \mid (\ell,r) \in D^P(x),\ \ell \le \bar{\ell},\ r \le \bar{r}\} \qquad (x \in \mathbb{R}^3_{++}) .$$

The ("constrained") solutions of (3.10) and (3.11) are denoted, respectively, by

$$\bar{L}^C(\bar{\ell},\bar{r};x) \ , \quad \bar{R}^C(\bar{\ell},\bar{r};x) \ ,$$

$$\bar{L}^P(\bar{\ell},\bar{r};x) \ , \quad \bar{R}^P(\bar{\ell},\bar{r};x) \ .$$

These solutions are similar to those considered by Drèze and also called Drèze demands and supplies.
Clearly, the solution of (3.10) is independent of the initial inventory y and the solution of (3.11) is independent of initial real money holding m in the consumption sector.
If neither of the constraints $\ell \le \bar{\ell}$ and $r \le \bar{r}$ is strictly active (see Section 2.2), the solutions of (3.10) and (3.11) are the "notional solutions" of the preceding section. Hence

$$\bar{L}^C(\infty,\infty;x) = \ell^{C*}(x) \ ,$$

etc. By definition of $\bar{L}^C$ we have

$$\bar{L}^C(\bar{\ell},\bar{r};x) \le \min\,[\bar{\ell},\ell^{C*}(x)] \ .$$

Therefore, Remark 3.6 implies that $\bar{L}^C(\bar{\ell},\bar{r};x)$ is finite. In this way it can be shown that the solutions of (3.10) and (3.11) exist.

At this moment, the definitions of a "voluntary trade" and "voluntary trade correspondences" can be given.

DEFINITION 3.7. *The voluntary trade correspondence* $H^C: \mathbb{R}^3_{++} \rightrightarrows \mathbb{R}^2_+$ *of the consumption sector is defined by*

$$H^C(x) := \{(\ell,r) \in \mathbb{R}^2_+ \mid \exists(\bar{\ell},\bar{r}) \in \mathbb{R}^2_+: \ell = \bar{L}^C(\bar{\ell},\bar{r};x) \wedge r = \bar{R}^C(\bar{\ell},\bar{r};x)\} .$$

An element of $H^C(x)$ *is called a voluntary trade for the consumption sector.*

The voluntary trade correspondence $H^P: \mathbb{R}^3_{++} \rightrightarrows \mathbb{R}^2_+$ *of the production sector is defined by*

$$H^P(x) := \{(\ell,r) \in \mathbb{R}^2_+ \mid \exists(\bar{\ell},\bar{r}) \in \mathbb{R}^2_+: \ell = \bar{L}^P(\bar{\ell},\bar{r};x) \wedge r = \bar{R}^P(\bar{\ell},\bar{r};x)\} .$$

An element of $H^P(x)$ *is called a voluntary trade for the production sector.*

A trade is called voluntary for a sector, if it is the optimal solution of the maximization problem of that sector for some pair of upper bounds $(\bar{\ell},\bar{r}) \in \mathbb{R}^2_+$. Since lower bounds are not considered, nobody is forced to buy or sell more than he wishes. A (potential) buyer is not forced to become a seller or vice versa, since the solutions of (3.10) and (3.11) are elements of the nonnegative orthant.

As a consequence, Definition 3.7 is compatible with the definition of "voluntary" given in Section 1.4.

From the solutions of (3.10) and (3.11) the following functions can be derived.

DEFINITION 3.8. *The effective labour supply function* $L^C: \mathbb{R}_+ \times \mathbb{R}^3_+ \to \mathbb{R}_+$ *is defined by*

$$L^C(r;x) := \bar{L}^C(\infty,r;x) .$$

The effective goods demand function $R^C: \mathbb{R}_+ \times \mathbb{R}^3_{++} \to \mathbb{R}_+$ *is defined by*

$$R^C(\ell;x) := \bar{R}^C(\ell,\infty;x) .$$

The effective labour demand function $L^P: \mathbb{R}_+ \times \mathbb{R}^3_+ \to \mathbb{R}_+$ *is defined by*

$$L^P(r;x) := \bar{L}^P(\infty,r;x) .$$

The effective goods supply function $R^P: \mathbb{R}_+ \times \mathbb{R}^3_+ \to \mathbb{R}_+$ *is defined by*

$$R^P(\ell;x) := \bar{R}^P(\ell,\infty;x) .$$

A synonym for "effective" demand (supply) is "Clower" demand (supply) called after Clower (1965).

The functions of Definition 3.8 are considered to represent the demands and supplies that are actually expressed on the markets, instead of the "notional" demands and supplies.
The effective demands and supplies play a role in Keynesian theory. Keynes stated that, since the demand of workers is based on wage income, the employment rate of the economy is important for the demands on the markets of consumption goods. If unemployment is large, the expenditure of the workers is low (cf. the "dual decision hypothesis" in Clower, 1965, and also Section 1.4). If consumption is low, the producers will hire few workers, so that unemployment prevails. Likewise, a lack of consumption goods supply may cause a decrease of labour supply and the production of goods may be low as a consequence of a shortage of labour input.
In each of these situations markets are influenced by a deficiency on another market. The functions of Definition 3.8 have a variable, corresponding with the other market, as an argument.
The relation of the effective demand and supply with the constrained demand and supply appears in the following lemma.

LEMMA 3.9. *Under Assumptions* As 1 *and* As 2, *if* $x \in \mathbb{R}^3_{++}$, *for every* $(\bar{\ell},\bar{r}) \in \mathbb{R}^2_+$

$$\bar{L}^C(\bar{\ell},\bar{r};x) = \min[\bar{\ell},L^C(\bar{r};x)] ,$$

$$\bar{R}^C(\bar{\ell},\bar{r};x) = \min[\bar{r},R^C(\bar{\ell};x)] .$$

Hence, the constrained (Drèze) demand (supply) equals the effective (Clower) one, unless there is a "strictly active" constraint (see Section 2.2) on the market of the same good.
With Lemma 3.9 the set of voluntary trades of the consumption sector can be expressed in terms of effective demand and supply functions.

THEOREM 3.10. *Under Assumptions* As 1 *and* As 2, *if* $x \in \mathbb{R}^3_{++}$, *the set of voluntary trades*

$$H^C(x) := \{(\ell,r) \in \mathbb{R}^2_+ \mid \exists(\bar{\ell},\bar{r}) \in \mathbb{R}^2_+ : \ell = \bar{L}^C(\bar{\ell},\bar{r};x), r = \bar{R}^C(\bar{\ell},\bar{r};x)\}$$

is identical to the set

$$\tilde{H}^C(x) := \{(\ell,r) \in \mathbb{R}^2_+ \mid \ell \le L^C(r;x),\ r \le R^C(\ell;x)\} .$$

Theorem 3.10 implies that a voluntary trade is identical to an "acceptable trade" as defined by Gepts (1977).

In Figure 3.1 an illustration of Theorem 3.10 is given.

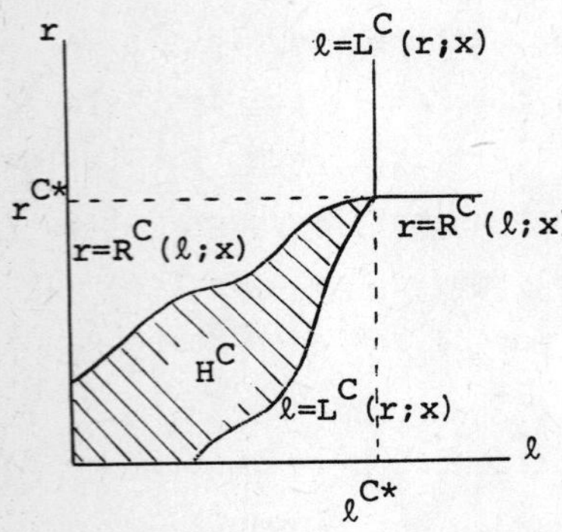

Figure 3.1.

Voluntary trades of the consumption sector.

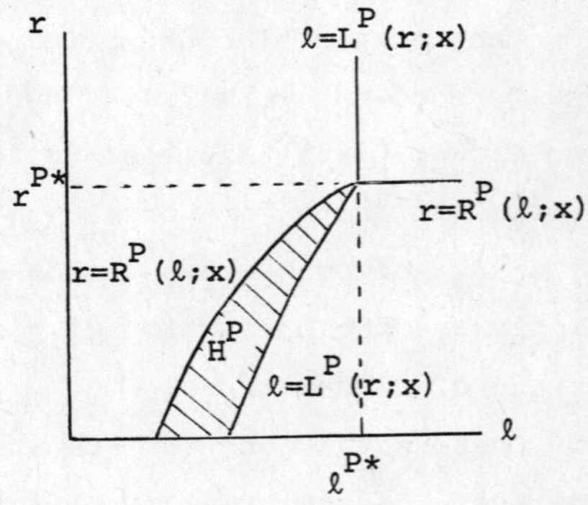

Figure 3.2.

Voluntary trades of the production sector.

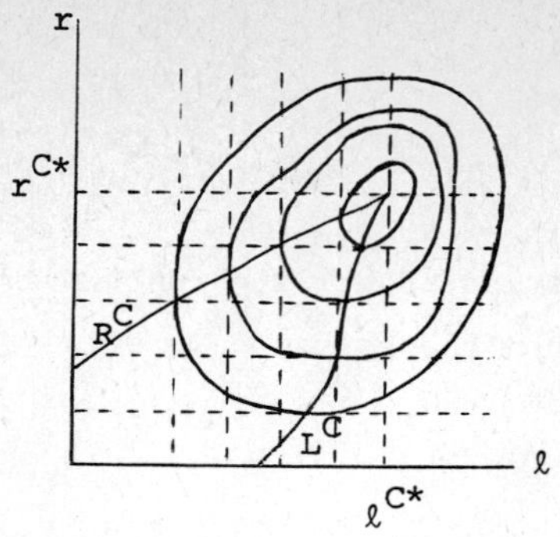

Figure 3.3.
Increasing effective demand and supply functions ($\tilde{U}_{r\ell} > 0$).

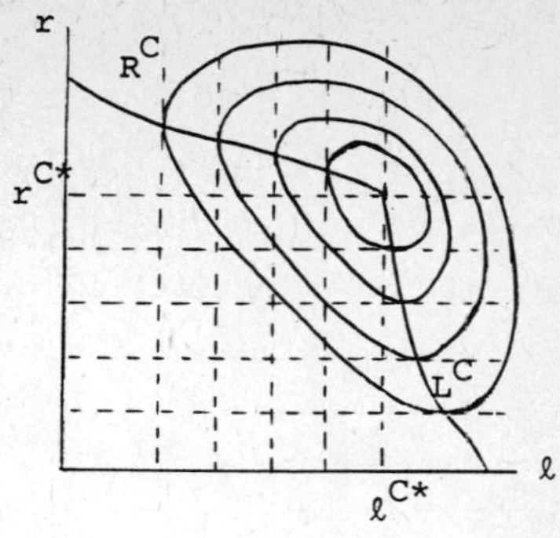

Figure 3.4.
Decreasing effective demand and supply functions ($\tilde{U}_{r\ell} < 0$).

Figures 3.1-3.3 are similar to figures in Böhm (1978) and Muellbauer and Portes (1978). In Figures 3.1 and 3.2 the "effective" functions defined in Definition 3.8 are represented. It should be noted that the arguments of the effective labour supply function L^C and the effective labour demand function L^P are on the vertical axis, while the function values are on the horizontal axis.
According to Theorem 3.10, a trade is voluntary for the consumption sector, if and only if the labour supply is smaller than the effective labour supply (given the goods demand) and the goods demand is smaller than the effective goods demand (given the labour supply).
In the Figures 3.3 and 3.4 it can be seen, how the effective demand and supply functions can be determined. For a labour volume $\bar{\ell} \in (0,\ell^{C*}(x))$ the effective demand $R^C(\bar{\ell};x)$ is the volume of r, where the line $\ell = \bar{\ell}$ is tangent to the contour curve of the restricted utility function $\tilde{U}$ defined in Definition 3.2.
The way to derive the effective demand and supply functions follows from the following corollary, which is straightforward from Lemma 3.9.

COROLLARY 3.11. *Under Assumptions* As 1 *and* As 2, *if* $x \in \mathbb{R}^3_{++}$ *and* $\bar{r} \in (0,r^{C*}(x))$, $L^C(\bar{r};x)$ *is the solution of*

$$\max_{\ell} \{\tilde{U}(\ell,\bar{r};x) \mid (\ell,\bar{r}) \in D^C(x)\} .$$

Analogously, if $\bar{\ell} \in (0,\ell^{C*}(x))$, $R^C(\bar{\ell};x)$ *is the solution of*

$$\max_r \{\tilde{U}(\bar{\ell},r;x) \mid (\bar{\ell},r) \in D^C(x)\} .$$

Remember the differentiability of the restricted utility function $\tilde{U}$ by Theorem 3.3. Hence, if $\bar{r} \in (0,r^{C*}(x))$, then the solution ℓ_0 of

$$\tilde{U}_\ell(\ell_0,\bar{r};x) = 0$$

can be considered, provided that $(\ell_0,\bar{r}) \in \text{int } D^C(x)$. Following Corollary 3.11 we then have

$$\ell_0 = L^C(\bar{r};x) .$$

A similar derivation can be given for the expression $R^C(\bar{\ell};x)$.

For the production sector, analogues can be formulated of Lemma 3.9, Theorem 3.10 and Corollary 3.11. These analogues can be proved in a similar way. The relation between Drèze and Clower demand and supply is given by:

LEMMA 3.12. *Under Assumptions* As 3-6, *if* $x \in \mathbb{R}^3_{++}$, *for any* $(\bar{\ell},\bar{r}) \in \mathbb{R}^2_+$

$$\bar{L}^P(\bar{\ell},\bar{r};x) := \min[\bar{\ell},L^P(\bar{r};x)] ,$$

$$\bar{R}^P(\bar{\ell},\bar{r};x) := \min[\bar{r},R^P(\bar{\ell};x)] .$$

Similar to Theorem 3.10 is the following theorem.

THEOREM 3.13. *Under Assumptions* As 3-6, *if* $x \in \mathbb{R}^3_{++}$, *the set of voluntary trades*

$$H^P(x) := \{(\ell,r) \in \mathbb{R}^2_+ \mid \exists(\bar{\ell},\bar{r}) \in \mathbb{R}^2_+ : \ell = \bar{L}^P(\bar{\ell},\bar{r};x) \wedge r = \bar{R}^P(\bar{\ell},\bar{r};x)$$

is identical to the set

$$H^P(x) := \{(\ell,r) \in \mathbb{R}^2_+ \mid \ell \le L^P(r;x) \wedge r \le R^P(\ell;x) .$$

In Figure 3.2 (see below Theorem 3.10) an illustration of Theorem 3.13 is given.

Finally, we have the analogue of Corollary 3.11.

COROLLARY 3.14. *Under Assumptions* As 3-6, *if* $x \in \mathbb{R}^3_{++}$, *for* $\bar{r} \in (0, r^{P*}(x))$, $L^P(\bar{r};x)$ *is equal to the solution of*

$$\max_{\ell} \{\tilde{V}(\ell,\bar{r};x) \mid (\ell,\bar{r}) \in D^P(x)\} .$$

Analogously, for $\bar{\ell} \in (0, \ell^{P*}(x)]$, $R^P(\bar{\ell};x)$ *equals the solution of*

$$\max_{r} \{\tilde{V}(\bar{\ell},r;x) \mid (\bar{\ell},r) \in D^P(x)\} .$$

It follows from Corollary 3.14 that the effective goods supply and labour demand functions can be derived from the restricted objective function $\tilde{V}$. Under $\ell_0 > 0$ and $F(\ell_0) > \bar{r} - y$, the effective labour demand $\ell_0 = L^P(\bar{r};x)$ is determined by the equality

$$\tilde{V}_\ell(\ell_0,\bar{r};x) = 0$$

(remember the function $\tilde{V}$ is differentiable by Theorem 3.5) and hence by

$$w - \underset{\sim}{Q}_q(y + F(\ell_0) - \bar{r}) \cdot F_\ell(\ell_0) = 0 .$$

The equality

$$\tilde{V}_r(\bar{\ell},r_0;x) = 0$$

yields

$$\underset{\sim}{Q}_q(y + F(\bar{\ell}) - r_0) = 1 .$$

The latter equality determines the *optimal inventory* y^* as well as the effective supply of goods $r_0 = R^P(\bar{\ell};x)$. The following relation holds:

$$(3.12) \qquad y^* = y + F(\bar{\ell}) - R^P(\bar{\ell};x) \; ,$$

cf. the inventory equation (3.5). Hence, the optimal inventory adds to the initial inventory the difference of production and effective goods supply.

Equality (3.12) and the definitions of ℓ^{P*}, r^{P*} and R^P imply

$$(3.13) \qquad y^* = y + F[\ell^{P*}(x)] - r^{P*}(x) .$$

Obviously, the optimal inventory level y^* is independent of the parameters m, w and y, as a consequence of the restrictiveness of Assumption As 4.

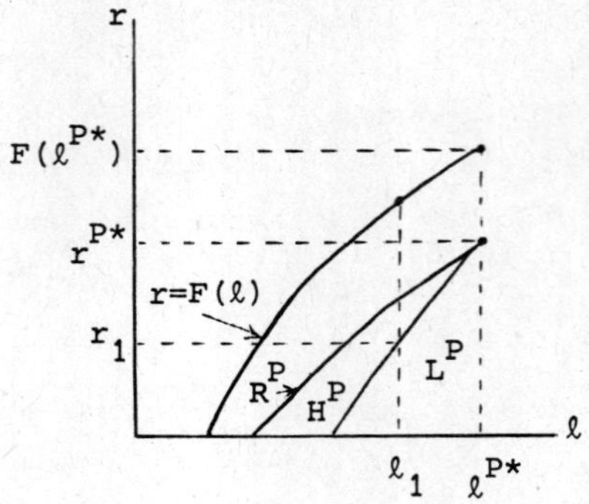

Figure 3.5.
Illustration of inventory change.

An illustration of the behaviour of the production sector with respect to the inventory is given in Figure 3.5. In the picture three curves are represented. The curves $r = R^P(\ell;x)$ and $\ell = L^P(r;x)$ limit the set of voluntary trades $H^P(x)$ of the production sector (see Theorem 3.13). The former represents the effective goods supply and the latter the effective labour demand. The third curve is given by $r = F(\ell)$ and corresponds with the production function. According to equality (3.12) the production function curve and the effective goods supply curve are vertically equidistant. The vertical distance is given by the difference $y^* - y$ of optimal and initial inventory. In the Figure the situation for $y^* > y$ is depicted. Clearly, for $y^* = y$ the relevant curves coincide. The case $y^* < y$ is left to the reader.
The valuation function of stock Q introduced in Assumption As 4 is responsible for the top angle of the "wedge" formed by the set $H^P(x)$. Two cases of inventory behaviour can be distinguished. In the point $(\ell,R^P(\ell_1;x))$ in Figure 3.5, where $\ell_1 < \ell^{P*}(x)$, the inventory change is ruled by

$$F(\ell_1) - R^P(\ell_1;x) = y^* - y ,$$

cf. (3.12). This point corresponds with a situation in which the production sector is unconstrained on the goods market. In the point (ℓ_1, r_1) with $\ell_1 = L^P(r_1;x)$, on the contrary, we have

$$F(\ell_1) - r_1 > y^* - y .$$

Now the production sector is constrained on the goods market and is bound to make an additional inventory.

If we consider the case of absent inventories in the production sector ($Q(q) \equiv 0$, $y = 0$), the set of voluntary trades $H^P(x)$ of the production sector degenerates to a part of a curve. In this case the functions L^P and R^P coincide with the production function for $\ell \in [0, \ell^{P*}(x)]$ and $r \in [0, r^{P*}(x)]$. A similar argument holds for the consumption sector, if the preference for money (in the utility function) disappears.

3.4. *Properties of demand and supply functions*

In the preceding sections, "notional" and "effective" demands and supplies have been introduced. The notional demands and supplies are functions of the parameters real initial money stock m, real wage rate w and initial inventory y. The effective demands and supplies are functions of these parameters and, in addition, of a constraint variable related with the other market. In this section it is investigated how the demand and supply functions depend on their arguments.

The values of the parameter vector $x = (m,w,y)'$ will be restricted to the sets defined by:

$$(3.14) \qquad X^C := \{x \in \mathbb{R}^3_{++} \mid \mathbb{R}^2_{++} \cap H^C(x) \subset \text{int } D^C(x)\} ,$$

$$(3.15) \qquad X^P := \{x \in \mathbb{R}^3_{++} \mid \mathbb{R}^2_{++} \cap H^P(x) \subset \text{int } D^P(x)\} ,$$

$$(3.16) \qquad X := \{x \in X^C \cap X^P \mid H^C(x) \cap H^P(x) \neq \emptyset\} .$$

The sets $H^C(x)$ and $H^P(x)$ in (3.14) - (3.16) are sets of voluntary trades (see Definition 3.7) for $x \in \mathbb{R}^3_{++}$. Also for $x \in \mathbb{R}^3_{++}$, the set $D^C(x)$ is the budget set of the consumption sector (cf. Definition 3.1) and $D^P(x)$ is the production set (cf. Assumption As 6). Thus the sets X^C, X^P and X are defined in such a way, that the positive voluntary

trades of the sectors are elements of (open) sets in which the corresponding objective functions $\tilde{U}$ and $\tilde{V}$ are continuously differentiable (see Theorems 3.3 and 3.5). The set X^C depends on the utility function U, as well as on the maximum labour supply ℓ_{max}. The set X^P depends on the production function F and the valuation function of stock Q. (Since, however, ℓ_{max}, U, F and Q are fixed, they are not denoted as arguments.)
The set X is defined in such a way, that for parameter values in X, trades exist that are voluntary for both sectors. This existence will be an important aspect in the following section, where we regard the interaction of the sectors.

The first theorem of this section concerns the notional and effective demand and supply functions of the consumption sector.

THEOREM 3.15. *Under Assumptions* As 1 *and* As 2

$$\ell^{C*} \mid X^C \in C'(X^C \to \mathbb{R}_+) \ ,$$

$$r^{C*} \mid X^C \in C'(X^C \to \mathbb{R}_+) \ .$$

The function L^C *is continuously differentiable in* x *on* X^C *and, if* $x \in X^C$*, in* r *on* $(0, r^{C*}(x)]$*, where we define*

$$(3.17) \qquad L^C_r(r^{C*}(x);x) := \lim_{\bar{r} \uparrow r^{C*}(x)} L^C_r(\bar{r};x) \ .$$

The function R^C *is continuously differentiable in* x *on* X^C *and, if* $x \in X^C$*, in* ℓ *on* $(0, \ell^{C*}(x)]$*, where we define*

$$(3.18) \qquad R^C_\ell(\ell^{C*}(x);x) := \lim_{\bar{\ell} \uparrow \ell^{C*}(x)} R^C_\ell(\bar{\ell};x) \ .$$

Furthermore, for $x \in X^C$

$$(3.19) \qquad \text{for } \bar{r} \in (0, r^{C*}(x)] : \ L^C_r(\bar{r};x) = -\frac{\tilde{U}_{\ell r}[L^C(\bar{r};x), \bar{r};x]}{\tilde{U}_{\ell\ell}[L^C(\bar{r};x), \bar{r};x]} \ ,$$

$$(3.20) \qquad \text{for } \bar{\ell} \in (0, \ell^{C*}(x)] : \ R^C_\ell(\bar{\ell};x) = -\frac{\tilde{U}_{r\ell}[\bar{\ell}, R^C(\bar{\ell};x);x]}{\tilde{U}_{rr}[\bar{\ell}, R^C(\bar{\ell};x);x]} \ .$$

The analogue of Theorem 3.15 for the production sector is:

THEOREM 3.16. *Under Assumptions* As 3-6,

$$\ell^{P*} \mid X^P \in C'(X^P \to \mathbb{R}_+)$$

$$r^{P*} \mid X^P \in C'(X^P \to \mathbb{R}_+) \ .$$

The function L^P *is continuously differentiable in* x *on* X^P *and, if* $x \in X^P$*, in* r *on* $(0, r^{P*}(x)]$*, where* $L^P_r(r^{P*}(x);x)$ *is defined similar to* (3.17)

The function R^P *is continuously differentiable in* x *on* X^P *and, if* $x \in X^P$*, in* ℓ *on* $(0, \ell^{P*}(x)]$*, where* $R^P_\ell(\ell^{P*}(x);x)$ *is defined similar to* (3.18)

Furthermore, if $x \in X^P$*:*

$$\text{for } \bar{r} \in (0, r^{P*}(x)] : \ L^P_r(\bar{r};x) = - \frac{\tilde{V}_{\ell r}[L^P(\bar{r};x), \bar{r};x]}{\tilde{V}_{\ell\ell}[L^P(\bar{r};x), \bar{r};x]} \ ,$$

$$\text{for } \bar{\ell} \in (0, \ell^{P*}(x)] : \ R^P_\ell(\bar{\ell};x) = - \frac{\tilde{V}_{r\ell}[\bar{\ell}, R^P(\bar{\ell};x);x]}{\tilde{V}_{rr}[\bar{\ell}, R^P(\bar{\ell};x);x]} = F_\ell(\bar{\ell}) \ .$$

Theorems 3.15 and 3.16 give differentiability properties of the functions introduced in the preceding section, both with respect to the variables ℓ and r and the parameters m, w and y. We shall first investigate when the effective demand and supply functions L^C, R^C, L^P and R^P are increasing in the variables ℓ and r, that correspond with the upper bounds in the other sector. In view of monotonicity of the function L^C in r and the function R^C in ℓ, we assume:

ASSUMPTION As 7.

For every $x \in X^C$ *and* $\bar{r} \in (0, r^{C*}(x)]$: $\tilde{U}_{\ell r}[L^C(\bar{r};x), \bar{r};x] > 0$.

For every $x \in X^C$ *and* $\bar{\ell} \in (0, \ell^{C*}(x)]$: $\tilde{U}_{r\ell}[\bar{\ell}, R^C(\bar{\ell};x);x] > 0$.

REMARK 3.17. Working out the differential $\tilde{U}_{\ell r}[\bar{\bar{\ell}}, \bar{r};x]$, where $\bar{\bar{\ell}} = L^C(\bar{r};x)$, yields

$$\tilde{U}_{\ell r}(\bar{\bar{\ell}},\bar{r};x) = U_{\ell r}(\bar{\bar{\ell}},\bar{r},z) - U_{\ell z}(\bar{\bar{\ell}},\bar{r},z) + w[U_{zr}(\bar{\bar{\ell}},\bar{r},z) - U_{zz}(\bar{\bar{\ell}},\bar{r},z)] .$$

With the help of Assumption As 7, it can be shown that the effective demand and supply functions L^C and R^C have the following monotonicity property (see also Figures 3.3 and 3.4).

THEOREM 3.18. *Under Assumptions* As 1, As 2 *and* As 7, *if* $x \in X^C$,
the function L^C *is increasing in* r *on* $(0,r^{C*}(x)]$,
the function R^C *is increasing in* ℓ *on* $(0,\ell^{C*}(x)]$.

The above result is assumed by Böhm instead of our Assumption As 7. For the production sector an analogue of Theorem 3.18 can be formulated, even without an additional assumption like Assumption As 7.

THEOREM 3.19. *Under Assumptions* As 3-6, *if* $x \in X^P$,
the function L^P *is increasing in* r *on* $(0,r^{P*}(x)]$,
the function R^P *is increasing in* ℓ *on* $(0,\ell^{P*}(x)]$.

The above theorem follows from Theorems 3.5 and 3.16.

For the production sector it can also be shown that the boundary of the set of voluntary trades $H^P(x)$, which corresponds with the function R^P, lies "above" the one corresponding with the function L^P. (The mutual locations of these two boundaries are, for instance, like the ones in Figure 3.2.) This property is a consequence of the following lemma.

LEMMA 3.20. *Under Assumptions* As 3-6, *if* $x \in X^P$,

$$\forall \bar{r} \in (0,r^{P*}(x)]: \; R^P_\ell[L^P(\bar{r};x);x] \cdot L^P_r(\bar{r};x) < 1 ,$$

$$\forall \bar{\ell} \in (0,\ell^{P*}(x)]: \; R^P_\ell(\bar{\ell};x) \cdot L^P_r[R^P_\ell(\bar{\ell};x);x] < 1 .$$

The rest of this section is devoted to the sensitivity analysis of the demand and supply functions for the parameters m, w and y. This sensitivity will be important in the next chapter. The relevant derivatives for the consumption sector can be expressed in terms of the bordered Hessian of the utility function U (see (3.4)). This way is followed by Veendorp (1975). However, the expressions in terms of the bordered

Hessian in our model are rather untransparant. Therefore we simply assume:

ASSUMPTION As 8.

For every $x \in X^C$: $\ell_m^{C*} < 0$, $\ell_w^{C*} > 0$, $r_m^{C*} > 0$, $r_w^{C*} > 0$;

for every $(r;x)$ *with* $x \in X^C$ *and* $r \in (0, r^{C*}(x)]$: $L_m^C < 0$, $L_w^C > 0$;

for every $(\ell;x)$ *with* $x \in X^C$ *and* $\ell \in (0, \ell^{C*}(x)]$: $R_m^C > 0$, $R_w^C > 0$.

If the real money stock m of the consumption sector increases, the labour supply decreases. An increase of the real wage rate w has an opposite effect. The demand for consumption goods goes up at an increase of m as well as an increase of w.
Assumption As 8 is compatible with Assumptions (C1) - (C2) in Böhm (1978).

An analogue of Assumption As 8 for the production sector is not necessary. The following property can be obtained.

THEOREM 3.21. *Let Assumptions* As 3-6 *hold. Evaluated at any* $x \in X^P$, *we have*

$$\ell_w^{P*} = 1/F_{\ell\ell}^* < 0\ ,\quad \ell_y^{P*} = 0\ ,\quad r_w^{P*} = w/F_{\ell\ell}^* < 0\ ,\quad r_y^{P*} = 1\ ,$$

where $F_{\ell\ell}^* := F_{\ell\ell}(\ell^{P*})$.
If $x \in X^P$ *and* $\bar{r} \in (0, r^{P*}(x)]$, *we have* $L_w^P(\bar{r};x) < 0$ *and* $L_y^P(\bar{r};x) = - L_r^P(\bar{r};x) < 0$.
If $x \in X^P$ *and* $\ell \in (0, \ell^{P*}(x)]$, *we have* $R_w^P(\ell;x) = 0$ *and* $R_y^P(\ell;x) = 0$.

We end this section with some special relations concerning the effective demand and supply functions, which hold if the derivatives are evaluated at the notional solutions (cf. Veendorp, 1975, relations C_A' and C_A''). In these relations Definitions (3.17) etc., are important.

THEOREM 3.22. *Let Assumptions* As 1 *and* As 2 *hold and* $x \in X^C$. *The following equalities are valid for the consumption sector, where the derivatives of* ℓ^{C*} *and* r^{C*} *are evaluated at* x *and those of* L^C *and* R^C*, respectively, at* $(r^{C*}(x);x)$ *and* $(\ell^{C*}(x);x)$*:*

$$L^C_m = \ell^{C*}_m - L^C_r \, r^{C*}_m \;,$$

$$L^C_w = \ell^{C*}_w - L^C_r \, r^{C*}_w \;,$$

$$R^C_m = r^{C*}_m - R^C_\ell \, \ell^{C*}_m \;,$$

$$R^C_w = r^{C*}_w - R^C_\ell \, \ell^{C*}_w \;.$$

THEOREM 3.23. *Let Assumptions* As 3-6 *hold and* $x \in X^P$. *The following equalities are valid for the production sector, where the derivatives of* ℓ^{P*} *and* r^{P*} *are evaluated at* x *and those of* L^P *and* R^P*, respectively, at* $(r^{P*}(x);x)$ *and* $(\ell^{P*}(x);x)$*:*

$$L^P_y = \ell^{P*}_y - L^P_r \, r^{P*}_y \;,$$

$$L^P_w = \ell^{P*}_w - L^P_r \, r^{P*}_w \;,$$

$$R^P_y = r^{P*}_y - R^P_\ell \, \ell^{P*}_y \;,$$

$$R^P_w = r^{P*}_w - R^P_\ell \, \ell^{P*}_w \;.$$

Furthermore, if $F^*_{\ell\ell} := F_{\ell\ell}(\ell^{P*})$, $Q^*_{qq} := Q_{qq}(y^*)$ *and* $x = (m, w_0, y)$

$$L^P_w = [Q^*_{qq} \, w_0^2 + F^*_{\ell\ell}]^{-1} < 0 \;,$$

$$L^P_r = - L^P_y = Q^*_{qq} \, w_0 [Q^*_{qq} \, w_0^2 + F^*_{\ell\ell}]^{-1} > 0 \;.$$

REMARK 3.24. The results of Theorems 3.22 and 3.23 can be expressed in terms of matrices. For instance,

$$\begin{pmatrix} R^C_m & R^C_w \\ L^C_m & L^C_w \end{pmatrix} = \begin{pmatrix} 1 & -R^C_\ell \\ -L^C_r & 1 \end{pmatrix} \begin{pmatrix} r^{C*}_m & r^{C*}_w \\ \ell^{C*}_m & \ell^{C*}_w \end{pmatrix} .$$

3.5. *Non-Walrasian Equilibrium states*

3.5.1. Definition and several types of Non-Walrasian Equilibrium states

The preceding sections were an investigation of the maximization problems of the sectors separately and the effective demand and supply functions that can be derived. Now, attention must be given to the trade, which is a result of the interaction between the sectors.
As mentioned in Subsection 1.4.1, a Non-Walrasian Equilibrium satisfies certain conditions. First, the corresponding trade has to be optimal for the agents within the constrained budget/production sets. Second, at most one side is rationed (the "long" side). Finally, the trade must be "voluntary".
The concept of "voluntary trade" is elaborated already and a specific definition is given for our model. In this section the conditions of "optimality" and "long side rationed only" are considered and a specific definition of a Non-Walrasian Equilibrium (state) is given.

A trade is considered to be *optimal* for a sector, if it is the solution of the maximization problem of the sector under the given quantity constraints. Hence, a condition that has to be imposed on the quantity constraints, perceived by the sectors, is that they generate the same solution for both maximization problems (3.10) and (3.11).
The concept of "optimality" is closely related to "voluntary" from Section 3.3. An optimal trade is also voluntary. Since we look for a trade which is optimal for both sectors, this trade must be an element of the intersection of the sets of voluntary trades for the given parameters.
The consumption sector is a demander of goods and a supplier of labour and the opposite holds for the production sector. If the two sectors were restricted on the same market, they could realize a trade which were better for both, if the demander would demand more and the supplier would supply more. For a Non-Walrasian Equilibrium it is required, that at most one of the sectors is rationed on each of the markets. This condition is called "*rationing on the long side only*", where the "long side" stands for the maximum of unequal demand and supply. This condition is a further restriction of the admissible rationing schemes.

The phenomenon "rationed on a market" can be described by a "strictly active" constraint (see Section 2.2). On both markets at least one of the sectors does not meet a strictly active constraint.

The above reflections lead us to the following definition.

DEFINITION 3.25. *A* *<u>Non-Walrasian Equilibrium state</u>* *<u>(NWE-state)</u>* *is a sequence* $\{x,(\hat{\ell},\hat{r}),(\bar{\ell}^C,\bar{r}^C),(\bar{\ell}^P,\bar{r}^P)\} \in \mathbb{R}^3_{++} \times \mathbb{R}^2_+ \times \bar{\mathbb{R}}^2_+ \times \bar{\mathbb{R}}^2_+$, *which satisfies*

1) $(\hat{\ell},\hat{r}) = (\bar{L}^C(\bar{\ell}^C,\bar{r}^C;x),\bar{R}^C(\bar{\ell}^C,\bar{r}^C;x)) = (\bar{L}^P(\bar{\ell}^P,\bar{r}^P;x),\bar{R}^P(\bar{\ell}^P,\bar{r}^P;x))$;

2) *at least one of the constraints* $\ell \le \bar{\ell}^C$ *and* $\ell \le \bar{\ell}^P$ *and at least one of the constraints* $r \le \bar{r}^C$ *and* $r \le \bar{r}^P$ *is not strictly active.*

The trade $(\hat{\ell},\hat{r})$ *of the sequence is called a* *<u>transaction</u>.*

The suffix "state" is used to avoid confusion with the concept of an "equilibrium" of a differential system.

There are nine types of NWE-states. Following the names given by Malinvaud (1977) and Muellbauer and Portes (1978), these states can be characterized as in Table 3.1 below. (In this table the argument x, which is the triple of parameters, is omitted).

TABLE 3.1. The types of NWE-states.

	$\hat{\ell}=\bar{\ell}^C=L^P(\bar{r}^P) < \ell^{C*}$ $\bar{\ell}^P \ge L^P(\bar{r}^P)$	$\bar{\ell}^C \ge L^C(\bar{r}^C)=\hat{\ell}$ $\bar{\ell}^P \ge L^P(\bar{r}^P)=\hat{\ell}$	$\bar{\ell}^C \ge L^C(\bar{r}^C)$ $\hat{\ell}=\bar{\ell}^P=L^C(\bar{r}^C) < \ell^{P*}$
$\hat{r}=\bar{r}^C=R^P(\bar{\ell}^P) < r^{C*}$ $\bar{r}^P \ge R^P(\bar{\ell}^P)$	Classical (unemployment) state	Classical/ inflation state	(Repressed) inflation state
$\bar{r}^C \ge R^C(\bar{\ell}^C)=\hat{r}$ $\bar{r}^P \ge R^P(\bar{\ell}^P)=\hat{r}$	Keynesian/ classical state	Walras Equilibrium state	inflation/ underconsumption state
$\bar{r}^C \ge R^C(\bar{\ell}^C)$ $\hat{r}=\bar{r}^P=R^C(\bar{\ell}^C) < r^{P*}$	Keynesian (unemployment) state	underconsumption/ Keynesian state	underconsumption state

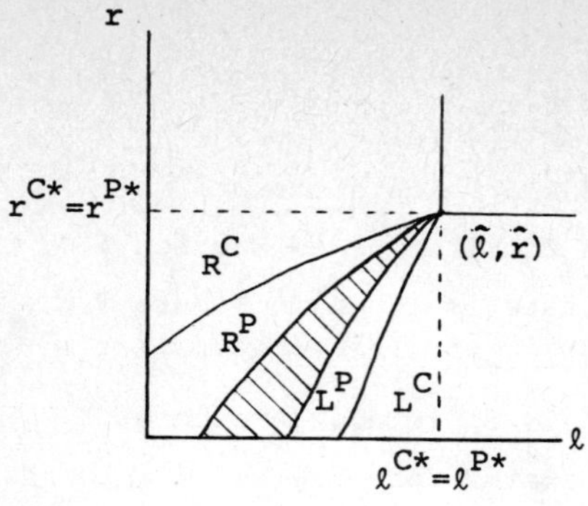

Figure 3.6.

Walras equilibrium.

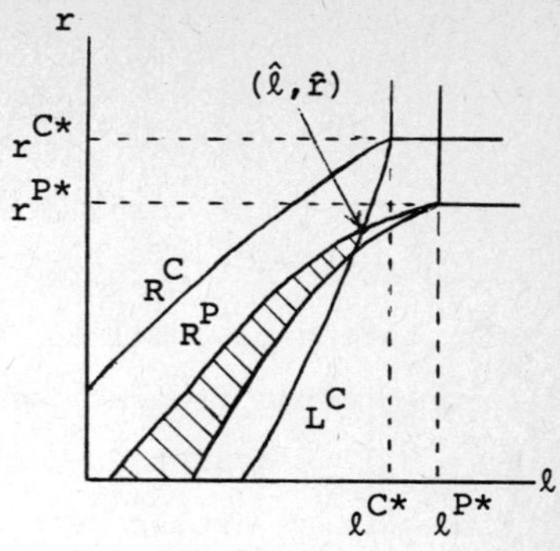

Figure 3.7.

Repressed Inflation.

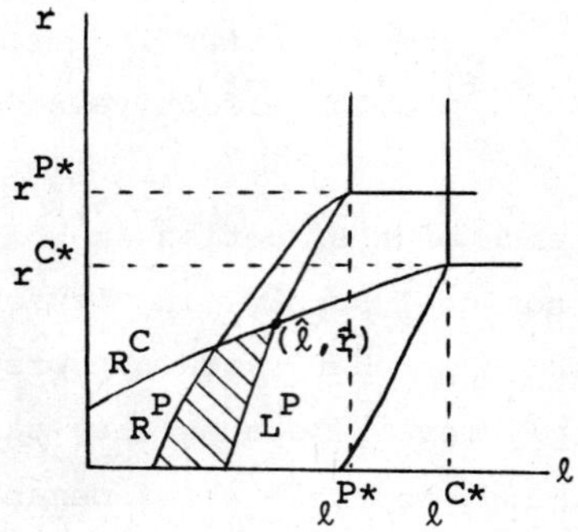

Figure 3.8.

Keynesian Unemployment.

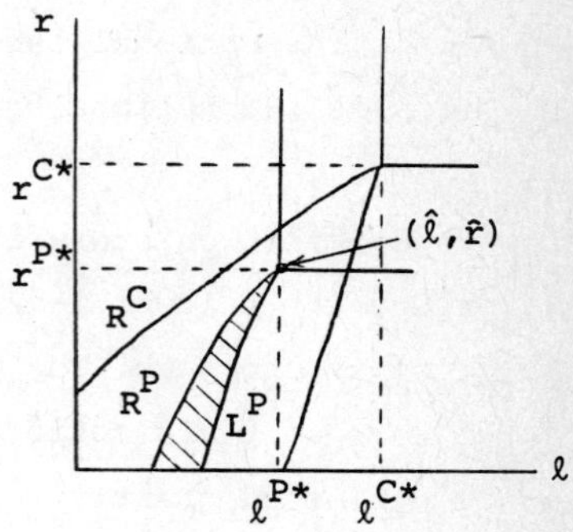

Figure 3.9.

Classical Unemployment.

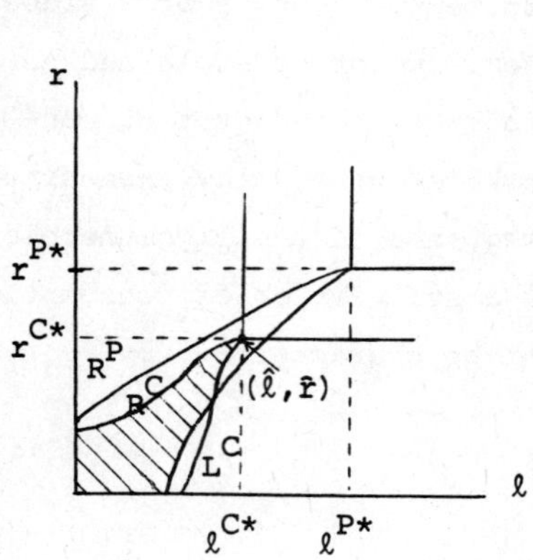

Figure 3.10.

Underconsumption.

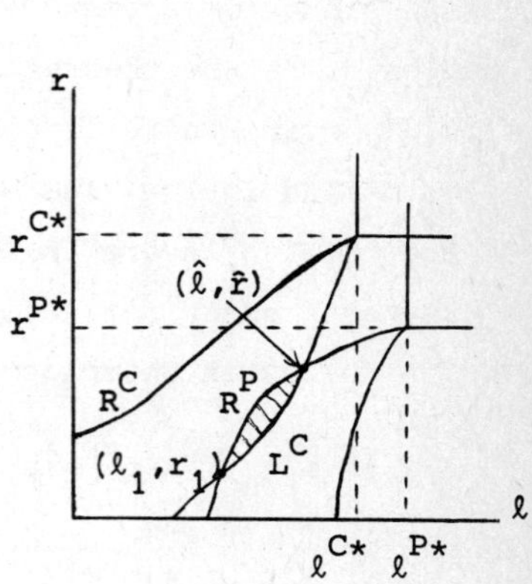

Figure 3.11.

Two transactions.

A *Walras Equilibrium state* is an NWE-state with no rationing. The transaction equals both notional solutions of the two sectors, i.e., it is the solution of both maximization problems (3.8) and (3.9) simultaneously. This formulation of a Walras Equilibrium state is compatible with the definition of a Walras Equilibrium in Section 1.3. A representation of a Walras Equilibrium state is given in Figure 3.6, where $(\hat{\ell},\hat{r})$ is the transaction.

In Figure 3.7 a *Repressed inflation state* is depicted. In such a state there is an excess demand on both markets. Formally,

$$\bar{\ell}^{P} = \hat{\ell}(x) = L^{C}[\hat{r}(x);x] < \ell^{P*}(x) ,$$

$$\bar{r}^{C} = \hat{r}(x) = R^{P}[\hat{\ell}(x);x] < r^{C*}(x) ,$$

where ℓ^{P*} is the notional labour demand, L^{C} is the effective labour supply, r^{C*} is the notional goods demand and R^{P} is the effective goods supply.

A Repressed inflation state is the consequence of a situation in which firms produce at a lower level than their notional supply, in view of a labour input shortage. The workers, on the other hand, are not prepared to work at their notional labour supply level, because they can buy only a limited quantity of goods. According to the "law of demand and supply", excess demands lead to price increases. As long as the prices are fixed, such increases are repressed, which explains the name.

In a *Keynesian unemployment state* (see Figure 3.8) both supply sides are rationed. In the theory of Keynes, unemployment is explained as follows. The firms hire little labour because of the fact that consumption demand is low. The consumers (workers) have a low expenditure, since their total income is low as a consequence of the high unemployment. Keynes' remedy for unemployment was a stimulation of consumption demand. A Keynesian Unemployment state can be characterized by

$$\bar{\ell}^{C} = \hat{\ell}(x) = L^{P}[\hat{r}(x);x] < \ell^{C*}(x)$$

$$\bar{r}^{P} = \hat{r}(x) = R^{C}[\hat{\ell}(x);x] < r^{P*}(x) .$$

Classical unemployment is the context in which the Classical economists used to place unemployment. The cause of this unemployment is much different from the Keynesian explanation. The producers choose for a relatively small production in view of the high real wage costs that make labour input expensive. Therefore the Classical economists emphasized the necessity of wage decreases.

In a Classical unemployment state (see Figure 3.9) the production sector reaches its notional solution and the consumption sector is rationed on both markets.

Underconsumption (see Figure 3.10) is the counterpart of Classical unemployment, i.e., the consumption sector is satisfied and the production sector is rationed on both markets.

In Figures 3.6 - 3.10, the intersection of the sets of voluntary trades is indicated by the shaded areas. It can be observed that a transaction is always an intersection of an "effective goods curve" and an "effective labour curve". For instance, for a Keynesian NWE-state $(x,(\hat{\ell},\hat{r}),(\bar{\ell}^C,\infty),(\infty,\bar{r}^P))$ the following equations hold:

$$(\hat{\ell},\hat{r}) = (\bar{L}^C(\bar{\ell}^C,\infty;x),\bar{R}^C(\bar{\ell}^C,\infty;x)) = (\bar{L}^P(\infty,\bar{r}^P;x),\bar{R}^P(\infty,\bar{r}^P;x)) \ ,$$

which can be reduced to

$$(\hat{\ell},\hat{r}) = (\bar{\ell}^C,R^C(\bar{\ell}^C;x)) = (L^P(\bar{r}^P;x),\bar{r}^P) \ .$$

3.5.2. Existence and uniqueness results

NWE-states depend on the parameters initial money stock m, real wage rate w and initial inventory y. Therefore, transactions are dependent of these three variables as well. A relevant question is whether NWE-states exist and are unique for a given triple $x = (m,w,y)'$.

The existence of NWE-states and transactions is warranted, if the intersection of the sets of voluntary trades $H^C(x)$ and $H^P(x)$ for the given $x \in \mathbb{R}^3_{++}$ is nonempty. A sufficient condition for existence is $x \in X$, where the set X is defined by (3.16).

However, the above condition does not imply uniqueness of NWE-states. In Figure 3.11 an example is given of two transactions for a given triple of parameters. The pairs (ℓ_1,r_1) and $(\hat{\ell},\hat{r})$ are both transactions related with a Repressed inflation state.

With respect to uniqueness, the following assumption is made (cf. Böhm, 1978, Assumption (A), (ii) and (iii)).

ASSUMPTION As 9. *For all* $x \in X$ *and* $\bar{\ell} \in (0, \ell^{P*}(x)]: -\tilde{U}_{r\ell}/\tilde{U}_{rr} < F_{\ell}(\bar{\ell})$, *where the derivatives of* $\tilde{U}$ *are evaluated at* $(\bar{\ell}, R^C(\bar{\ell};x);x)$.
For all $x \in X$ *and* $\bar{r} \in (0, r^{P*}(x)]: \tilde{U}_{\ell r}/\tilde{U}_{\ell\ell} > \tilde{V}_{\ell r}/\tilde{V}_{\ell\ell}$, *where the derivatives of* $\tilde{U}$ *are evaluated at* $(L^C(\bar{r};x), \bar{r};x)$ *and those of* $\tilde{V}$ *at* $(L^P(\bar{r};x), \bar{r};x)$.

In view of Theorems 3.15 and 3.16, Assumption As 9 states that the effective demand and supply functions of the production sector with respect to the constraints on the other markets are steeper than the ones of the consumption sector.
As a consequence of Assumption As 9, the following theorem can be obtained, which is proved by Böhm, 1978, Theorem 1.

THEOREM 3.26. *Under Assumptions* As 1-9, *there is a unique NWE-state for every* $x \in X$ *and the set* X *of parameters can be subdivided in disjoint sets, that cover* X *and are defined as follows: The set* WE *is the set of triples that have a Walrasian Equilibrium state as the corresponding NWE-state. Similarly, the following sets are defined:*

C *corresponds with a Classical state,*
I *with an Inflation state,*
U *with an Underconsumption state,*
K *with a Keynesian state,*
CI *with a Classical/Inflation state,*
IU *with an Inflation/Underconsumption state,*
UK *with an Underconsumption/Classical state,*
KC *with a Keynesian/Classical state.*

It is important to notice that Theorem 3.26 implies not only the unicity of a transaction, but also the unequivocal determination of the strictly active constraints (see Section 2.2) for any $x \in X$. In other words, there is a one-to-one relation between parameters and NWE-states.
As a consequence of the restriction to elements of the set X, the differentiability properties of Theorems 3.15 and 3.16 hold for every x in the sets defined in Theorem 3.26.
A direct consequence of the definitions of the sets in Theorem 3.26 is the following.

THEOREM 3.27. *Under Assumptions* As 1-9,

$$X \cap \text{cl } C = C \cup CI \cup KC \cup WE$$

$$X \cap \text{cl } I = I \cup CI \cup IU \cup WE$$

$$X \cap \text{cl } U = U \cup UK \cup IU \cup WE$$

$$X \cap \text{cl } K = K \cup UK \cup KC \cup WE$$

$$\text{cl } I \cap \text{cl } K = WE$$

$$\text{cl } C \cap \text{cl } U = WE \ .$$

The above theorem is an elaboration of the relations among the sets introduced in Theorem 3.26 and the way in which the set X from (3.16) is subdivided. This topic will be analyzed further in Section 3.6.

In addition to Theorem 3.26, we can prove the following existence and uniqueness theorem for Walras Equilibrium states.

THEOREM 3.28. *Let Assumptions* As 1-9 *hold.*
For every y *there is at most one pair* (m,w)*, such that* $(m,w,y)' \in WE$*,*
for every w *there is at most one pair* (m,y)*, such that* $(m,w,y)' \in WE$*,*
for every m *there is at most one pair* (w,y)*, such that* $(m,w,y)' \in WE$*.*

PROOF. Let y be fixed on the value y_0. Define the functions $\Phi^{\ell}: \mathbb{R}^2_+ \to \mathbb{R}$ and $\Phi^{r}: \mathbb{R}^2_+ \to \mathbb{R}$ by

$$\Phi^{\ell}(m,w) := \ell^{C*}(m,w,y_0) - \ell^{P*}(m,w,y_0) \ ,$$

$$\Phi^{r}(m,w) := r^{C*}(m,w,y_0) - r^{P*}(m,w,y_0) \ .$$

The definition of the set WE (see Theorem 3.26) implies, for $x_0 = (m_0,w_0,y_0)'$,

$$(m_0,w_0,y_0)' \in WE \iff \Phi^{\ell}(m_0,w_0) = \Phi^{r}(m_0,w_0) = 0$$

and $x_0 \in X^C$ and $x_0 \in X^P$.
For $x_0 \in X^C$ the derivatives $\ell^{C*}(x_0)$, etc., exist (see Theorem 3.15). Analogously, $x_0 \in X^P$ implies the existence of the derivatives $\ell^{P*}(x_0)$, etc. (see Theorem 3.16).

Let the functions w^ℓ and w^r be implicitly defined by

$$\Phi^\ell[m,w^\ell(m)] = 0 \ , \quad \Phi^r[m,w^r(m)] = 0$$

and consider the derivatives $\frac{dw^\ell}{dm}$ and $\frac{dw^r}{dm}$. With the aid of the implicit function theorem (Theorem 2.2), it can be found that the first derivative is

$$\frac{dw^\ell}{dm} = - \frac{\ell_m^{C*}}{\ell_w^{C*} - \ell_w^{P*}} ,$$

which is positive (cf. Assumption As 8 and Theorem 3.21), and the second derivative is

$$\frac{dw^r}{dm} = - \frac{r_m^{C*}}{r_w^{C*} - r_w^{P*}} ,$$

which is negative.
Therefore, at most one pair (m,w) can exist for which $\Phi^\ell(m,w) = \Phi^r(m,w) = 0$ holds. The other two assertions can be proved in a similar way. □

Theorem 3.28 states that a plane perpendicular to one of the axes contains at most one Walras Equilibrium. This result is also important for the locations of the different sets in the parameter space (see Section 3.6).

3.5.3. Differentiability of transactions with respect to the parameters

It can be concluded from Theorem 3.26 that the transaction is a function of the vector x of parameters. In this subsection we investigate differentiability properties of this function. For that purpose the following lemma is useful. It is a consequence of Assumption As 9 and Lemma 3.19.

LEMMA 3.29. *Under Assumptions* As 1-6 *and* As 9, *the functions* χ_I: $X \cap \text{cl}\, I \to \mathbb{R}$ *and* χ_K: $X \cap \text{cl}\, K \to \mathbb{R}$, *defined by*

$$\chi_I(x) := 1 - L_r^C[\hat{r}(x);x] \cdot F_\ell[\hat{\ell}(x)] \;,$$

$$\chi_K(x) := 1 - L_r^P[\hat{r}(x);x] \cdot R_\ell^C[\hat{\ell}(x);x]$$

where $(\hat{\ell},\hat{r})$ *is the transaction, have positive values.*

The value of $\chi_I(x)$ corresponds with the difference of the slopes of the functions that determine the Inflation transaction $(\hat{\ell}(x),\hat{r}(x))$. A zero value of χ_I is related with coinciding tangents to the graphs of these functions. The value of χ_K has a similar interpretation.

In the main theorem of this subsection it is proved that the transaction, under the "uniqueness assumption" As 9, is a continuously differentiable function of the parameter vector $x = (m,w,y)'$ on subsets of the set X. Since these subsets are non-open, Definition 2.7 of continuous differentiability is used. The derivatives of the transaction $(\hat{\ell},\hat{r})$ with respect to the parameters m, w and y on the common boundaries of these subsets are defined with the aid of the functions R^{C*}, L^C, etc., which are differentiable in x on the whole set X (see Theorems 3.15 and 3.16). Furthermore, the transaction is a continuous function of x on the whole set X.

THEOREM 3.30. *Under Assumptions* As 1-9, *for the transaction* $(\hat{\ell},\hat{r})$ *the following relations hold:*

$$\hat{\ell} \in C(X \to \mathbb{R}_+) \;, \quad \hat{r} \in C(X \to \mathbb{R}_+) \;,$$

$$\hat{\ell} \,|\, (X \cap \text{cl}\, Z) \in C'(X \cap \text{cl}\, Z \to \mathbb{R}_+) \;,$$

$$\hat{r} \,|\, (X \cap \text{cl}\, Z) \in C'(X \cap \text{cl}\, Z \to \mathbb{R}_+) \;,$$

for $Z = C, I, U, K$.

For $x \in X \cap \text{cl}\, I$:

$$\hat{\ell}_m = L^C_m / \chi_I < 0 ,$$

$$\hat{\ell}_w = L^C_w / \chi_I > 0 ,$$

$$\hat{\ell}_y = L^C_r / \chi_I > 0 ,$$

$$\hat{r}_m = L^C_m F_\ell / \chi_I < 0 ,$$

$$\hat{r}_w = L^C_w F_\ell / \chi_I > 0 ,$$

$$\hat{r}_y = 1 / \chi_I > 0 ,$$

where χ_I *is defined as in Lemma* 3.29, *the derivatives of* $\hat{\ell}$ *and* $\hat{r}$ *are evaluated at* x, *the derivatives of* L^C *at* $[\hat{r}(x);x]$ *and those of* F *at* $\hat{\ell}(x)$.

For $x \in X \cap \text{cl } K$:

$$\hat{\ell}_m = L^P_r \cdot R^C_m / \chi_K > 0 ,$$

$$\hat{\ell}_w = (L^P_r \cdot R^C_w + L^P_w) / \chi_K ,$$

$$\hat{\ell}_y = L^P_y / \chi_K < 0 ,$$

$$\hat{r}_m = R^C_m / \chi_K > 0 ,$$

$$\hat{r}_w = (L^P_w \cdot R^C_\ell + R^C_w) / \chi_K ,$$

$$\hat{r}_y = L^P_y \cdot R^C_\ell / \chi_K < 0 ,$$

where χ_K *is defined as in Lemma* 3.29, *the derivatives of* $\hat{\ell}$ *and* $\hat{r}$ *are evaluated at* x, *the derivatives of* R^C *at* $[\hat{\ell}(x);x]$ *and those of* L^P *at* $[\hat{r}(x);x]$.

PROOF. The transactions can be subdivided, in the sense of Theorem 3.26, in Classical transactions, etc.

For $x \in \text{cl } C$:

$$\hat{\ell}(x) = \ell^{P*}(x) \wedge \hat{r}(x) = r^{P*}(x) .$$

For $x \in \text{cl}\ \mathcal{I}$:

$$\hat{\ell}(x) = L^C[\hat{r}(x);x] ,$$

$$r(x) = R^P[\hat{\ell}(x);x] .$$

For $x \in \text{cl}\ \mathcal{U}$:

$$\hat{\ell}(x) = \ell^{C*}(x) \wedge \hat{r}(x) = r^{C*}(x) .$$

For $x \in \text{cl}\ \mathcal{K}$:

$$\hat{\ell}(x) = L^P[\hat{r}(x);x] ,$$

$$\hat{r}(x) = R^C[\hat{\ell}(x);x] .$$

Specifications on the boundaries are compatible and lead to a single value of $(\hat{\ell},\hat{r})$ as a function of x. Continuity of this function on $\mathcal{X}$ follows from continuity of the functions ℓ^{P*}, etc., on the corresponding sets (see Theorems 3.15 and 3.16). Together, this gives the continuity of $\hat{\ell}$ and $\hat{r}$ as functions of x.

Continuous differentiability follows from the above specifications and continuous differentiability of the functions ℓ^{P*}, L^C, etc. (see Theorems 3.15 and 3.16).

For $x \in \mathcal{X} \cap \text{cl}\ \mathcal{I}$, for example, the value of $\hat{\ell}$ can be determined by solving

$$H(\hat{\ell},m) = 0$$

where

$$H(\hat{\ell},m) := \hat{\ell} - L^C[R^P(\hat{\ell};x);x] .$$

With the help of the implicit function theorem (Theorem 2.2), the derivative $\hat{\ell}_m$ can be found:

$$\hat{\ell}_m = - H_m / H_{\hat{\ell}} = L^C_m / \chi_I ,$$

where χ_I is positive by Lemma 3.29.

Each of the other derivatives can be found in a similar way. The signs are a result of Assumption As 8 and Theorems 3.17-19. □

REMARK 3.31. For $x \in \mathcal{X} \cap \text{cl}\ \mathcal{U}$ the signs of the derivatives $\hat{\ell}_m$ etc., follow from Assumption As 8. For $x \in \mathcal{X} \cap \text{cl}\ \mathcal{C}$ these signs are given by Theorem 3.21.

3.6. *Locations in the parameter space*

We shall regard the locations of the sets KC, CI, IU and UK in (m,w,y)-space when, successively, the parameter y is fixed at a level y_0, w at w_0 and m at m_0. It will be assumed that Assumptions As 1-9 hold.
Let y be fixed at the level y_0. Then the set KC is determined by the equation

$$R^C[\ell^{P*}(x);m,w,y_0] = F[\ell^{P*}(x)] + y_0 - y^* \qquad (x \in X)$$

where $x = (m,w,y_0)'$.
It can be noted that the notional labour demand is independent of the parameters y (see Theorem 3.21) and m. Furthermore, the effective goods demand R^C does not depend on the inventory y.
Let $w^{KC}(m)$ be defined in such a way that $(m,w^{KC}(m),y_0) \in KC$. Then we can write, omitting all irrelevant arguments,

$$R^C[\ell^{P*}[w^{KC}(m)];m,w^{KC}(m)] - F(\ell^{P*}[w^{KC}(m)]) - y_0 + y^* = 0 \qquad (x \in X) .$$

By the implicit function theorem (Theorem 2.2) the following equality can be found for $x \in X$ with $x_3 = y_0$,

$$w_m^{KC} = - R_m^C \cdot [R_w^C + \ell_w^{P*} \; (R_\ell^C - F_\ell)]^{-1}$$

where R_m^C is evaluated at $[\ell^{P*}(x);x]$, etc.
It follows from Assumptions As 8 and As 9 and Theorem 3.21 that the derivative w_m^{KC} is negative.
In analogous terms the slopes of the curves corresponding with the intersections of the sets CI, IU and UK with the plane $y = y_0$ can be determined. Thus we find

$$w_m^{CI} = - L_m^C \cdot [L_w^C - \ell_w^{P*} \cdot \chi_I]^{-1}$$

where χ_I is defined as in Lemma 3.29. Assumption As 8, Lemma 3.29 and Theorem 3.21 imply that the derivative w_m^{CI} is positive.

$$w_m^{IU} = (r_m^{C*} - F_\ell \cdot \ell_m^{C*}) \cdot (F_\ell \cdot \ell_w^{C*} - r_w^{C*})^{-1} .$$

The term $r_m^{C*} - F_\ell \cdot \ell_m^{C*}$ is positive, but the sign of w_m^{IU} is indefinite.

$$w_m^{UK} = (\ell_m^{C*} - L_r^P \cdot r_m^{C*}) \cdot (L_r^P \cdot r_w^{C*} + L_w^P - \ell_w^{C*})^{-1} \ .$$

Now, the term $L_r^P \cdot r_w^{C*} + L_w^P - \ell_w^{C*}$ is negative.
Figure 3.12 is a representation of the relevant sets in the plane $y = y_0$.

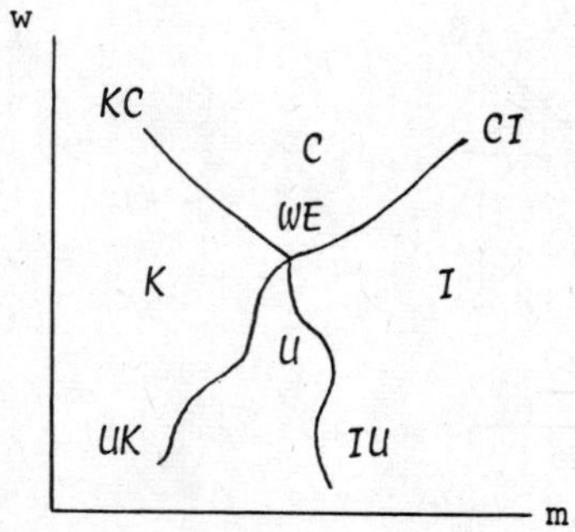

Figure 3.12.
Situation of the regimes for $y = y_0$

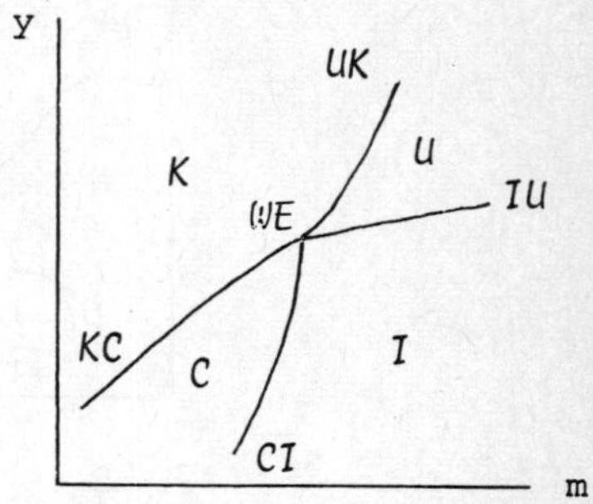

Figure 3.13.
Situation of the regimes for $w = w_0$.

Similar results can be derived for the plane $w = w_0$ (see Figure 3.13):

$$y_m^{KC} = R_m^C > 0 \ ,$$

$$y_m^{CI} = - L_m^C / L_r^C > 0 \ ,$$

$$y_m^{IU} = r_m^{C*} - F_\ell \cdot \ell_m^{C*} > 0 \ ,$$

$$y_m^{UK} = (\ell_m^{C*} - L_r^P \cdot r_m^{C*}) / L_y^P > 0 \ .$$

Finally, in the $m = m_0$ - plane (see Figure 3.14):

$$y_w^{KC} = R_w^C + \ell_w^{P*} (R_\ell^C - F_\ell) > 0 \ ,$$

$$y_w^{CI} = (\ell_w^{P*} \chi_I - L_w^C) / L_r^C < 0 \ ,$$

$$y_w^{IU} = r_w^{C*} - F_\ell \cdot \ell_w^{C*} \ ,$$

$$y_w^{UK} = (L_w^P - L_r^P \cdot r_w^{C*} - \ell_w^{C*}) / L_y^P \ .$$

It can be observed that, if the curve in Figure 3.12 corresponding with the set *UK* has a positive slope, it has a negative slope in Figure 3.14. The same goes for the set *IU*.

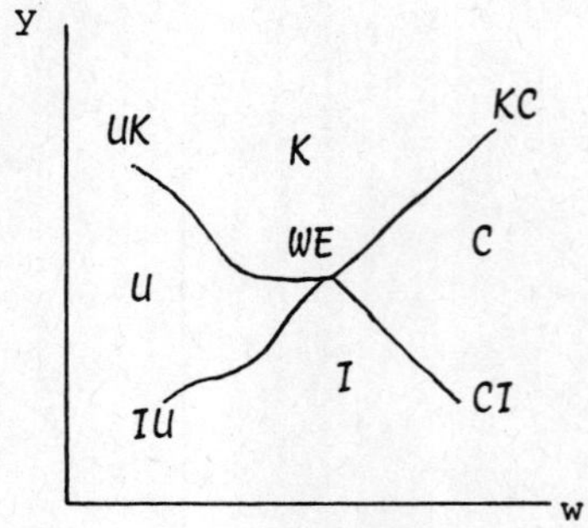

Figure 3.14.
Situation of the regimes
for $m = m_0$.

It is important to investigate what happens with the location of the subsets *C*, *I*, *K* and *U*, if the preferences for stocks tend to zero.
If the importance of money in the utility function of the consumption sector disappears, the boundaries *KC* and *CI* are going to coincide. The new boundary of the sets *K* and *I* can be represented by a vertical half line in Figure 3.12 and a horizontal half line in Figure 3.14.
If the valuation of stock in the production sector tends to zero, the boundary *UK* tends to the boundary *IU*. The latter is independent of the valuation of stock.
If the preferences for both money stocks and stocks of goods disappear, the model becomes inconsistent (see Muellbauer and Portes, 1978).

3.7. *Extensions*

In this section little attention has been paid to the intertemporal character of the models. Since the sectors have to decide about two periods, present and future, expectations with respect to prices, consumption, etc., are very important. Until this far, these expectations are assumed to be implicit in the objective functions U and V. The specification of the expectations, however, causes many difficulties (see Muellbauer and Portes, 1978). An intertemporal treatment of stock can be found in Schittko and Eckwert (1981). An introduction of foreign trade into a model comparable to the one of this section is given in Schittko (1981).

There are many possibilities with relation to the stocks in the models. For instance, the money stocks of the production sector may be regarded. The consumption sector can be given a possibility to hold an inventory of goods, etc.

Not much is said until this far about the destination of profits. In this thesis profits are not paid to the consumption sector, but, for instance, taxed away completely by the government. One could think of several other possibilities with relation to the profits.

APPENDIX: *Proofs with respect to Sections 3.2 - 3.4*

PROOF OF THEOREM 3.3.

$\tilde{U} \in C^2(\text{int } D^C(x) \to \mathbb{R}_+)$, for given $x \in \mathbb{R}^3_{++}$, is implied by Assumption As 2 and the definition of $\tilde{U}$ (Definition 3.2).

The Hessian of the function $\tilde{U}$ with respect to (ℓ,r) on int $D^C(x)$ satisfies

$$\begin{bmatrix} \tilde{U}_{\ell\ell} & \tilde{U}_{\ell r} \\ \tilde{U}_{r\ell} & \tilde{U}_{rr} \end{bmatrix} = \begin{bmatrix} 0 & 1 & 0 & w \\ 0 & 0 & 1 & -1 \end{bmatrix} \begin{bmatrix} 0 & U_\ell & U_r & U_z \\ U_\ell & U_{\ell\ell} & U_{\ell r} & U_{\ell z} \\ U_r & U_{r\ell} & U_{rr} & U_{rz} \\ U_z & U_{z\ell} & U_{zr} & U_{zz} \end{bmatrix} \begin{bmatrix} 0 & 0 \\ 1 & 0 \\ 0 & 1 \\ w & -1 \end{bmatrix}.$$

This Hessian is thus also negative definite by Assumption As 2.2. □

PROOF OF THEOREM 3.5.

For the Hessian of the function $\tilde{V}$ with respect to (ℓ, r) the following equality holds. Evaluated at $(\ell_0, r_0) \in \text{int } D^P(x)$

$$\begin{pmatrix} \tilde{V}_{\ell\ell} & \tilde{V}_{\ell r} \\ \tilde{V}_{r\ell} & \tilde{V}_{rr} \end{pmatrix} = \begin{pmatrix} Q_{qq}(F_\ell)^2 + Q_q F_{\ell\ell} & -Q_{qq}F_\ell \\ -Q_{qq}F_\ell & Q_{qq} \end{pmatrix}$$

where the derivatives of F are evaluated at ℓ_0 and those of Q at $y + F(\ell_0) - r_0$. Hence we have the equalities

$$(\ell \quad r)\begin{pmatrix} \tilde{V}_{\ell\ell} & \tilde{V}_{\ell r} \\ \tilde{V}_{r\ell} & \tilde{V}_{rr} \end{pmatrix}\begin{pmatrix} \ell \\ r \end{pmatrix} = \{Q_{qq}(F_\ell)^2 + Q_q F_{\ell\ell}\}\ell^2 - 2(Q_{qq}F_\ell)\ell r + Q_{qq}r^2 =$$

$$= Q_q F_{\ell\ell}\ell^2 + Q_{qq}(F_\ell \ell - r)^2 \quad .$$

This latter expression is negative, since $Q_q > 0$, $F_{\ell\ell} < 0$ and $Q_{qq} < 0$ (see Assumptions As 3, As 4). Therefore the function V has a negative definite Hessian with respect to (ℓ, r). □

PROOF OF LEMMA 3.9.

In this proof the argument x is omitted from the notation. Let $\bar{\ell} \le L^C(\bar{r})$. Suppose $\bar{L}^C(\bar{\ell}, \bar{r}) < \bar{\ell}$. Note that the following inequality will always be true:

$$\text{(A1)} \qquad \tilde{U}[\bar{L}^C(\bar{\ell},\bar{r}), \bar{R}^C(\bar{\ell},\bar{r})] \le \tilde{U}[\bar{L}^C(\infty,\bar{r}), \bar{R}^C(\infty,\bar{r})] \ .$$

Consider the convex combination

$$(\ell_1, r_1) := \lambda_1(\bar{L}^C(\bar{\ell},\bar{r}), \bar{R}^C(\bar{\ell},\bar{r})) + (1-\lambda_1)(\bar{L}^C(\infty,\bar{r}), \bar{R}^C(\infty,\bar{r}))$$

and note that there will be real numbers $\lambda_1 \in (0,1)$ such that $L^C(\bar{\ell},\bar{r}) < \ell_1 < \bar{\ell}$.

Since furthermore, $r_1 \le r$ and $m + w\ell_1 - r_1 \ge 0$, the convex combination (ℓ_1, r_1) is a point in the feasible region of the maximization problem (3.10).

From inequality (A1) and strict concavity of $\tilde{U}$ it follows that

$$\tilde{U}(\bar{L}^C(\bar{\ell},\bar{r}), \bar{R}^C(\bar{\ell},\bar{r})) < \tilde{U}(\ell_1, r_1) \ .$$

This is a contradiction to the fact that $(\bar{L}^C(\bar{\ell},\bar{r}),\bar{R}^C(\bar{\ell},\bar{r}))$ is the optimal solution of (3.10). Therefore, $\bar{L}^C(\bar{\ell},\bar{r}) \geq \bar{\ell}$.
If $\bar{\ell} > \bar{L}^C(\infty,\bar{r})$, then the point $((\bar{L}^C(\infty,\bar{r}),\bar{R}^C(\infty,\bar{r}))$ lies in the feasible region of the maximization problem (3.10) and therefore will be the solution of (3.10). The first equality of Lemma 3.9 is proved now. The proof of the second one is analogous. □

PROOF OF THEOREM 3.10.

In this proof the argument x is omitted from the notation.
Let $(\ell,r) \in \tilde{H}^C$. Then by Lemma 3.9 it follows that $L^C(\ell,r) = \ell$ and $\bar{R}^C(\ell,r) = r$. Therefore, $(\ell,r) \in H^C$.
Let $(\ell,r) \in H^C$. Then there exists a pair $(\bar{\ell},\bar{r}) \in \mathbb{R}^2_+$ such that (ℓ,r) is the solution of the maximization problem

$$\max \{\tilde{U}(\tilde{\ell},\tilde{r}) \mid (\tilde{\ell},\tilde{r}) \in D^C \wedge \tilde{\ell} \leq \bar{\ell} \wedge \tilde{r} \leq \bar{r}\} ,$$

see Theorem 3.3. The pair (ℓ,r) is then also the solution of the maximization problem

$$\max \{\tilde{U}(\tilde{\ell},\tilde{r}) \mid (\tilde{\ell},\tilde{r}) \in D^C \wedge \tilde{\ell} \leq \bar{\ell} \wedge \tilde{r} \leq r\} .$$

Hence, by definition of $\bar{L}^C$, we have $\ell = \bar{L}^C(\bar{\ell},r)$.
Therefore, since $\bar{L}^C(\bar{\ell},r) \leq \bar{L}^C(\infty,r) = L^C(r)$, the inequality $\ell \leq L^C(r)$ holds.
Similarly, it can be proved that $r \leq R^C(\ell)$, so that $(\ell,r) \in \tilde{H}^C$ and the equality $H^C = \tilde{H}^C$ is proved. □

PROOF OF LEMMA 3.12: similar to Lemma 3.9.

PROOF OF THEOREM 3.13: similar to Theorem 3.10.

PROOF OF THEOREM 3.15

This theorem is an application of Theorem 2.3. The choice of x in the set X^C and $\bar{r} \in (0,r^{C*}(x)]$ imply $(L^C(\bar{r};x),\bar{r}) \in \text{int } D^C(x)$. Furthermore, by Corollary 3.11, $L^C(\bar{r};x)$ is the solution of

$$\max_{\ell} \{\tilde{U}(\ell,\bar{r};x) \mid (\ell,\bar{r}) \in D^C(x)\} .$$

By Theorem 3.3, $\tilde{U} \in C^2(\text{int } D^C(x) \to \mathbb{R}_+)$, hence

(A2) $\quad \tilde{U}_{\ell}[L^C(\bar{r};x),\bar{r};x] = 0$.

Strict concavity of the function $\tilde{U}$ (see Theorem 3.3) implies

(A3) $\quad \tilde{U}_{\ell\ell}[L^C(\bar{r};x),\bar{r};x] < 0$.

The implicit function theorem (Theorem 2.2) applied on (A2) together with (A3) implies that $L_r^C(\bar{r};x)$ exists and satisfies (3.19). The other assertions can be proved in a similar way. □

PROOF OF THEOREM 3.16.

The equality (3.12) implies $R_{\ell}^P = F_{\ell}$. The rest of the proof is similar to the proof of Theorem 3.15. □

PROOF OF THEOREM 3.18.

(3.19) and (A3) imply that for every $x \in X^C$ the function L^C is increasing on $(0,r^{C*}(x)]$ if

$$\tilde{U}_{\ell r}[L^C(\bar{r};x),\bar{r};x] > 0 .$$

Hence, the function L^C is increasing on $(0,r^{C*}(x)]$ under Assumption As 7.
A similar proof can be applied to show that the function R^C is increasing in ℓ on $(0,\ell^{C*}(x)]$. □

PROOF OF LEMMA 3.20.

Observe that the relevant derivatives exist according to Theorem 3.16 (even for $\bar{r} = r^{P*}$ and $\bar{\ell} = \ell^{P*}$). It follows from Theorem 3.16 and the proof of Theorem 3.5 that

$$L_r^P(\bar{r};x) = Q_{qq} F_{\ell} [Q_{qq}(F_{\ell})^2 + Q_q F_{\ell\ell}]^{-1} ,$$

where the derivatives of Q are evaluated at $y + F[L^P(\bar{r};x)] - \bar{r}$ and those of F at $L^P(r;x)$. By the Assumptions As 3 and As 4, the term $Q_q F_{\ell\ell}$ is negative. Furthermore, Theorem 3.16 implies $F_{\ell} = R_{\ell}^P$. Now the first assertion can easily be derived. The proof of the second one is similar. □

PROOF OF THEOREM 3.21.

The solution $\ell^{P*}(x)$ is determined by

$$F_\ell(\ell^{P*}) = w .$$

With the implicit function theorem (Theorem 2.3) we find $\ell_w^{P*}(x) = 1/F_{\ell\ell}^*$, which is negative by Assumption As 3. Clearly, $\ell_y^{P*}(x) = 0$. The relations $r_w^{P*}(x) = w/F_{\ell\ell}^* < 0$ and $r_y^{P*} = 1$ follow easily from (3.13). Likewise, (3.12) implies $R_w^P(\ell;x) = 0$ and $R_y^P(\ell;x) = 0$, if $x \in X^P$ and $\ell \in (0,\ell^{P*}(x)]$.

For $\bar{x} = (\bar{m},\bar{w},\bar{y})' \in X^P$ and $\bar{r} \in (0,r^{P*}(\bar{x})]$, the function L^P is determined by ℓ in the following equation:

$$Q_q[\bar{y} + F(\ell) - \bar{r}] \cdot F_\ell(\ell) - \bar{w} = 0 .$$

With the implicit function theorem (Theorem 2.2) and the Assumptions As 3 and As 4, we find

$$L_w^P(\bar{r};\bar{x}) = [Q_{qq}(F_\ell)^2 + Q_q F_{\ell\ell}]^{-1} < 0 , \tag{A4}$$

$$L_y^P(\bar{r};\bar{x}) = -Q_{qq} F_\ell \cdot [Q_{qq}(F_\ell)^2 + Q_q F_{\ell\ell}]^{-1} < 0 , \tag{A5}$$

$$L_r^P(\bar{r};\bar{x}) = Q_{qq} F_\ell \cdot [Q_{qq}(F_\ell)^2 + Q_q F_{\ell\ell}]^{-1} > 0 , \tag{A6}$$

where the derivatives of F are evaluated at $L^P(\bar{r};\bar{x})$ and those of Q at $\bar{y} + F[L^P(\bar{r};\bar{x})] - \bar{r}$. □

PROOF OF THEOREM 3.22.

The following equation holds by definition

$$L^C(r^{C*};x) = \ell^{C*}(x) .$$

Differentiation of the left-hand side with respect to m yields

$$L_m^C + L_r^C r_m^{C*} .$$

This expression equals the derivative with respect to m of the right-hand side, i.e., ℓ_m^{C*}. Therefore

$$L_m^C = \ell_m^{C*} - L_r^C \, r_m^{C*} \ .$$

The other equalities can be proved in a similar way. □

PROOF OF THEOREM 3.23.

The derivatives L_w^P, L_r^P and L_Y^P immediately follow, if we substitute $F_\ell = w$, $Q_{qq} = Q_{qq}^*$, $Q_q = 1$ and $F_{\ell\ell} = F_{\ell\ell}^*$ in relations (A4)-(A6) in Theorem 3.21. The other assertions can be checked easily with the results of Theorem 3.21. □

4. DYNAMIC MODEL

4.1. Introduction

In the preceding chapter the models covered a period, during which the price of goods and the wage rate were fixed. The present chapter contains an analysis of a somewhat longer term, in which prices are variable (capital and investments, however, are still neglected).
A continuous time is introduced. Stocks and prices adjust over time in the following way.
To begin with, it is assumed that the process of quantity rationing, leading to a transaction, is infinitely faster than adjustments of stocks and prices. This assumption is usual in literature on dynamics of disequilibria, cf. Hicks (1946) ("fix-price method"), Barro and Grossman (1971), Benassy (1975), Veendorp (1975) and Grandmont (1977b).
A disequilibrium transaction initiates adjustments in stocks and prices. On the one hand, it may lead to (dis-)savings and changes of inventory. On the other hand, the differences in demand and supply give rise to an increase or a decrease in prices, according to the "law of demand and supply".
The adjustments of stocks and prices reflect the uncertainty of the agents, which is implicit in the model, i.e., worked up in the preferences (see Section 3.1).

Dynamic models with quantity rationing have been investigated by Veendorp (1975), Dehez and Jaskold Gabszewicz (1977), Böhm (1978), Honkapohja (1979), Picard (1979), Laroque (1981b), Eckalbar (1980), a.o. Böhm (1978) and Dehez and Jaskold Gabszewicz (1977) introduce discrete time models in which money holdings are variable, but prices remain fixed. In Veendorp (1975), Picard (1979), Laroque (1981b) and Eckalbar (1980), on the other hand, time is continuous and the prices of two of the three goods are varying, while stocks are neglected (Picard also considers investments and capital accumulation). Honkapohja's continu-

ous time approach includes both price and (money) stocks dynamics. However, Honkapohja does not investigate Walrasian states. It is our goal to combine the mentioned models in a continuous time context and add a varying inventory in the production sector. We will integrate both stock and price dynamics (and examine stationary Walrasian equilibria as well as Non-Walrasian equilibria in the next chapter).
A formulation of dynamic stock and price relations can be found in Section 4.2. The stock and price adjustment functions are analyzed in Section 4.3. In Section 4.4 special attention will be devoted to Walras Equilibria and their relations to stock adjustments. Section 4.5 is the analogue of Section 3.6 for the continuous time models. In Section 4.6 we consider the consequences of the omission of the possibility of an inventory of goods. Finally, some extensions are mentioned in Section 4.7.

4.2. *Formulation of a dynamic system*

4.2.1. Adjustments of stocks

In this section the adjustments of the stocks and the prices over time are described. It is assumed that the preferences and the technology are constant over time.

ASSUMPTION As 10. *The utility function* U*, the production function* F *and the valuation function of stock* Q *are constant over time.*

As a result of Assumption As 10 the transaction $(\hat{\ell},\hat{r})$ (see Definition 3.26) is a time-independent function of $x = (m,w,y)'$. The objective function V of the production sector is constant as well.
Assumption As 10 implies that technical progress is absent and that price expectations are constant. The latter obviously is a severe restriction.
Henceforth time indices will be omitted, if this will not lead to misunderstandings.

The model of the preceding chapter is reformulated in a dynamic model with continuous time. The budget equation is now assumed to be given by

$$(4.1) \qquad z_n = m_n + k_m(w_n \ell - pr) \qquad (k_m > 0) \ .$$

The consumers assume that the present flow of nominal savings $w_n \ell - pr$ will be constant over some arbitrary time interval k_m. They base their decisions on the fictitious money stock given by (4.1). It can be seen that the dimension of k_m is such that the dimension of $k_m(w_n \ell - pr)$ is compatible with the one of the nominal money stock m_n. The variable z_n in (4.1) must be nonnegative:

$$(4.2) \qquad m_n + k_m(w_n \ell - pr) \geq 0 \ .$$

For negative savings, (4.2) is an expression of the consumers' wish to "keep it up" with their money holdings a period of k_m time units. (4.1) can, of course, be given in real terms as well:

$$(4.3) \qquad z = m + k_m(w\ell - r) \ .$$

Similarly, the inventory equation in the new model is

$$(4.4) \qquad q = y + k_y[F(\ell) - r] \qquad (k_y > 0) \ ,$$

where

$$y + k_y[F(\ell) - r] \geq 0 \ .$$

The unconstrained maximization problem of the consumption sector becomes

$$\max \{U(\ell,r,z) \mid (\ell,r,z) \in \Delta \wedge z = m + k_m(w\ell - r)\} \ ,$$

where Δ is the consumption set (see Assumption As 1). The unconstrained maximization problem of the production sector can be found in a similar way.

The following functions will play a role in the sequel. It is assumed that Assumption As 9 holds, so that the transaction defined in Definition 3.26 is a function of x.

DEFINITION 4.1. *Let Assumption* As 9 *hold.*
The *__real savings function__* $S\colon X \to \mathbb{R}$ *is defined by*

$$S(x) := w\hat{\ell}(x) - \hat{r}(x)$$

where $(\hat{\ell},\hat{r})$ *is the transaction and* X *is defined in* (3.16).

The <u>*inventory adjustment function*</u> $Y: \mathcal{X} \to \mathbb{R}$ *is defined by*

$$Y(x) := F[\hat{\ell}(x)] - \hat{r}(x) .$$

Since savings and inventory adjustment are determined by the transaction $(\hat{\ell},\hat{r})$, the functions S and Y have different specifications on the sets $\mathcal{C}$, $\mathcal{I}$, $\mathcal{U}$ and $\mathcal{K}$, as have the functions $\hat{\ell}$ and $\hat{r}$.

REMARK 4.2. If $\pi: \mathcal{X} \to \mathbb{R}$ denotes the real profits of the production sector excluding government demand $-F(0)$, the following equality holds:

$$S(x) + \pi(x) + F(0) = 0 \quad (x \in \mathcal{X}) .$$

The stock adjustments are formalized as follows:

$$\text{(4.5)} \qquad \overset{\circ}{m}_n = pS(x) \quad (x \in \mathcal{X}) ,$$

$$\text{(4.6)} \qquad \overset{\circ}{y} = Y(x) \quad (x \in \mathcal{X}) .$$

If the production sector is not rationed on the goods market, i.e., if $x \in \text{cl}(\mathcal{C} \cup \mathcal{I})$, then the following equation holds, cf. (3.12),

$$\text{(4.7)} \qquad \hat{r}(x) = F[\hat{\ell}(x)] + k_y^{-1}(y - y^*) .$$

Hence, by (4.6), the inventory change is given by

$$\overset{\circ}{y} = k_y^{-1}(y^* - y) .$$

The solution of IVP$(Y,y_0,0)$ with $Y(y) = k_y^{-1}(y^* - y)$ is given by

$$y(t) = (y_0 - y^*) \exp[-t/k_y] + y^* .$$

As long as the production sector is unconstrained on the goods market, it adjusts its inventory continuously upto the optimal inventory level y^*. For the initial value $y_0 = y^*$ the inventory is kept constant, of course.

For a point $x \in \mathcal{K} \cup \mathcal{UK} \cup \mathcal{U}$, related to an NWE-state, in which the production sector is rationed on the goods market, we have:

$$R^P[\hat{\ell}(x);x] - \hat{r}(x) > 0$$

(cf. (ℓ_1,r_1) in Figure 3.5). The vertical distance between the curves of the production function and effective goods supply function is now $k_y^{-1}(y^*-y)$. Hence, we find

$$\overset{\circ}{y} = F[\hat{\ell}(x)] - \hat{r}(x) =$$

$$= k_y^{-1}(y^*-y) + R^P[\hat{\ell}(x);x] - \hat{r}(x)$$

and therefore, if $x \in K \cup UK \cup U$,

$$\overset{\circ}{y} > k_y^{-1}(y^*-y)$$

which represents an additional accumulation of stocks.

4.2.2. Adjustments of prices

We have met some specifications of price adjustments in economic theory in Section 1.5. In the present subsection we will confine ourselves to neoclassical adjustments of the two prices (the price of goods and the nominal wage rate). Hence, it is assumed that these adjustments are based on excess demands.
We introduce *excess demand functions* E^{rC}, E^{rP}, $E^{\ell C}$ and $E^{\ell P}$ defined on the set X (see (3.16)) and into $\mathbb{R}$. These functions are supposed to represent the excess demands. The upper indices correspond with the market and the constrained sector. It is assumed that the dynamic behaviour of the price of goods and the nominal wage rate depend on the excess demand functions in the following way:

$$\overset{\circ}{p}/p = k^{rC}\, E^{rC}(x) - k^{rP}\, E^{rP}(x) \qquad (x \in X)\ , \tag{4.8}$$

$$\overset{\circ}{w}_n/w_n = k^{\ell P}\, E^{\ell P}(x) - k^{\ell C}\, E^{\ell C}(x) \qquad (x \in X)\ . \tag{4.9}$$

The positive scalars k^{rC}, k^{rP}, $k^{\ell P}$ and $k^{\ell C}$ are *weight factors*, corresponding with the adjustment speeds of the price changing process. If the agents are easily prepared to make concessions in the determination of a price, then the corresponding weight factor is large.

Some examples of excess demand functions are given that are to be evaluated in the next chapter:

$$(4.10)\quad \begin{cases} E^{rC}(x) = R^{C}[\hat{\ell}(x);x] - \hat{r}(x) & (x \in \mathcal{X}) , \\ E^{\ell P}(x) = L^{P}[\hat{r}(x);x] - \hat{\ell}(x) & (x \in \mathcal{X}) , \\ E^{rP}(x) = R^{P}[\hat{\ell}(x);x] - \hat{r}(x) & (x \in \mathcal{X}) , \\ E^{\ell C}(x) = L^{C}[\hat{r}(x);x] - \hat{\ell}(x) & (x \in \mathcal{X}) , \end{cases}$$

where $(\hat{\ell},\hat{r})$ is the transaction at x, R^{C} is the effective goods demand function and L^{P} is the effective labour demand function, etc.

$$(4.11)\quad \begin{cases} E^{rC}(x) = R^{C}[\hat{\ell}(x);x] / \hat{r}(x) - 1 & (x \in \mathcal{X}) \ (\hat{r}(x) > 0) , \\ E^{\ell P}(x) = L^{P}[\hat{r}(x);x] / \hat{\ell}(x) - 1 & (x \in \mathcal{X}) \ (\hat{\ell}(x) > 0) , \\ E^{rP}(x) = R^{P}[\hat{\ell}(x);x] / \hat{r}(x) - 1 & (x \in \mathcal{X}) \ (\hat{r}(x) > 0) , \\ E^{\ell C}(x) = L^{C}[\hat{r}(x);x] / \hat{\ell}(x) - 1 & (x \in \mathcal{X}) \ (\hat{\ell}(x) > 0) ; \end{cases}$$

$$(4.12)\quad \begin{cases} E^{rC}(x) = r^{C*}(x) - \hat{r}(x) & \text{for } x \in \mathcal{X} \cap \text{cl } \mathcal{I} , \\ \phantom{E^{rC}(x)} = R^{C}[\hat{\ell}(x);x] - \hat{r}(x) & \text{elsewhere,} \\ E^{\ell P}(x) = \ell^{P*}(x) - \hat{\ell}(x) & \text{for } x \in \mathcal{X} \cap \text{cl } \mathcal{I} , \\ \phantom{E^{\ell P}(x)} = L^{P}[\hat{r}(x);x] - \hat{\ell}(x) & \text{elsewhere,} \\ E^{rP}(x) = r^{P*}(x) - \hat{r}(x) & \text{for } x \in \mathcal{X} \cap \text{cl } \mathcal{K} , \\ \phantom{E^{rP}(x)} = R^{P}[\hat{\ell}(x);x] - \hat{r}(x) & \text{elsewhere,} \\ E^{\ell C}(x) = \ell^{C*}(x) - \hat{\ell}(x) & \text{for } x \in \mathcal{X} \cap \text{cl } \mathcal{K} , \\ \phantom{E^{\ell C}(x)} = L^{C}[\hat{r}(x);x] - \hat{\ell}(x) & \text{elsewhere.} \end{cases}$$

In the examples (4.10)-(4.12) the value $E^{rC}(x)$ is positive for $x \in \mathcal{C} \cup \mathcal{CI} \cup \mathcal{I}$, i.e., if the consumption sector is rationed on the goods market. Its value is zero for $x \in \mathcal{C} \cup \mathcal{CI} \cup \mathcal{I}$. Since only one side of the market can be constrained in an NWE-state, at most one value of the pair $(E^{rC}(x),E^{rP}(x))$ can be positive. The same goes to the pair $(E^{\ell P}(x),E^{\ell C}(x))$.

We consider the following equivalencies to be necessary conditions for excess demand functions:

(4.13) $\quad x \in \mathcal{WE} \Longleftrightarrow \overset{\circ}{p} = \overset{\circ}{w}_n = 0$,

(4.14) $\quad x \in \mathcal{C} \Longleftrightarrow \overset{\circ}{p} > 0 \wedge \overset{\circ}{w}_n < 0$,

(4.15) $\quad x \in \mathcal{U} \Longleftrightarrow \overset{\circ}{p} < 0 \wedge \overset{\circ}{w}_n > 0$.

Furthermore, the price p must be constant on the set $\mathcal{KC} \cup \mathcal{WE} \cup \mathcal{IU}$ and the nominal wage rate constant on the set $\mathcal{UK} \cup \mathcal{WE} \cup \mathcal{CI}$.
These necessary conditions can be stated alternatively. The sets $\mathcal{C}$, $\mathcal{I}$, $\mathcal{U}$ and $\mathcal{K}$ can be expressed in terms of the excess demand functions:

$$\mathcal{C} = \{x \in \mathcal{X} \mid E^{\ell C}(x) > 0 \wedge E^{rC}(x) > 0\} ,$$

$$\mathcal{I} = \{x \in \mathcal{X} \mid E^{\ell P}(x) > 0 \wedge E^{rC}(x) > 0\} ,$$

$$\mathcal{U} = \{x \in \mathcal{X} \mid E^{\ell P}(x) > 0 \wedge E^{rP}(x) > 0\} ,$$

$$\mathcal{K} = \{x \in \mathcal{X} \mid E^{\ell C}(x) > 0 \wedge E^{rP}(x) > 0\} .$$

In a similar way, the boundaries and the set $\mathcal{WE}$ can be expressed with the help of equalities and inequalities.

A distinction can be made between (4.10) and (4.11) on the one hand and (4.12) on the other hand. (4.10) and (4.11) define *continuous excess demand functions* on $\mathcal{X}$, while (4.11) is the specification of a *discontinuous excess demand function* on $\mathcal{X}$. For instance, the function E^{rC} is discontinuous, due to the specification on the boundary $\mathcal{CI}$.
We shall come back on this distinction several times.
Specification (4.12) is basically the same as the one in Veendorp (1975).

4.2.3. A differential system describing the dynamic model

Since the following equalities hold

(4.16) $\quad \overset{\circ}{m}/m = \overset{\circ}{m}_n/m_n - \overset{\circ}{p}/p$,

(4.17) $\quad \overset{\circ}{w}/w = \overset{\circ}{w}_n/w_n - \overset{\circ}{p}/p$, the equations (4.6)-(4.9) can be written in terms of $x = (m,w,y)'$. Let the functions $M: X \to \mathbb{R}$ and $W: X \to \mathbb{R}$ be defined by

$$(4.18) \qquad M(x) := S(x) + m[-k^{rC} E^{rC}(x) + k^{rP} E^{rP}(x)] \ ,$$

$$(4.19) \qquad W(x) := w[k^{\ell P} E^{\ell P}(x) - k^{\ell C} E^{\ell C}(x) - k^{rC} E^{rC}(x) + k^{rP} E^{rP}(x)] \ .$$

Then the dynamic behaviour of the model can be represented by the following autonomous system of first order differential equations:

$$(4.20) \qquad \begin{cases} \overset{\circ}{m} = M(m,w,y) \\ \overset{\circ}{w} = W(m,w,y) \qquad (m,w,y)' \in X \ . \\ \overset{\circ}{y} = Y(m,w,y) \end{cases}$$

System (4.20) is not necessarily continuous (see Definition 2.9). It can be observed that the specifications (4.10) and (4.11) lead to continuity of the right-hand sides of (4.8) and (4.9), and hence of system (4.20), on the whole domain. Veendorp's adjustment (4.12), however, leads to discontinuities on the boundaries.

4.3. *Analysis of the adjustment functions*

4.3.1. Adjustments of stocks

In this section continuity and differentiability properties of the adjustment functions are investigated. We start with the functions that correspond with the stocks, i.e., the real savings functions S and the inventory adjustment function Y, both defined in Definition 4.1. It is not a restriction to take the arbitrary intervals k_m and k_y from Section 4.2 as unity.

ASSUMPTION As 11. $k_m = k_y = 1$.

An alternative way to formulate Assumption As 11 is to say that the periods k_m and k_y, considered by the consumption sector, respectively the production sector, are equal. Then the time units can be chosen in such a way that both constants are unity. Due to Assumption As 11, the theorems of Chapter 3 still hold unchanged.

The restriction $S \mid (X \cap \mathrm{cl}\ C)$ will be denoted by S^C. In a similar way, the functions S^I, S^U, S^K, Y^C, Y^I, Y^U and Y^K can be defined. The following theorem can be proved.

THEOREM 4.3. *Under Assumptions* As 1-11, *the following properties hold:*

(i) $S \in C(X)$ and $Y \in C(X)$.

(ii) $S^Z \in C'(X \cap \mathrm{cl}\ Z)$ and $Y^Z \in C'(X \cap \mathrm{cl}\ Z)$ $\quad Z = C, I, U, K.$

(iii) *Signs or values of derivatives are given by the following table:*

S	*in interior of regime* m	*in interior of regime* y	*at Walras Equilibrium* m	*at Walras Equilibrium* w	*at Walras Equilibrium* y
upper index C	0	-1	0	ℓ^*	-1
I	+	–	0	ℓ^*	-1
U	–	+	–		0
K	–		–		–

Y	m	w	y
upper index C	0	0	-1
I	0	0	-1
U	–		0
K	–	–	–

Furthermore, evaluated at $x_0 = (m_0, w_0, y_0)' \in WE$,

$$S_m^U = Y_m^U = w_0 \ell_m^{C*} - r_m^{C*} ,$$

$$S_w^U - \ell^* = Y_w^U = w_0 \ell_w^{C*} - r_w^{C*} ,$$

$$S_m^K = Y_m^K = - F_{\ell\ell}^* L_w^P R_m^C / \chi_K$$

$$S_y^K = Y_y^K = L_w^P Q_{qq}^* w_0 (R_\ell^C - w_0) / \chi_K ,$$

where $\ell^* := \ell^{C*}(x_0) = \ell^{P*}(x_0)$, $r^* := r^{C*}(x_0) = r^{P*}(x_0)$, $F^*_{\ell\ell} := F_{\ell\ell}(\ell^*)$, $Q^*_{qq} := Q_{qq}(y^*)$, L^P_w *is evaluated at* $(r^*;x_0)$ *and the derivatives of* R^C *at* $(\ell^*;x_0)$ *and other functions at* x_0. *The function* χ_K *is defined as in Lemma* 3.29.

PROOF. The properties (i) and (ii) are immediate consequences of Theorem 3.31. For $x \in \mathcal{X} \cap \mathrm{cl}\,\mathcal{C}$ the following equalities hold:

$$S^{\mathcal{C}}(x) = w\ell^{P*}(x) - r^{P*}(x) \wedge Y^{\mathcal{C}}(x) = y^* - y \;.$$

Therefore, by Theorem 3.21, $S^{\mathcal{C}}_m = 0$ and $S^{\mathcal{C}}_y = w\ell^{P*}_y - r^{P*}_y = -1$ and obviously, $Y^{\mathcal{C}}_m = Y^{\mathcal{C}}_w = 0$ and $Y^{\mathcal{C}}_y = -1$, where all the derivatives are evaluated at $x \in \mathcal{X} \cap \mathrm{cl}\,\mathcal{C}$.

For $x \in \mathcal{X} \cap \mathrm{cl}\,\mathcal{K}$ we have

$$S^{\mathcal{K}}_m(x) = w\hat{\ell}_m(x) - \hat{r}_m(x) \;.$$

Application of Theorem 3.30 yields

$$S^{\mathcal{K}}_m(x) = [wL^P_r(\hat{r}(x);x) - 1] \cdot R^C_m[\hat{\ell}(x);x] \,/\, \chi_K(x) \;.$$

The "decreasing returns"-Assumption As 3.3 implies $w \le F_\ell[\hat{\ell}(x)]$. Hence by Lemma 3.20

$$wL^P_r - 1 \le F_\ell L^P_r - 1 = R^P_\ell L^P_r - 1 < 0$$

where L^P_r is evaluated at $(\hat{r}(x);x)$, F_ℓ at $\hat{\ell}(x)$ and R^P_ℓ at $(\hat{\ell}(x);x)$. This implies, together with Assumption As 8 and Lemma 3.29, that $S_m(x) < 0$. In addition, the value of this derivative in a Walras Equilibrium can be determined. Let $x_0 \in \mathcal{WE}$. Theorem 3.23 implies

$$w_0 L^P_r(r^*;x_0) - 1 = w_0^2\, Q^*_{qq}\, [Q^*_{qq} w_0^2 + F^*_{\ell\ell}]^{-1} - 1 = -F^*_{\ell\ell} \cdot L^P_w(r^*;x_0) \;.$$

In a similar way it can be found that

for $x \in \mathcal{X} \cap \mathrm{cl}\,\mathcal{K}$:

$$Y^{\mathcal{K}}_m = (F_\ell L^P_r - 1) R^C_m \,/\, \chi_K < 0 \;,$$

$$Y^{\mathcal{K}}_w = [\,(F_\ell L^P_r - 1) R^C_w + (F_\ell - R^C_\ell) L^P_w] \,/\, \chi_K < 0 \;,$$

$$Y^{\mathcal{K}}_y = (F_\ell - R^C_\ell) L^P_y \,/\, \chi_K < 0 \;;$$

for $x \in \mathcal{X} \cap \text{cl}\, \mathcal{I}$:

$$S_m^{\mathcal{I}} = (w - F_\ell) L_m^C / \chi_I \geq 0 ,$$

$$S_y^{\mathcal{I}} = (wL_r^C - 1) / \chi_I \leq (F_\ell L_r^C - 1) / \chi_I = -1 ,$$

where L_r^P is evaluated at $(\hat{r}(x);x)$, etc.

For $x \in \mathcal{I}$: the derivatives of the function Y are the same as those for $x \in \mathcal{C}$.

Finally, we have, evaluated at $x \in \mathcal{X} \cap \text{cl}\, \mathcal{U}$:

$$S_m^{\mathcal{U}} = w\ell_m^{C*} - r_m^{C*} < 0 ,$$

$$Y_m^{\mathcal{U}} = F_\ell \ell_m^{C*} - r_m^{C*} < 0 ,$$

$$Y_y^{\mathcal{U}} = F_\ell \ell_y^{C*} - r_y^{C*} = 0 .$$

The assertions that are not proved yet can be found in a similar way. □

According to the theorem above, the stock adjustment functions S and Y are continuous and piecewise continuously differentiable on the domain $\mathcal{X}$. The continuous differentiability of the restrictions $S^{\mathcal{C}}$, etc., is in the sense of Definition 2.7. The derivatives of these restrictions are defined by Definition 2.7. Thus the derivatives in a Walras Equilibrium are defined as well. Suppose there is a sequence of points in the interior of a regime and with a Walras Equilibrium as a limit. This sequence generates a sequence of derivatives, evaluated at the elements of the first sequence. The limit of the sequence of derivatives must be equal to a derivative evaluated at the Walras Equilibrium. It is noticeable that in the interior of the Inflation regime, we have $S_m^{\mathcal{I}} > 0$ and at a Walras Equilibrium $S_m^{\mathcal{I}} = 0$. In each of the other cases, the sign of the limit derivative is the same as the sign in the interior of the corresponding regime.

The signs that are not given in Theorem 4.3 are indefinite under our assumptions.

For all $x \in \mathcal{X}$

$$S_w(x) = \hat{\ell}(x) + w\hat{\ell}_w(x) - \hat{r}_w(x) .$$

The sign of the value $S_w(x)$ depends on the labour level $\hat{\ell}$ as well as on the derivatives $\hat{\ell}_w$ and $\hat{r}_w$. It seems reasonable that $S_w(x)$ is positive.

4.3.2. Adjustments of prices

The right-hand sides of the specifications of the excess demand functions, as, for instance, in (4.10)-(4.12), are supposed to be continuous functions, defined on the whole set $\mathcal{X}$, Furthermore, we assume that these right-hand sides are continuously differentiable on the sets $\mathcal{X} \cap \mathrm{cl}\ \mathcal{Z}$, $\mathcal{Z} = \mathcal{C}, \mathcal{I}, \mathcal{U}, \mathcal{K}$.
The restriction of the right-hand side of the specification of the function E^{rC} to the set $\mathcal{X} \cap \mathrm{cl}\ \mathcal{C}$ is denoted by $E^{rC\mathcal{C}}$.
The functions $E^{rC\mathcal{I}}$, $E^{\ell C\mathcal{C}}$, etc., are given similarly. Thus the notation of the restrictions $S^{\mathcal{C}}$, etc., is analogous to the notation given above: the (extra) upper index $\mathcal{Z}$, $\mathcal{Z} = \mathcal{C}, \mathcal{I}, \mathcal{U}, \mathcal{K}$, denotes the domain $\mathcal{X} \cap \mathrm{cl}\ \mathcal{Z}$.
The assumption which is made above already can now be expressed as follows.

ASSUMPTION As 12.

$$E^{rC\mathcal{C}} \in C'(\mathcal{X} \cap \mathrm{cl}\ \mathcal{C}) , \quad E^{rC\mathcal{I}} \in C'(\mathcal{X} \cap \mathrm{cl}\ \mathcal{I}) ,$$

$$E^{\ell C\mathcal{C}} \in C'(\mathcal{X} \cap \mathrm{cl}\ \mathcal{C}) , \quad E^{\ell C\mathcal{K}} \in C'(\mathcal{X} \cap \mathrm{cl}\ \mathcal{K}) ,$$

$$E^{\ell P\mathcal{I}} \in C'(\mathcal{X} \cap \mathrm{cl}\ \mathcal{I}) , \quad E^{\ell P\mathcal{U}} \in C'(\mathcal{X} \cap \mathrm{cl}\ \mathcal{U}) ,$$

$$E^{rP\mathcal{K}} \in C'(\mathcal{X} \cap \mathrm{cl}\ \mathcal{K}) , \quad E^{rP\mathcal{U}} \in C'(\mathcal{X} \cap \mathrm{cl}\ \mathcal{U}) .$$

The derivatives in Assumption As 12 are defined by Definition 2.7.

The given examples of excess demand functions satisfy this assumption. This is a consequence of Theorems 3.15, 3.16 and 3.30.

PROPOSITION 4.4. *Under Assumptions* As 1-10, *the specifications* (4.10)-(4.12) *satisfy Assumption* As 12.

Proposition 4.4 shows that Assumption As 12 is reasonable.

4.3.3. The differentiability of the system

In the two preceding subsections, continuity and differentiability of the stock adjustment functions and the excess demand functions are dealt with. Now we can regard the right-hand side of system (4.20) which is built up of these functions.
Following the restrictions of the stock adjustment functions and excess demand functions, which are denoted with an (extra) upper index. we define the following functions:

$$
(4.21) \quad \begin{aligned} M^{\mathcal{C}}(x) &:= S^{\mathcal{C}}(x) - m\,k^{rC}\,E^{rC\mathcal{C}}(x) \ , \\ W^{\mathcal{C}}(x) &:= -w\,[k^{\ell C}\,E^{\ell C\mathcal{C}}(x) + k^{rC}\,E^{rC\mathcal{C}}(x)] \qquad (x \in \mathcal{X} \cap \mathrm{cl}\ \mathcal{C}) \ ; \end{aligned}
$$

$$
(4.22) \quad \begin{aligned} M^{\mathcal{I}}(x) &:= S^{\mathcal{I}}(x) - m\,k^{rC}\,E^{rC\mathcal{I}}(x) \ , \\ W^{\mathcal{I}}(x) &:= w[k^{\ell P}\,E^{\ell P\mathcal{I}}(x) - k^{rC}\,E^{rC\mathcal{I}}(x)] \qquad (x \in \mathcal{X} \cap \mathrm{cl}\ \mathcal{I}) \ ; \end{aligned}
$$

$$
(4.23) \quad \begin{aligned} M^{\mathcal{U}}(x) &:= S^{\mathcal{U}}(x) + m\,k^{rP}\,E^{rP\mathcal{U}}(x) \ , \\ W^{\mathcal{U}}(x) &:= w[k^{\ell P}\,E^{\ell P\mathcal{U}}(x) + k^{rP}\,E^{rP\mathcal{U}}(x)] \qquad (x \in \mathcal{X} \cap \mathrm{cl}\ \mathcal{U}) \ ; \end{aligned}
$$

$$
(4.24) \quad \begin{aligned} M^{\mathcal{K}}(x) &:= S^{\mathcal{K}}(x) + m\,k^{rP}\,E^{rP\mathcal{K}}(x) \ , \\ W^{\mathcal{K}}(x) &:= w[-k^{\ell C}\,E^{\ell C\mathcal{K}}(x) + k^{rP}\,E^{rP\mathcal{K}}(x)] \qquad (x \in \mathcal{X} \cap \mathrm{cl}\ \mathcal{K}) \ . \end{aligned}
$$

Due to definitions (4.21)-(4.24), Assumption As 12 and Theorem 4.3, the restrictions of M and W in the right-hand side of system (4.20) are continuously differentiable on the intersections of the set $\mathcal{X}$ with the closures of the sets $\mathcal{C}$, $\mathcal{I}$, $\mathcal{U}$ and $\mathcal{K}$.

THEOREM 4.5. *Under Assumptions* As 1-10 *and* As 12,

$$
M^{\mathcal{Z}} \in C'(\mathcal{X} \cap \mathrm{cl}\ \mathcal{Z}) \quad \textit{and} \quad W^{\mathcal{Z}} \in C'(\mathcal{X} \cap \mathrm{cl}\ \mathcal{Z}) \quad \textit{for}\ \mathcal{Z} = \mathcal{C}, \mathcal{I}, \mathcal{U}, \mathcal{K} .
$$

Hence, the right-hand side of system (4.20) is (although not necessarily continuous) piecewise continuously differentiable.

4.4. *Walras Equilibria in the dynamic model*

A Walras Equilibrium state is defined in Section 3.5 as an NWE-state without strictly active constraints. Therefore, with the price adjustments (4.8) and (4.9) nominal wage rate w_n and price p of consumption goods are constant. Hence also real wage rate w is constant.
In this section, Walras Equilibria are related to changes in stocks.

DEFINITION 4.6. *The sets MWE, IWE and SWE are defined by*

$$MWE := \{x \in WE \mid S(x) = 0\} ,$$

$$IWE := \{x \in WE \mid Y(x) = 0\} ,$$

$$SWE := MWE \cap SWE .$$

An element of the set MWE will be called a <u>*Money Walras Equilibrium*</u>.
An element of the set IWE will be called an <u>*Inventory Walras Equilibrium*</u>.
An element of the set SWE will be called a <u>*Stationary Walras Equilibrium*</u>.

In a Money Walras Equilibrium the money stock m and the price p are constant. Hence, the real money stock m is constant. Therefore, an element of the set SWE is an equilibrium of system (4.20) (see Definition 2.13).

PROPOSITION 4.7. *Under Assumptions* As 1-10, *the following relations hold, where* y^* *is the optimal inventory (see Section* 3.3*),*

$$x \in IWE \Rightarrow y = y^* ,$$

$$y = y^* \Rightarrow \text{there is at most one pair } (m,w) \text{ such that } x \in IWE .$$

PROOF. The first relation follows directly from Definition 4.1 and the equalities (4.5) and (4.6).
The second relation follows immediately from Theorem 3.28. □

Hence, it is a necessary condition that an Inventory Walras Equilibrium and therefore also a Stationary Walras Equilibrium has an optimal inventory level. Furthermore, for such an optimal inventory level existence of an Inventory Walras Equilibrium immediately implies uniqueness.

In Proposition 4.7 we have had use of the fact that the optimal inventory q^* (see Section 3.2) is independent of the parameters m, w and y.

$$(4.25) \qquad \forall x \in X: \ q^*(x) = y^* .$$

There is no counterpart of (4.25) for real savings. The analogue of Proposition 4.7 can be formulated as follows.

PROPOSITION 4.8. *Under Assumptions* As 1-10, *the following relations hold, where* z^* *is the optimal money stock level (see Section* 3.2*)*,

$$x \in MWE \Rightarrow m = z^*(x) ,$$

$$m = z^*(x) \Rightarrow \textit{there is at most one } y \in \mathbb{R}_{++} \textit{ such that } x \in MWE .$$

4.5. *Locations in the parameter space*

For a more complete understanding of the dynamic models it is necessary to determine in (m,w,y)-space the loci where the variables remain constant over time.
Thus we will try to find the sets where, respectively,

$$\mathring{p} = 0 , \ \mathring{w}_n = 0 , \ \mathring{m}_n = 0 , \ \mathring{m} = 0 , \ \mathring{w} = 0 , \ \mathring{y} = 0 .$$

In Subsection 4.2.2 it is mentioned that the set of points in the set X, where $\mathring{p} = 0$, coincides with the set $KC \cup WE \cup IU$. Analogously, the points in X where $\mathring{w}_n = 0$ are the elements of the set $UK \cup WE \cup CI$.

For the set $\{x \in X \mid \mathring{m}_n = 0\}$ the following properties are implied by Theorem 4.3(iii).

PROPOSITION 4.9. *Let Assumptions* As 1-10 *hold.*

(i) *If for* $(m,w,y) \in K \cup UK \cup U$ *the equality* $\mathring{m}_n = 0$ *holds, then for* $(\tilde{m},w,y) \in K \cup UK \cup U$ *we have*

$$\mathring{m}_n < 0 \quad \textit{if } \tilde{m} > m ,$$

$$\mathring{m}_n > 0 \quad \textit{if } \tilde{m} < m .$$

(ii) *If for* $(m,w,y) \in I$ *the equality* $\overset{\circ}{m}_n = 0$ *holds, then for* $(\tilde{m},w,y) \in I$ *we have*

$$\overset{\circ}{m}_n > 0 \quad \text{if } \tilde{m} > m ,$$

$$\overset{\circ}{m}_n < 0 \quad \text{if } \tilde{m} < m .$$

(iii) *If for* $(m,w,y) \in C$, $\overset{\circ}{m}_n = 0$, *then this equality holds for* $(\tilde{m},w,y) \in C$ *as well.*

(iv) *If for* $(m,w,y) \in C \cup CI \cup I$ *the equality* $\overset{\circ}{m}_n = 0$ *holds, then for* $(m,w,\tilde{y}) \in C \cup CI \cup I$ *we have*

$$\overset{\circ}{m}_n > 0 \quad \text{if } \tilde{y} < y ,$$

$$\overset{\circ}{m}_n < 0 \quad \text{if } \tilde{y} > y .$$

(v) *If for* $(m,w,y) \in U$ *the equality* $\overset{\circ}{m}_n = 0$ *holds, then it holds for* $(m,w,\tilde{y}) \in U$ *as well.*

In the Keynesian regime starting in a point with a constant nominal money stock a higher value of real money stock m implies a decrease of the nominal money stock. In the Inflationary regime the reverse holds. In the set C the points with a constant nominal money stock are situated in a plane parallel to the m-axis. The interpretation of this location is that in the Classical situation the production sector determines the sales and purchases and hence the savings of the consumption sector. Since the latter variable is not relevant for the production sector, the location of the points of constant nominal money stock is independent of the real money stock.
A similar argument holds for the independency of the stock variable in the Underconsumption regime (v), where the consumption sector determines the savings. Finally, it is stated in (iv) that if the production sector is unconstrained on the goods market an increase of the inventory implies a decrease of the nominal money stock.

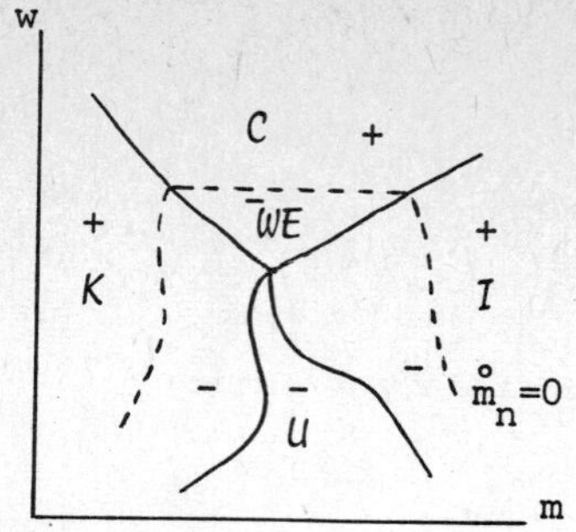

Figure 4.1.
Points with $\mathring{m}_n = 0$ in a plane $y = y_1$.

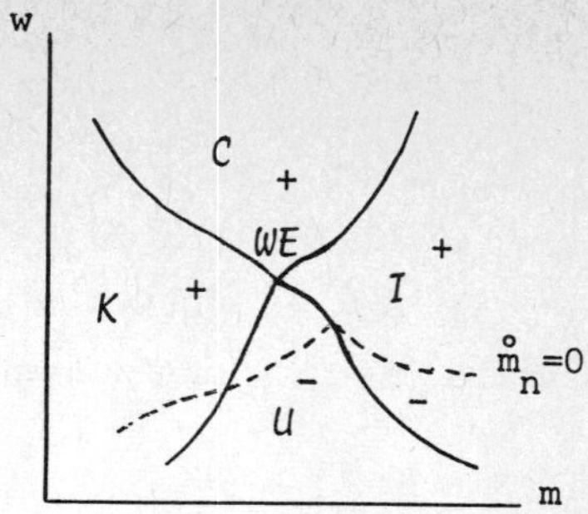

Figure 4.2.
Points with $\mathring{m}_n = 0$ in a plane $y = y_2$.

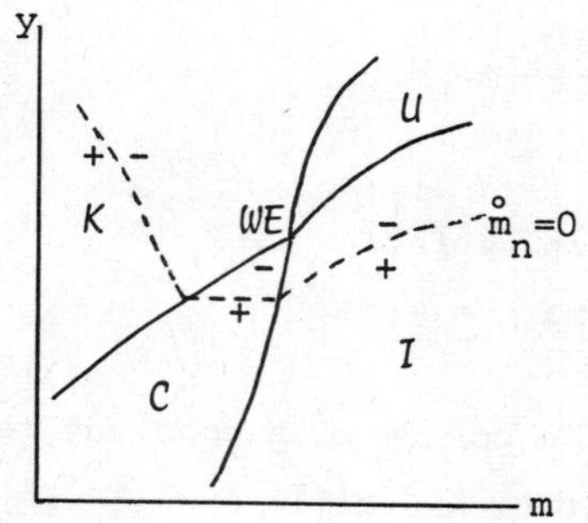

Figure 4.3.
Points with $\mathring{m}_n = 0$ in a plane $w = w_1$

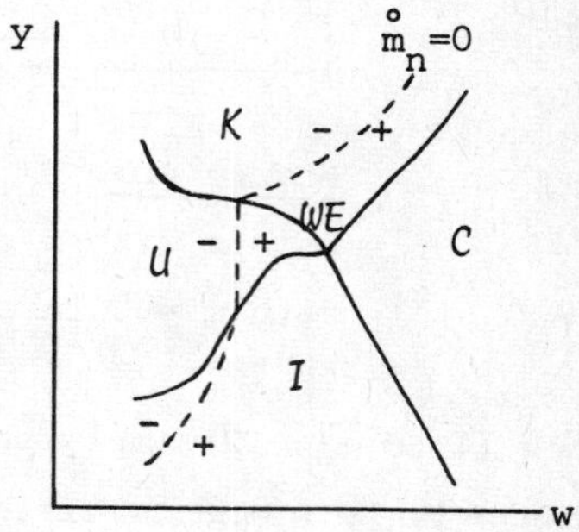

Figure 4.4.
Points with $\mathring{m}_n = 0$ in a plane $m = m_1$.

Proposition 4.9 is illustrated in Figures 4.1 - 4.4.

Now attention will be paid to the set of points, where real money stocks are constant. The set $\{x \in X \mid \mathring{m} = 0\}$ coincides with the set $\{x \in X \mid \mathring{m}_n = 0\}$ on the set $KC \cup WE \cup IU$, where the price p is constant. That is the point on the latter set, where real wage rate w reaches its maximum level (see Figures 4.1 and 4.2), cf. Proposition 4.9(i),(ii).

PROPOSITION 4.10. *Under Assumptions* As 1-10,

for $x \in K \cup UK \cup U$, $\mathring{m} = 0$ *implies* $\mathring{m}_n < 0$,

for $x \in C \cup CI \cup I$, $\mathring{m} = 0$ *implies* $\mathring{m}_n > 0$.

PROOF. The assertion follows immediately from equation (4.16) and the fact that $\mathring{p} < 0$ for $x \in K \cup UK \cup U$ and $\mathring{p} > 0$ for $x \in C \cup CI \cup I$.

Figure 4.5 is an illustration of Proposition 4.10. In the (m,w)-plane in the set K the curve $\mathring{m} = 0$ is located below the curve $\mathring{m}_n = 0$. The reverse is valid in the Classical and Inflationary regimes.

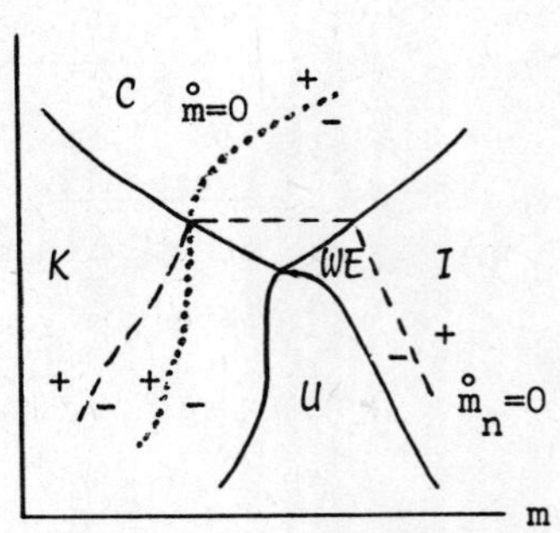

Figure 4.5.
Points with $\mathring{m}_n = 0$ and points with $\mathring{m} = 0$ in a plane $y = y_1$.

The relations (4.10)-(4.12) imply that the points with constant real wage rate can only be elements of the set cl K ∪ cl I:

$$\mathring{w} = 0 \Rightarrow x \in \text{cl } K \cup \text{cl } I$$

Finally, the set of triples with a constant inventory can be examined. For a point $x \in X \cap \text{cl}(C \cup I)$, where the production sector is unconstrained on the goods market, $\mathring{y} = y^* - y$ holds.

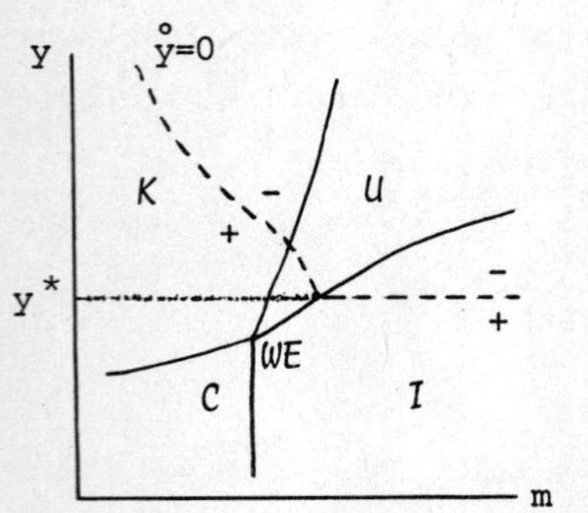

Figure 4.6.
Points with $\mathring{y} = 0$ in a plane $w = w_1$.

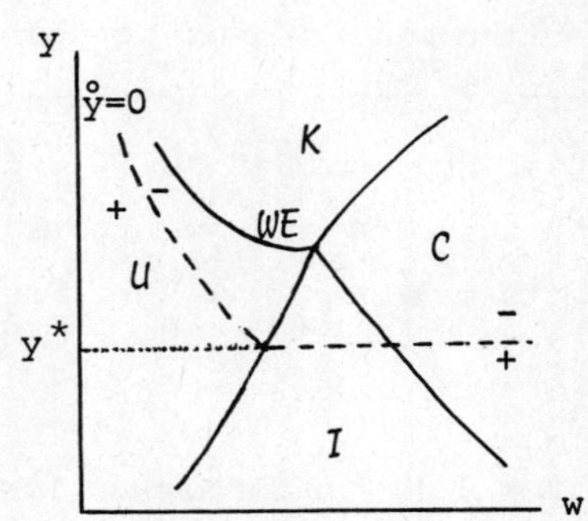

Figure 4.7.
Points with $\mathring{y} = 0$ in a plane $m = m_1$.

For such a point the equalities $\overset{\circ}{y} = 0$ and $y = y^*$ are equivalent.
For a point $x \in K \cup UK \cup U$ ($x \notin \mathrm{cl}(C \cup I)$), we have $\overset{\circ}{y} > y^* - y$ (cf. Subsection 4.2.1). Therefore, the inventory can only be constant in x, if the inventory in x exceeds the optimal inventory y^* (see Figures 4.6 and 4.7).

4.6. The BGM-model

Before investigating the stability properties of system (4.20), the next chapter will start with the analysis of the (original) Barro and Grossman/Malinvaud model. We shall refer to the model of this chapter with the exception of the possibility of an inventory of consumption goods as the "*BGM-model*".
In the BGM-model Assumption As 4 is not made. We have

$$Q(q) \equiv 0 \quad \text{and} \quad y \equiv 0 \; ,$$

where q is inventory, y is initial inventory and Q is the valuation function of stock.
For any function f defined in Chapters 3 and 4, which has the arguments m, w and y, we will omit the argument y in the notation and write f(m,w) instead of f(m,w,0). The pair (m,w)' again will be denoted by x.

For the BGM-model the graphs of the effective demand and supply functions of the production sector in (ℓ,r)-space coincide with the graph of the production function (for labour inputs that do not exceed the notional labour demand). A consequence for the effective labour demand function is

$$L_r^P(r^{P*}(x);x) = 1/w \; ,$$

which is the reciprocal of the value of the real wage rate.
The set of voluntary trades of the production sector for a given pair of parameters $x = (m,w)' \in \mathbb{R}^2_{++}$ degenerates to a part of a curve. With the help of Theorem 3.13 we find

$$H^P(x) = \{(\ell,r) \in \mathbb{R}^2_+ \mid r = F(\ell),\ \ell \le \ell^{P*}(x)\} \quad (x \in \mathbb{R}^2_{++}) \; . \tag{4.26}$$

The set of voluntary trades of the consumption sector for the parameters m and w is still given by Theorem 3.10.

The analogues of (3.14)-(3.16) in the BGM-model are the following definitions:

(4.27) $\quad X_b^C := \{x \in \mathbb{R}_{++}^2 \mid \mathbb{R}_{++}^2 \cap H^C(x) \subset D^C(x)\}$,

(4.28) $\quad X_b^P := \{x \quad \mathbb{R}_{++}^2 \mid \ell^{P*}(x) > 0 \wedge r^{P*}(x) > 0\}$,

(4.29) $\quad X_b := \{x \in X_b^C \cap X_b^P \mid H^C(x) \cap H^P(x) \neq 0\}$.

It can be observed that $x = (m,w)'$ is an element of the set X_b^P only if $\lim_{\bar{\ell}\downarrow 0} F_\ell(\bar{\ell}) < w$.

The BGM-model can be described by the following system:

$$(4.30) \quad \begin{cases} \overset{\circ}{m} = M(m,w) \\ \overset{\circ}{w} = W(m,w) \end{cases} \qquad (m,w)' \in X_b ,$$

where the functions M and W are specified as in (4.18) and (4.19). System (4.30) has not got an Underconsumption regime as a consequence of the fact that the set $H^P(x)$ of voluntary trades for the production sector has an empty interior. For the BGM-model the following set will be defined:

(4.31) $\quad KI := (\text{cl } K \cap \text{cl } I) \setminus WE$.

The NWE-state corresponding with an element of KI is called a Keynesian/Inflation state.

Furthermore, since there is no inventory of goods in the BGM-model, the following equalities hold (see Definition 4.6):

$$IWE = WE \wedge MWE = SWE .$$

Clearly, the production sector is constrained in a Keynesian/Inflation state (see (4.31)). Nevertheless, it can be checked that

$$\text{for } x \in \text{cl } K\text{: } R^P[\hat{\ell}(x);x] - \hat{r}(x) = 0 ;$$

$$\text{for } x \in \text{cl } I\text{: } L^P[\hat{r}(x);x] - \hat{\ell}(x) = 0 .$$

Therefore, the excess demand specifications (4.10) and (4.11) do not signalize the restriction of the production sector in a Keynesian/ Inflation state. That makes these specifications unrealistic. Furthermore, the derivatives related with the production sector $E_m^{\ell P}$, $E_w^{\ell P}$, E_m^{rP} and E_w^{rP} are all equal to zero. These objections hold for every continuous excess demand specification.

4.7. *Extensions*

In this chapter it is assumed explicitly that the preferences of the sectors are constant over time (Assumption As 10). This assumption implies that expectations of both sectors are constant. Hence a lot of information about the price formation in the past is ignored. It should be more realistic if, for instance, the sectors would take account of a price increase in a situation of Repressed Inflation. Such expectations could be incorporated in the model, buth then the differential system would not be of first order anymore.

Dynamic models can be introduced with discrete time as well. Instead of (4.1) we then get

$$m_n(t+1) = m_n(t) + w_n(t) \cdot \hat{\ell}[m(t),w(t),y(t)] - p(t) \cdot \hat{r}[m(t),w(t),y(t)] ,$$

in which $w_n(t)$ and $p(t)$ are the nominal wage rate and the price of consumption good, both fixed during period t. The terms $m_n(t)$ and $y(t)$ denote the stocks of nominal money and goods at the beginning of period t. Real money holdings and real wage rate are given by $m(t)$ and $w(t)$. The values of $\hat{\ell}$ and $\hat{r}$ are the quantities of labour and the consumption good, that are traded among the sectors during period t. The nominal money holdings at the end of period t (beginning of period t + 1) are denoted by $m_n(t+1)$. Prices are adjusted at the beginning of the new period. For instance,

$$p(t+1) = p(t) + p(t)\,[k^{rC} E^{rC}(m(t),w(t),y(t)) - k^{rP} E^{rP}(m(t),w(t),y(t))] .$$

In this way a difference system can be obtained.

5. STABILITY PROPERTIES OF THE DIFFERENT TYPES OF EQUILIBRIA

5.1. Possible types of equilibria in the dynamic model

In this chapter some stability properties of equilibria of the models from the preceding section will be investigated.
The system

$$(4.20)\qquad \begin{cases} \overset{\circ}{m} = M(m,w,y) \\ \overset{\circ}{w} = W(m,w,y) \qquad (m,w,y)' \in X \\ \overset{\circ}{y} = Y(m,w,y) \end{cases}$$

has several types of equilibria. As already pointed out in Section 4.5, for any element of the sets C and U the inequality $\overset{\circ}{w} \neq 0$ holds. So, equilibria of system (4.20) within these sets are impossible. There may be equilibria in the sets cl K and cl I. Equilibria in the sets K and I will be called Keynesian and Inflation equilibria, respectively. In an Inflation equilibrium the price of the good, the nominal wage rate w_n and the nominal money stocks m_n grow at the same rate. This inflation, however, does not affect the traded quantities of labour $\hat{\ell}$ and goods $\hat{r}$, that are constant over time. In a Keynesian equilibrium the variables p, w_n and m_n decrease proportionally, so that there is a constant deflation and the quantities $\hat{\ell}$ and $\hat{r}$ are constant again.
An equilibrium of system (4.20), which is an element of the set WE of Walras Equilibria is also an element of the set SWE of Stationary Walras Equilibria (see Definition 4.6). In the latter set money and goods stocks are constant over time, as well as the price p of goods, the nominal wage rate w_n and the transaction $(\hat{\ell},\hat{r})$.

In the next section we will start with the analysis of equilibria in the BGM-model (see Section 4.6). It will be assumed to be impossible for the production sector to hold an inventory of goods, so that the model can be described by the two-dimensional system

$$(4.30)\quad \begin{cases} \overset{\circ}{m} = M(m,w) \\ \overset{\circ}{w} = W(m,w) \end{cases} \qquad (m,w)' \in \mathcal{X}_b ,$$

which has the same three types of equilibria as system (4.20). Stationary Walras Equilibria will be investigated in Section 5.3. Inflation and Keynesian equilibria of system (4.30) have been studied by Honkapohja (1979) and are also the subject of the Subsections 5.3.3 and 5.3.4.

In Sections 5.4 and 5.5 also the inventory of consumption goods in the production sector will be considered, as we study the stability properties of system (4.20).

In this chapter much attention will be paid to the weight factors k^{rc} etc., in the price adjustment relations (4.8) and (4.9) and their influence on stability.

It will be assumed henceforth that the set *IWE* of Inventory Walras Equilibria (see Definition 4.6) is nonempty. Since this set contains at most one element by Proposition 4.7, this assumption implies that the set *IWE* contains a single element denoted, respectively, by $x^* = (m^*,w^*,y^*)'$ and $x^* = (m^*,w^*)'$.

We select a translation such that x^* is the origin of the new coordinate system. The same notation will be used for the variables with regard to the new coordinate system. Hence, m with regard to the new coordinate system corresponds with $m+m^*$ with regard to the old one.

5.2. *Walras Equilibria in* $\mathbb{R}^2$

5.2.1. Introduction.

In the present and the next section we consider the BGM-model and system (4.30) (see Section 4.6). In this section the case of zero savings at the origin will be investigated. So it will be assumed that the origin is an equilibrium of system (4.30). System (4.30) is a discontinuous, piecewise differentiable system (see Section 2.4).

Even for continuous excess demand functions the right-hand side of system (4.30) might be discontinuous on the boundary $\mathcal{KI}$. We start with an investigation of the subsystems. Henceforth, derivatives evaluated at the origin will be denoted without arguments.

5.2.2. Linearization of regimes and right-hand sides

The sets $\mathcal{C}$, $\mathcal{I}$ and $\mathcal{K}$ will be approximated by tangent cones (see Definition 2.5). It follows from the conditions concerning the effective demand functions in Subsection 4.2.2 that these sets can be represented as follows:

$$\mathcal{C} = \{x \in \mathcal{X}_b \mid E^{\ell C}(x) > 0 \wedge E^{rC}(x) > 0\} \text{ ,}$$

$$\mathcal{I} = \{x \in \mathcal{X}_b \mid E^{\ell P}(x) > 0 \wedge E^{rC}(x) > 0\} \text{ ,}$$

$$\mathcal{K} = \{x \in \mathcal{X}_b \mid E^{\ell C}(x) > 0 \wedge E^{rP}(x) > 0\} \text{ ,}$$

where the set $\mathcal{X}_b$ is defined in (4. 29).
By writing the regimes in this way, the tangent cones can be found with the aid of Theorem 2.8. The tangent cones can be expressed in terms of the gradients of the effective demand functions evaluated at the origin.

As an example the common boundary of the tangent cones $\mathrm{Co}(\mathcal{C})$ and $\mathrm{Co}(\mathcal{I})$ is taken. This common boundary is equal to the set $\mathrm{Co}(\mathcal{CI})$. The common boundary of the sets $\mathcal{C}$ and $\mathcal{I}$ is characterized by the fact that for its elements (cf. Subsection 4.3.2)

$$E^{\ell C\mathcal{C}}(x) = E^{\ell P\mathcal{I}}(x) = 0 \text{ .}$$

The gradients of the functions $E^{\ell C\mathcal{C}}$ and $E^{\ell P\mathcal{I}}$, both evaluated at the origin, are dependent, but their directions are opposite. These gradients can be found easily from the equation

$$\ell^{P*}(x) - L^C[r^{P*}(x),x] = 0$$

which determines the common boundary $\mathcal{CI}$, where $(\ell^{P*}(x),r^{P*}(x))$ is the notional solution of the production sector and L^C is the effective labour supply function (cf. Section 3.6).

The gradient of the left-hand side of the above equation evaluated at the origin is defined by

$$(5.1)\qquad b^{CI} := -\,(L^C_m\,,\,L^C_w + r^{P*}_w L^C_r - \ell^{P*}_w)\ ,$$

where the derivatives of L^C are evaluated at the Walras Equilibrium. Similarly, the gradients b^{KI} and b^{KC} are defined:

$$(5.2)\qquad b^{KI} := (w^*\ell^{C*}_m - r^{C*}_m\,,\,w^*\ell^{C*}_m - r^{C*}_m)\ ,$$

$$(5.3)\qquad b^{KC} := (R^C_m\,,\,R^C_w + R^C_\ell\,\ell^{P*}_w - r^{P*}_w)\ ,$$

where $(\ell^{C*}(x), r^{C*}(x))$ is the notional solution of the consumption sector and R^C is the effective goods demand function. With respect to (5.2) it can be recalled that in the BGM-model for the production sector the following equalities hold:

$$(5.4)\qquad R^P_\ell[\ell^{P*}(x);x] = F_\ell[\ell^{P*}(x)] = 1\,/\,L^P_r[r^{P*}(x);x] = w$$

which is valid for all $x = (m,w)' \in X_b$.

If the two by two matrix Z is defined by

$$(5.5)\qquad Z := \begin{pmatrix} r^{C*}_m - r^{P*}_m & r^{C*}_w - r^{P*}_w \\ \ell^{C*}_m - \ell^{P*}_m & \ell^{C*}_w - \ell^{P*}_w \end{pmatrix}$$

where, under our assumptions, $\ell^{P*}_m = r^{P*}_m = 0$, then the gradients b^{CI}, b^{KI} and b^{KC} can be written as follows (cf. (5.4) and Theorems 3.21-3.23):

$$(5.6)\qquad b^{CI} = (L^C_r,-1)Z\ ,\quad b^{KI} = (-1,w^*)Z\ ,\quad b^{KC} = (1,-R^C_\ell)Z\ .$$

Furthermore, we have the following dependencies

$$b^{CI} = -\,\zeta_1(E^{\ell CC}_m, E^{\ell CC}_w) = \zeta_2(E^{\ell PI}_m, E^{\ell PI}_w)\ ,$$

$$b^{KI} = -\,\zeta_3(E^{rCI}_m, E^{rCI}_w) = \zeta_4(E^{\ell CK}_m, E^{\ell CK}_w)\ ,$$

$$b^{KC} = -\,\zeta_5(E^{rPK}_m, E^{rPK}_w) = \zeta_6(E^{rCC}_m, E^{rCC}_w)\ ,$$

where ζ_i, i = 1,...,6, are certain positive numbers.

These equalities together with (5.1)-(5.3), Assumptions As 7 and As 8 and Theorem 3.21, lead to the sign pattern of the derivatives of the excess demand functions at Walras Equilibria.

PROPOSITION 5.1. *Under Assumptions* As 1-3, As 5-10 *and* As 12, *in the BGM-model the signs of the derivatives evaluated at the Walras Equilibrium are given by Table* 5.1.

TABLE 5.1. The sign pattern of the derivatives of the excess demand functions evaluated at the Walras Equilibrium in the BGM-model.

	$E^{\ell C}$	m	w	E^{rC}	m	w
third upper index	C	−	+	C	+	+
	K	−		I	+	

	$E^{\ell P}$	m	w	E^{rP}	m	w
third upper index	I	+	−	K	−	−

The derivative $E_m^{\ell CC}$ appears in the first row, first column, etc. The signs of the derivatives $E_w^{\ell CK}$ and E_w^{rCI} are indefinite. Under the assumptions of Proposition 5.1 we have

$$\text{(5.7)} \qquad \operatorname{sgn} E_w^{\ell CK} = - \operatorname{sgn} E_w^{rCI} = \operatorname{sgn}(w\ell_w^{C*} - r_w^{C*}) .$$

In the sequel the signs will be often denoted under the derivatives.

The vectors that generate the tangent cones can be found in a simple way. Let $P := \begin{pmatrix} 0 & 1 \\ -1 & 0 \end{pmatrix}$. We define

$$\text{(5.8)} \qquad (q^{CI})' := b^{CI} P, \quad (q^{KI})' := b^{KI} P, \quad (q^{KC})' := b^{KC} P.$$

The vector q^{CI} generates the half line $\text{Co}(CI)$, etc. (see Figure 5.1).

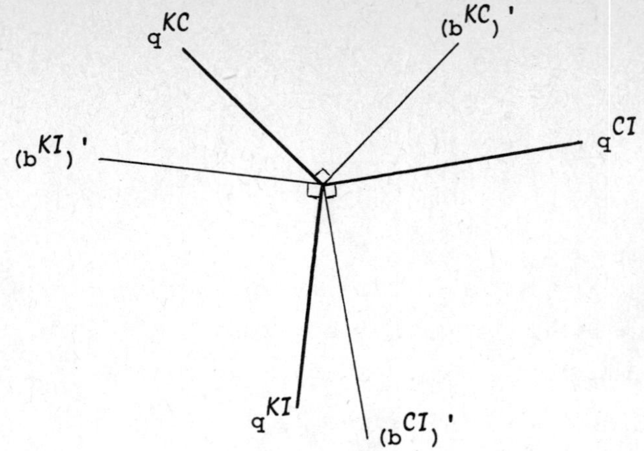

<u>Figure 5.1</u>.

Vectors generating the linearizations of the regimes of system (4.30).

It is important to remark that the vectors in Figure 5.1 can be described by (5.1)-(5.3) and (5.8), independent of the specification of the excess demand functions (under the necessary conditions for excess demand functions mentioned in Subsection 4.2.2)! Hence, these vectors are unequivocally determined for both continuous and discontinuous excess demand functions.

We continue the analysis of the linearized regimes of system (4.30). For that purpose we define the following two by two matrices

$$\text{(5.9)}\qquad \underline{B}^{C} := \begin{pmatrix} b^{KC} \\ -b^{CI} \end{pmatrix}, \quad \underline{B}^{I} := \begin{pmatrix} -b^{KI} \\ b^{CI} \end{pmatrix}, \quad \underline{B}^{K} := \begin{pmatrix} -b^{KC} \\ b^{KI} \end{pmatrix}.$$

Each of the matrices in (5.9) has rank 2. According to Theorem 2.8 the tangent cones of the set C, I and K are the following sets

$$\text{Co}(C) = \{x \in \mathbb{R}^2 \mid \underline{B}^{C} x \geq 0\},$$

$$\text{Co}(I) = \{x \in \mathbb{R}^2 \mid \underline{B}^{I} x \geq 0\},$$

$$\text{Co}(K) = \{x \in \mathbb{R}^2 \mid \underline{B}^{K} x \geq 0\}.$$

The cone $\text{Co}(C)$ is also the convex cone generated by the vectors q^{KC} and q^{CI}, etc.

It is obvious from (5.6) and (5.9) that we can write (cf. Laroque, 1978)

$$\underline{B}^{C} = \begin{pmatrix} 1 & -R_{\ell}^{C} \\ -L_{r}^{C} & 1 \end{pmatrix} Z \ , \quad \underline{B}^{I} = \begin{pmatrix} 1 & -w^{*} \\ L_{r}^{C} & -1 \end{pmatrix} Z \ , \quad \underline{B}^{K} = \begin{pmatrix} -1 & R_{\ell}^{C} \\ -1 & w^{*} \end{pmatrix} Z \ .$$

Under Assumptions As 1-3, As 5,6 and As 8 the determinants $|Z|$ and $|\underline{B}^{C}|$ are positive. If, additionally, the "unicity assumption" As 9 holds, then $|B^{I}|$ and $|\underline{B}^{K}|$ are negative. Moreover, the next proposition is valid.

PROPOSITION 5.2. *Under Assumptions* As 1-6, As 8 *and* As 9,

$$b^{KC}\, q^{CI} = -\, b^{CI}\, q^{KC} = |\underline{B}^{C}| = (1 - R_{\ell}^{C}\, L^{C}) \cdot |Z| > 0 \ ,$$

$$b^{CI}\, q^{KI} = -\, b^{KI}\, q^{CI} = -\, |\underline{B}^{I}| = (1 - w^{*} L_{r}^{C}) \cdot |Z| > 0 \ ,$$

$$b^{KI}\, q^{KC} = -\, b^{KC}\, q^{KI} = -\, |\underline{B}^{K}| = (w^{*} - R_{\ell}^{C}) \cdot |Z| > 0 \ .$$

where R_{ℓ}^{C} *and* L_{r}^{C} *are the slopes of the effective demand and supply functions of the consumption sector at the Walras Equilibrium and where* b^{KC}, q^{CI}, *etc., are defined by* (5.1)-(5.3) *and* (5.8) *and* Z *by* (5.5).

Obviously, the top angles of the tangent cones Co(C), Co(I) and Co(K) are determined by the slopes of the effective demand and supply functions at the Walras Equilibrium.

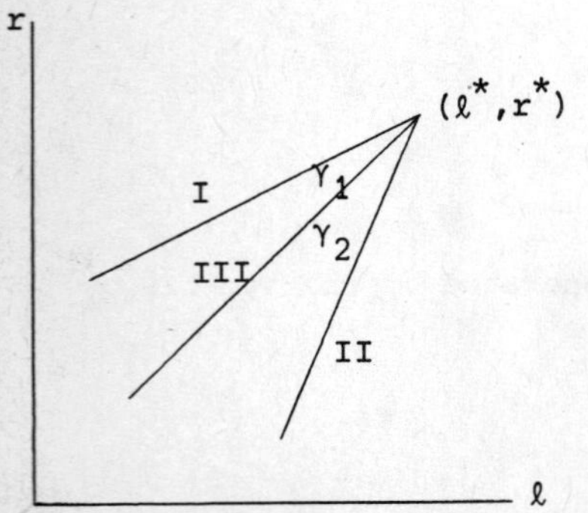

Figure 5.2

Linearization of the effective demand and supply functions at the Walras Equilibrium.

Figure 5.2 represents the slopes of the effective demand and supply functions at the Walras Equilibrium. Line I is the tangent of the effective goods demand function, line II of the effective labour supply function and line III of the production function, all at the Walras Equilibrium (ℓ^*, r^*). The slope of the production function is w^* (cf. (5.4)). It can be checked that the angle γ_1 corresponds with the term $w^* - R_\ell^C$, γ_2 with $1 - w^* L_r^C$ and $\gamma_1 + \gamma_2$ with $1 - R_\ell^C L_r^C$.
It is important to notice that Figure 5.2 is depicted under Assumption As 9, the unicity assumption. Due to this assumption the terms between brackets in Proposition 5.2 are positive.

After the linearization of the regimes, the subsystems of system (4.30) can be linearized as well. We shall analyze the matrices

$$B^Z := \begin{pmatrix} M_m^Z & M_w^Z \\ W_m^Z & W_w^Z \end{pmatrix}, \quad Z = C, I, K,$$

where the functions in the right-hand side are defined by (4.21), (4.22) and (4.24) and where the derivatives are evaluated at the origin. The matrices B^C, B^I and B^K are the Jacobian matrices of the right-hand sides of the subsystems of system (4.30) in the regimes C, I and K, respectively, and evaluated at the origin.
With the aid of (4.21), (4.22) and (4.24) and Theorem 4.3(iii) we find

$$(5.10) \qquad B^C = \begin{pmatrix} 0 & \ell^* \\ 0 & 0 \end{pmatrix} - \begin{pmatrix} m^* k^{rC} & 0 \\ w^* k^{rC} & w^* k^{\ell C} \end{pmatrix} \begin{pmatrix} \underset{+}{E_m^{rC}} & \underset{+}{E_w^{rC}} \\ \underset{-}{E_m^{\ell C}} & \underset{+}{E_w^{\ell C}} \end{pmatrix},$$

$$(5.11) \qquad B^I = \begin{pmatrix} 0 & \ell^* \\ 0 & 0 \end{pmatrix} + \begin{pmatrix} -m^* k^{rC} & 0 \\ -w^* k^{rC} & w^* k^{\ell P} \end{pmatrix} \begin{pmatrix} \underset{+}{E_m^{rCI}} & E_w^{rCI} \\ \underset{+}{E_m^{\ell PI}} & \underset{-}{E_w^{\ell PI}} \end{pmatrix},$$

$$(5.12) \qquad B^K = \begin{pmatrix} S_m^K & S_w^K \\ 0 & 0 \end{pmatrix} + \begin{pmatrix} m^* k^{rP} & 0 \\ w^* k^{rP} & -w^* k^{\ell C} \end{pmatrix} \begin{pmatrix} \underset{-}{E_m^{rPK}} & \underset{-}{E_w^{rPK}} \\ \underset{-}{E_m^{\ell CK}} & E_w^{\ell CK} \end{pmatrix},$$

where ℓ^* is the Walrasian labour level.

With respect to the first row of B^{K} the following can be noticed. According to Theorem 4.3, the vector $(S_m^K, S_w^K) - (0,\ell^*)$ is dependent of the gradient b^{KC} (see (5.3)). By Assumption As 3, Theorem 3.21 and Lemma 3.29 these two vectors have the same direction.

Now, the matrices B^{C}, B^{I} and B^{K} can be expressed alternatively as

(5.13) $$B^{C} = \begin{pmatrix} 0 & \ell^* \\ 0 & 0 \end{pmatrix} - \begin{pmatrix} \beta_1 & 0 \\ \beta_2 & \beta_3 \end{pmatrix} \underline{B}^{C},$$

(5.14) $$B^{I} = \begin{pmatrix} 0 & \ell^* \\ 0 & 0 \end{pmatrix} - \begin{pmatrix} \beta_4 & 0 \\ \beta_5 & -\beta_6 \end{pmatrix} \underline{B}^{I},$$

(5.15) $$B^{K} = \begin{pmatrix} 0 & \ell^* \\ 0 & 0 \end{pmatrix} - \begin{pmatrix} -\beta_7 & 0 \\ -\beta_8 & \beta_9 \end{pmatrix} \underline{B}^{K},$$

where $\beta_i > 0$, $i = 1,\ldots,9$, and the matrices $\underline{B}^{C}$, $\underline{B}^{I}$ and $\underline{B}^{K}$ are given by (5.9). It can be observed that the terms M_m^C, M_m^I, M_m^K as well as W_w^C are negative.

It has already been noticed that the matrices $\underline{B}^{C}$, $\underline{B}^{I}$ and $\underline{B}^{K}$ determine the tangent cones of the regimes of system (4.30). In the case of absence of stock adjustments, these three matrices rule the right-hand side of system (4.30).

5.2.3. Stability of the subsystems

According to Corollary 2.18, the asymptotic stability of the origin as an equilibrium of the subsystems depends on the traces and determinants of the Jacobian matrices B^{C}, B^{I} and B^{K}. The traces are given by (cf. (5.10)-(5.12))

(5.16) $$\mathrm{tr}\, B^{C} = -\, m^* k^{rC} \underset{+}{E_m^{rCC}} - w^* k^{rC} \underset{+}{E_w^{rCC}} - w^* k^{\ell C} \underset{+}{E_w^{\ell CC}},$$

(5.17) $$\mathrm{tr}\, B^{I} = -\, m^* k^{rC} \underset{+}{E_m^{rCI}} - w^* k^{rC} \underset{?}{E_w^{rCI}} + w^* k^{\ell P} \underset{-}{E_w^{\ell PI}},$$

(5.18) $$\mathrm{tr}\, B^{K} = \underset{-}{S_m} + m^* k^{rP} \underset{-}{E_m^{rPK}} - w^* k^{\ell C} \underset{?}{E_w^{\ell CK}} + w^* k^{rP} \underset{-}{E_w^{rPK}}.$$

Obviously, tr $B^C < 0$. In the right-hand sides of the latter two equalities there can be at most one positive term. Due to (5.7) we have

$$\operatorname{tr} B^I < 0 \vee \operatorname{tr} B^K < 0 .$$

Even if the derivative E_w^{rCI} is negative, tr B^I is negative, if the weight factor $k^{\ell P}$ is sufficiently large relative to k^{rC}. If, on the other hand, the derivative $E_w^{\ell CK}$ is negative, then tr B^K is negative, if the weight factor k^{rP} is sufficiently large relative to $k^{\ell C}$. Hence a sufficient condition for negativity of the traces is that the wage and price adjustments in the case the producers are rationed are more rapid than in the case the consumers are rationed. This condition, however, is by no means necessary.
The determinants of the matrices B^C, B^I and B^K can be investigated as well. We can write

$$|B^C| = \lambda_1\beta_2 + \lambda_2\beta_3 + \beta_1\beta_3|\underline{B}^C| \qquad (\lambda_1,\lambda_2 \in \mathbb{R}) ,$$

$$|B^I| = \lambda_3\beta_5 + \lambda_4\beta_6 - \beta_4\beta_6|\underline{B}^I| \qquad (\lambda_3,\lambda_4 \in \mathbb{R}) ,$$

$$|B^K| = \lambda_5\beta_8 + \lambda_6\beta_9 - \beta_7\beta_9|\underline{B}^K| \qquad (\lambda_5,\lambda_6 \in \mathbb{R}) ,$$

for certain values of the scalars λ_i, $i = 1,\dots,6$.
For large values of the weight factors of the excess demand functions the positive scalars β_i, $i = 1,2,\dots,9$ are also large. Hence, for large values of the weight factors the terms that are quadratic in the β_i's dominate. Then the sign of the determinant $|\underline{B}^C$ determines the sign of $|B^C|$, etc. The signs of the determinants $|\underline{B}^C|$, $|\underline{B}^I|$ and $|\underline{B}^K|$ are determined by Proposition 5.2. It can be observed that the coefficients of the quadratic terms $\beta_1\beta_3$, $\beta_4\beta_6$ and $\beta_7\beta_9$ in the above equations are all positive. Hence, it can be concluded that for sufficiently large values of the weight factors the determinants $|B^C|$, $|B^I|$ and $|B^K|$ are positive.
If the weight factors of the excess demand functions are zero, that is if there are no price adjustments at all, then it can be seen in (5.13)-(5.15) that

$$B^{C} = B^{I} = \begin{pmatrix} 0 & \ell^* \\ 0 & 0 \end{pmatrix} , \quad B^{K} = \begin{pmatrix} s_m^K & s_w^K \\ 0 & 0 \end{pmatrix} .$$

Since each of these matrices has at least one eigenvalue which is equal to zero, the subsystems of system (4.30) are not asymptotically stable in this case. Obviously, price adjustments are necessary to obtain asymptotically stable subsystems.

The conclusion of this subsection can be represented formally as follows.

THEOREM 5.3. *Let in system* (4.30) *the equality* $S(0) = 0$ *hold. Under Assumptions* As 1-3 *and* As 5-7, *there are nonnegative scalars* α, β, γ *and* δ *such that if*

$$k^{\ell P} \geq \alpha k^{rC} \geq \gamma$$

$$k^{rP} \geq \beta k^{\ell C} \geq \delta$$

then the origin is an asymptotically stable equilibrium of each of the subsystems of system (4.30).

It should be noted that $k^{\ell P}$ and k^{rP} must be sufficiently large compared with k^{rC} and $k^{\ell C}$ to ensure negativity of the traces of the matrices B^{I} and B^{K}, respectively.
Thus, especially in the case the producers are rationed, a flexible price adjustment behaviour is favourable for stability of the subsystems.
Our conclusion is weaker than the conclusion of Veendorp (1975) with respect to a model without a (money) stock. Veendorp shows the asymptotic stability of his subsystems, which is independent of the weight factors under his gross substitutability assumption.

5.2.4. Stability of the total system

For the stability of the total system the following theorem follows immediately from Theorem 2.38.

THEOREM 5.4. *Let in system* (4.30) *the equality* $S(0) = 0$ *hold. Under Assumptions* As 1-3 *and* As 5-12 *and if*

$$\text{(1)}\quad \operatorname{tr} B^{C} < 0,\ \operatorname{tr} B^{I} < 0,\ \operatorname{tr} B^{K} < 0,\ |B^{C}| > 0,\ |B^{I}| > 0,\ |B^{K}| > 0,$$

and in the case (4.30) *is discontinuous, also*

$$\text{(2)}\quad b^{CI} B^{C} q^{CI} \cdot b^{CI} B^{I} q^{CI} > 0,$$

$$b^{KI} B^{I} q^{KI} \cdot b^{KI} B^{K} q^{KI} > 0,$$

$$b^{KC} B^{K} q^{KC} \cdot b^{KC} B^{C} q^{KC} > 0,$$

$$\text{(3)}\quad \mathcal{E}(x) \neq 0 \text{ for all } x \neq 0 \Rightarrow b^{CI} B^{C} q^{CI} \geq b^{CI} B^{I} q^{CI},$$

$$b^{KI} B^{I} q^{KI} \geq b^{KI} B^{K} q^{KI},$$

$$b^{KC} B^{K} q^{KC} \geq b^{KC} B^{C} q^{KC},$$

where b^{CI} *etc. are given by* (5.1)-(5.3), q^{CI} *etc. are given by* (5.8) *and* $\mathcal{E}: \mathbb{R}^2 \to \mathbb{R}$ *is defined by*

$$\begin{aligned} \mathcal{E}(x) &= |x, B^{C}x| \quad \text{for} \quad x \in \{0\} \cup [\mathrm{Co}(C) \setminus \mathrm{Co}(K)] \\ &= |x, B^{I}x| \quad \text{for} \quad x \in \{0\} \cup [\mathrm{Co}(I) \setminus \mathrm{Co}(C)] \\ &= |x, B^{K}x| \quad \text{for} \quad x \in \{0\} \cup [\mathrm{Co}(K) \setminus \mathrm{Co}(I)], \end{aligned}$$

then the origin is an asymptotically stable equilibrium of system (4.30).

If system (4.30) is continuous, then the conditions (2) and (3) can be ignored. However, it has been noticed in Section 4.6 already that this continuity is not very realistic.
Condition (1) requires that the three subsystems of system (4.30) have the Stationary Walras Equilibrium as an asymptotically stable equilibrium. This asymptotic stability is dealt with in Theorem 5.3 in the preceding subsection. Hence, condition (1) is satisfied if the weight factors of the excess demand functions are sufficiently large and the weight factors related to the production sector are sufficiently large relative to those of the consumption sector.
Condition (2) is the condition of the existence of solutions of a discontinuous system (4.30) in a neighbourhood of the equilibrium.

Condition (3) is a sufficient condition under which the function $|\pounds|$ attaching the absolute value of $\pounds$ to x, is a generalized Liapunov function. The terms in conditions (2) and (3) are worked out below:

$$(5.19)\qquad b^{CI}B^{C}q^{CI} = \ell^{*}(b_1^{CI})^2 - (m^{*}b_1^{CI} + w^{*}b_2^{CI})(1 - R_{\ell}^{C}L_r^{C})\cdot|Z|\cdot k^{rC}/\|b^{KC}\|$$

$$(5.20)\qquad b^{CI}B^{I}q^{CI} = \ell^{*}(b_1^{CI})^2 - (m^{*}b_1^{CI} + w^{*}b_2^{CI})(1 - w^{*}L_r^{C})\cdot|Z|\cdot k^{rC}/\|b^{KI}\|$$

$$(5.21)\qquad b^{KI}B^{I}q^{KI} = \ell^{*}(b_1^{KI})^2 - w^{*}b_2^{KI}(1 - w^{*}L_r^{C})\cdot|Z|\cdot k^{\ell P}/\|b^{CI}\|$$

$$(5.22)\qquad b^{KI}B^{K}q^{KI} = \ell^{*}(b_1^{KI})^2 - (m^{*}b_1^{KI} + w^{*}b_2^{KI})(w^{*} - R_{\ell}^{C})\cdot|Z|\cdot k^{rP}/\|b^{KC}\|$$

$$(5.23)\qquad b^{KC}B^{K}q^{KC} = \ell^{*}(b_1^{KC})^2 - w^{*}b_2^{KC}(w^{*} - R_{\ell}^{C})\cdot|Z|\cdot k^{\ell C}/\|b^{KI}\|$$

$$(5.24)\qquad b^{KC}B^{C}q^{KC} = \ell^{*}(b_1^{KC})^2 - w^{*}b_2^{KC}(1 - R_{\ell}^{C}L_r^{C})\cdot|Z|\cdot k^{\ell C}/\|b^{CI}\|$$

where the matrix Z is given by (5.5), b^{CI} etc. by (5.1)-(5.3) and where the subindices of the vectors represent the components.
Clearly, the terms in Proposition 5.2 play a role in (5.19)-(5.24). The right-hand sides of (5.19)-(5.24) are linear functions in the weight factors of excess demand functions (k^{rC} etc.). For small values of these weight factors the left-hand sides of (5.19)-(5.24) are positive. This positivity corresponds with a clockwise motion of trajectories of system (4.30). However, for small values of the weight factors the conditions of Theorem 5.3 may be violated. The coefficients of $k^{\ell C}$ in (5.23) and (5.24) are negative. Hence, for sufficiently large values of $k^{\ell C}$ the motion of trajectories crossing the tangent cone Co(KC) is anti-clockwise. The signs of the coefficients of k^{rC}, $k^{\ell P}$ and k^{rP} are indefinite. Nevertheless, the signs of the coefficients of k^{rC} in (5.19) and (5.20) are equal. It can be observed that the following terms, respectively, determine the validity of the inequalities in condition (3):

$$(1 - R_{\ell}^{C}L_r^{C})\cdot\|b^{KI}\| - (1 - w^{*}L_r^{C})\cdot\|b^{KC}\|$$

$$k^{\ell P}w^{*}b_2^{KI}(1 - w^{*}L_r^{C})\cdot\|b^{KC}\| - k^{rP}(m^{*}b_1^{KI} + w^{*}b_2^{KI})(w^{*} - R_{\ell}^{C})\cdot\|b^{CI}\|$$

$$(w^{*} - R_{\ell}^{C})\cdot\|b^{CI}\| - (1 - R_{\ell}^{C}L_r^{C})\cdot\|b^{KI}\| .$$

The calculation of these terms is very unattractive.
It has been shown by Laroque (1981b) that discontinuities in the stockless model of Veendorp (1975) do not cause any existence problems related with solutions of the corresponding system. However, this conclusion does not hold in the present model with a money stock. The existence of solutions depends on the sizes of the weight factors of the excess demand functions.
Summarizing, we can say: The conditions in Theorem 5.4 depend on the flexibility of the price of consumption goods and the nominal wage rate and therefore on the price adjustment behaviour. Furthermore, in conditions (2) and (3) the sensitivity of effective demand and supply functions with respect to the constraints on the other market and the sensitivities of the notional solutions with respect to m and w, play a role (see Proposition 5.2). Especially the relevance of the top angles of the cones $Co(\mathcal{C})$, $Co(\mathcal{I})$ and $Co(\mathcal{K})$ (cf. Figure 5.1) for condition (3) is noticeable.

5.2.5. An alternative approach

Since condition (3) of Theorem 5.4 has not led us to a very satisfactory result, an alternative approach will be followed for discontinuous systems (4.30). This approach is similar to the one of Veendorp. We will make use of the special structure of system (4.30). The regimes $\mathcal{C}$, $\mathcal{I}$ and $\mathcal{K}$ can be characterized by the signs of the changes of the price p and the nominal wage rate w_n in the dynamic models. It is also possible to consider the signs of changes of real money stock m and real wage rate w. Then the following definitions can be made (see also Figure 5.3), in which the set $\mathcal{X}_b$ is defined by (4.29):

$$\Phi_{++} := \{x \in \mathcal{X}_b \mid M(x) > 0 \wedge W(x) > 0\} ,$$

$$\Phi_{+-} := \{x \in \mathcal{X}_b \mid M(x) > 0 \wedge W(x) < 0\} ,$$

$$\Phi_{-+} := \{x \in \mathcal{X}_b \mid M(x) < 0 \wedge W(x) > 0\} ,$$

$$\Phi_{--} := \{x \in \mathcal{X}_b \mid M(x) < 0 \wedge W(x) < 0\} .$$

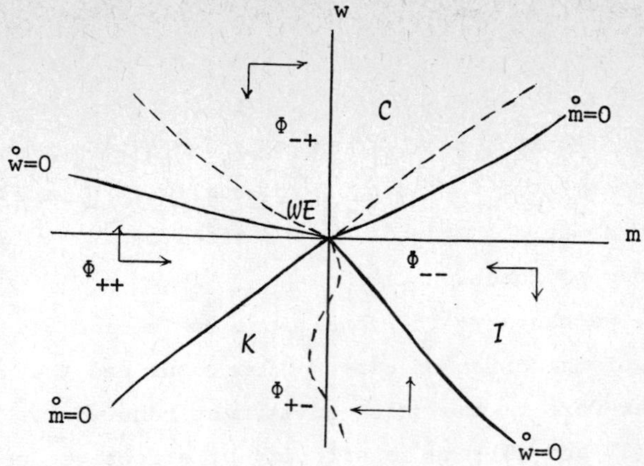

<u>Figure 5.3</u>

Possible representation of the sets where $\mathring{m} = 0$ and $\mathring{w} = 0$.

System (4.30) is not necessarily continuous on the sets Φ_{++}, etc. Since the origin is a Stationary Walras Equilibrium, it is surrounded by the above four sets. The goal of the new approach is to relate trajectories of system (4.30) with the slopes of the boundaries of the sets Φ_{++}, etc. It will be shown that these trajectories stay within clockwise spirals.

The real wage rate is increasing in the set KI and decreasing in the set C (cf. (4.14), (4.15)). It will be assumed provisionally, that the real money stock is decreasing in KI and increasing in C. This is equivalent to

(5.25) $\quad KI \subset \Phi_{-+} \quad$ and $\quad C \subset \Phi_{+-}$.

In Subsection 5.2.3 it has been investigated under which conditions the traces of the matrices B^C, B^I and B^K are negative (cf. (5.16)-(5.18)). If the price and wage flexibility of the production sector (related with the weight factors $k^{\ell P}$ and k^{rP}) is sufficiently large compared with the one of the consumption sector ($k^{\ell C}$ and k^{rC}), then we have

(5.26) $\quad W^I_w < 0 \quad$ and $\quad W^K_w < 0$.

Under (5.26), each of the elements on the main diagonals of the matrices B^C, B^I and B^K is negative and hence the traces are negative (see (5.16)-(5.18)). (5.26) can be expressed in terms of the inequalities in Theorem 5.3.

A possible representation of the sets Φ_{++}, etc., satisfying (5.25) is given in figure 5.3. This figure corresponds to Veendorp's Figure 1. Veendorp, however, considers the regimes based on only price adjustments.

If (5.25) holds, the boundaries of the sets Φ_{++}, etc., are given, at least in a neighbourhood of the origin, by

$$\{x \in I \mid M(x) = 0\} ,$$

$$\{x \in I \mid W(x) = 0\} ,$$

$$\{x \in K \mid M(x) = 0\} ,$$

$$\{x \in K \mid W(x) = 0\} .$$

Making use of the implicit function theorem (Theorem 2.2) and Assumption As 12 and (5.26), these sets coincide with differentiable half curves and the tangents to these half curves in the origin exist and they can be represented by expressions of the following form:

$$m = -(M_w^K / M_m^K)w : \text{ tangent to } \{(m,w) \in K \mid M(m,w) = 0\} \text{ in } (0,0) ,$$

etc. A possible representation of these tangents is depicted in Figure 5.4.

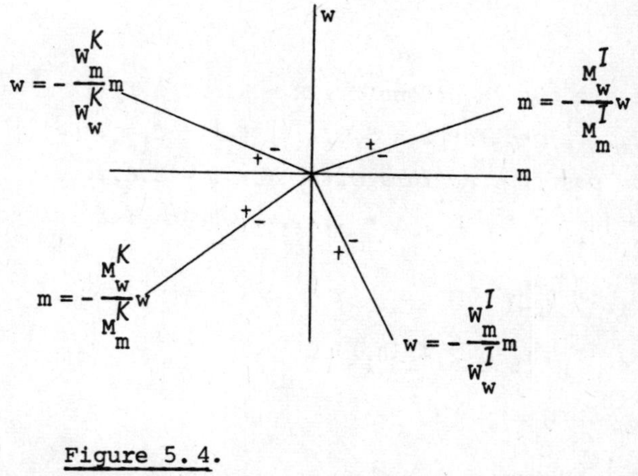

Figure 5.4.
Sign pattern of $(\overset{\circ}{m},\overset{\circ}{w})$ in the origin.

We will have use for a property which is based on the slopes of the tangents mentioned above and the sign pattern of (m,w) as it is represented in Figure 5.4. Let a trajectory of system (4.30) start in a point $(m_0,w_0)' \in \Phi_{++}$. As long as this trajectory has not left Φ_{++}, it will stay on the right-hand side of a vertical line through $(m_0,w_0)'$. If the sign pattern of $(\overset{\circ}{m},\overset{\circ}{w})$ near the origin can be represented by Figure 5.4, then such a trajectory will cross the curve determined by $\overset{\circ}{w} = 0$. Then the trajectory shows a clockwise motion and stays within a spiral, which is defined in the following lemma (see also Figure 5.5).

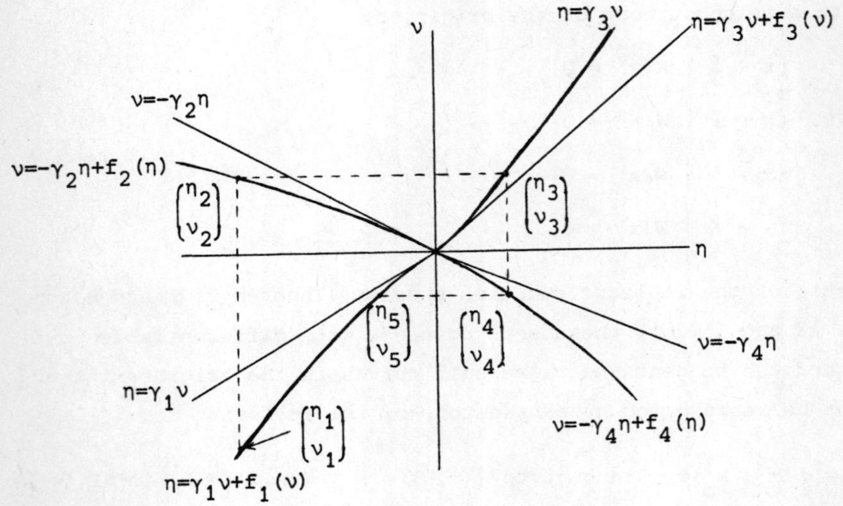

<u>Figure 5.5</u>.
Convergence of the sequence $(\eta_i,\nu_i)'$, $i = 1,2,3,\ldots$.

LEMMA 5.5. *Given are the functions* $f_i: \mathbb{R} \to \mathbb{R}$, *with* $f_i(\xi) = o(\xi)$ $(\xi \to 0)$, $i = 1,2,\ldots$, *and for* $i = 5,6,\ldots$, $f_i := f_{i-4}$. *Let* γ_i, $i = 1,2,3,\ldots$, *be positive scalars with, for* $i = 5,6,\ldots$, $\gamma_i := \gamma_{i-4}$. *Let the sequence* $(\eta_i,\nu_i)' \in \mathbb{R}^2$, $i = 1,2,\ldots$, *be defined as follows:*

If i *is even:*
$$\eta_i := \eta_{i-1}$$
$$\nu_i := -\gamma_i \eta_i + f_i(\eta_i).$$

If i *is odd:*
$$\nu_i := \nu_{i-1}$$
$$\eta_i := \gamma_i \nu_i + f_i(\nu_i).$$

If $\gamma_1\gamma_2\gamma_3\gamma_4 < 1$*, then there is a positive real number* δ*, such that*

$$|\eta_1| < \delta \Rightarrow \lim_{i\to\infty} \| (\eta_i,\nu_i)' \| = 0 \,.$$

PROOF. The elements of the sequence can be determined as follows:

$$\eta_2 = \eta_1 \,,$$

$$\nu_2 = -\gamma_2\eta_1 + f_1(\eta_1) \,,$$

$$\eta_3 = -\gamma_3\gamma_2\eta_1 + o(\eta_1) + f_2[-\gamma_2\eta_1 + f_1(\eta_1)] \quad (\eta_1 \to 0) \,.$$

Since the following equalities hold:

$$\lim_{\eta_1\to 0} \frac{|f_2[-\gamma_2\eta_1 + f_1(\eta_1)]|}{\eta_1}$$

$$= \lim_{\eta_1\to 0} \frac{|f_2[-\gamma_2\eta_1 + f_1(\eta_1)]|}{-\gamma_2\eta_1 + f_1(\eta_1)} \cdot \frac{-\gamma_2\eta_1 + f_1(\eta_1)}{\eta_1}$$

$$= \qquad 0 \qquad \cdot (-\gamma_2) = 0$$

we have

$$\eta_3 = -\gamma_3\gamma_2\eta_1 + o(\eta_1) \quad (\eta_1 \to 0) \,.$$

Proceeding in the same way yields

$$\eta_5 = \gamma_1\gamma_2\gamma_3\gamma_4\eta_1 + o(\eta_1) \quad (\eta_1 \to 0) \,,$$

$$\eta_{1+4k} = (\gamma_1\gamma_2\gamma_3\gamma_4)^k \eta_1 + o(\eta_1) \quad (\eta_1 \to 0) \,,$$

such that, if η_1 is sufficiently close to 0, since $\gamma_1\gamma_2\gamma_3\gamma_4 < 1$,

$$\lim_{k\to\infty} \eta_{1+4k} = 0 \,.$$

Analogously, it can be proved that ν_{1+4k} and $\| (\eta_{j+4k},\nu_{j+4k})' \|$ for $j = 2,3,4$, converge to zero if $|\eta_1| < \delta$ and δ is sufficiently small. □

Lemma 5.5 shows that the slopes of the tangents to the sets $\{x \in I \mid M(x) = 0\}$, etc., are related to the stability of system (4.30). This is the essence of the following lemma.

LEMMA 5.6. *Under* (5.25) *and* (5.26), *in Theorem* 5.4 *condition* (3) *can be replaced by the following condition:*

$$(3') \qquad \left.\begin{array}{l} M_w^K > 0 \\ W_m^I < 0 \\ W_m^K < 0 \end{array}\right\} \Rightarrow \frac{M_w^K W_m^K M_w^I W_m^I}{M_m^K W_w^K M_m^I W_w^I} < 1 \; .$$

PROOF. It should be noted first that the inequality $M_w^I > 0$ holds, since the boundary CI has a positive slope (see Section 3.6), which exceeds the slope $-M_w^I / M_m^I$ (with $M_m^I < 0$).
On the basis of the antecedence of implication (3') two cases can be distinguished.

Case I. Let the antecedence in (3') be false. Suppose, $W_m^K \geq 0$, $W_m^I < 0$ and $M_w^K > 0$. Since $|B^K| > 0$ and hence $W_m^K / W_w^K > M_m^K / M_w^K$ in this situation we have

$$Co(\Phi_{++}) \subset -\mathbb{R}_+^2 \; .$$

Hence, in a neighbourhood of the origin a trajectory of system (4.30) which is in the cone $Co(\Phi_{++})$ cannot leave this cone and converges to the origin. It can be checked with the help of phase diagrams, that all trajectories end up in the cone $Co(\Phi_{++})$, likewise to the cone K in Lemma 2.30.
As a consequence of the fact that $M_w^I > 0$, in each of the subcases of Case I there exists at least one cone in which trajectories are "captured" and forced to converge to the origin. Therefore, in Case I the origin is an asymptotically stable equilibrium of system (4.30).

Case II. Let the antecedence of (3') be true. Then trajectories of system (4.30) show clockwise motions, so that Lemma 5.5 is applicable. It can be seen easily, that a trajectory beginning with $(m_1, w_1)'$, sufficiently close to the origin, stays within a spiral as constructed in Lemma 5.5 with $\gamma_1 = M_w^K / M_m^K$, etc. Therefore, under (3'), such a trajectory converges to the origin and the origin is an asymptotically stable equilibrium of system (4.30). □

The construction of the spiral in Case II comes to the same thing as the construction of a Liapunov function of system (4.30). In comparison with Theorem 2.31, Case I of the above proof corresponds with the case that there exists an eigenvector of the matrix A_i in the cone $Co(S_i)$, such that the equality $\mathcal{E}(x) = 0$ holds for some $x \neq 0$. Case II corresponds with the situation $\mathcal{E}(x) < 0$ for $x \neq 0$ in Theorem 2.31.
In fact, it is not necessary in Lemma 5.6 to impose conditions with respect to the Classical regime. This corresponds with the fact that the real wage rate is decreasing in the set C, which makes Classical Unemployment a transitory phenomenon.

Another important remark is that the clockwise motions appearing in Case II of Lemma 5.6 imply that condition (2) of Theorem 5.4 is satisfied (see also Theorem 2.35). Hence, in Case II existence of solutions of system (4.30) in a neighbourhood of the origin is warranted.

The main theorem of this subsection can be formulated as follows.

THEOREM 5.7. *Let in system* (4.30) *the equality* $S(0) = 0$ *hold. Under Assumptions* As 1-3 *and* As 5-12 *there are nonnegative scalars* α, β, γ *and* δ *such that if*

$$k^{\ell P} \geq k^{rC} \geq \gamma ,$$

$$k^{rP} \geq k^{\ell C} \geq \delta ,$$

and the existence condition (2) *of Theorem* 5.4 *holds, then the origin is an asymptotically stable equilibrium of system* (4.30).

PROOF. In the case that system (4.30) is continuous, existence of solutions in a neighbourhood of the origin is warranted. If (4.30) is discontinuous, this condition is ensured by condition (2) of Theorem 5.4 (cf. Theorem 2.35).
Following Theorem 5.3, there exist nonnegative scalars α, β, γ and δ such that, if the inequalities in Theorem 5.7 are satisfied, the subsystems of system (4.30) have the origin as an asymptotically stable equilibrium, which by Corollary 2.18 is equivalent to condition (1) of Theorem 5.4. Similarly to Theorem 5.3 the traces of the matrices B^I and B^K must be negative (negativity of trace B^C is satisfied already).

If (5.25) and (5.26) hold in some neighbourhood of the origin instead of condition (3) of Theorem 5.4, condition (3') in Lemma 5.6 can be taken. Under (5.25), it can be noticed that high values of the weight factors yield low values of M_w^K, M_m^K, M_w^I and M_m^I, such that either $M_w^K \leq 0$ or the consequence of implication (3') is true (remember $M_w^I > 0$, $M_m^K, M_m^I < 0$).

If there is no neighbourhood of the origin in which (5.25) and (5.26) hold, the following is done. If, for instance, the set $Co(\{x \in C \mid \overset{\circ}{m} = 0\})$ is non-empty, the slope $-M_w^I / M_m^I$ in condition (3') can be replaced either by $-M_w^C / M_m^C$ or by the slope of the half line $Co(CI)$. Then we get an alternative form for Lemma 5.6 in which condition (3') is satisfied for sufficiently high values of the weight factors as well.

Now, the assertion is proved straightforwardly. □

Following Theorem 5.7, a flexible price and wage adjustment behaviour is favourable for stability. Especially if there is a large propensity to rise the wage rate in the case of Inflation and lower the price in the case of Keynesian unemployment, asymptotic stability of the Stationary Walras Equilibrium prevails (cf. Subsection 5.2.3).

The merit of Theorem 5.7 compared with Theorem 5.4 is that the role of the weight factors comes out even more: It is not so clear in Theorem 5.4 that high weight factors are favourable. We can now dispense with a condition like condition (3) in Theorem 5.4. Furthermore, in Theorem 5.7 we make use of the fact that under Assumptions As 1-3 and As 5-12 the determinants of the matrices B^C, B^I and B^K are positive for sufficiently large weight factors. On the other hand, we cannot dispense with the existence condition (2) of Theorem 5.4.

Finally, it can be remarked that the directions of trajectories for large weight factors may be counterclockwise, so that Lemma 5.5 cannot be applied. However, that does not matter, since for large values of the weight factors the antecedence of implication (3') in Lemma 5.6 is false, so that implication (3') itself is true.

5.3. *Stability of other Equilibria in* $\mathbb{R}^2$

5.3.1. Introduction

In this section the stability properties of Inflation and Keynesian equilibria of system (4.30) will be analyzed. In these equilibria the right-hand side of (4.30) is continuously differentiable. The stability properties can be derived from the analysis of the Jacobian matrix of the right-hand side of system (4.30), evaluated at the equilibrium. Assumption As 14 and Theorem 4.3 are important for the determination of the signs of the elements of this Jacobian matrix.

5.3.2. An assumption concerning the signs of the derivatives of the excess demand functions

For the analysis of the Jacobian matrices mentioned in the above introduction more knowledge is necessary with respect to the derivatives of the excess demand functions. In the previous section the signs of these derivatives have been determined if these are evaluated at the Walras Equilibrium (see Proposition 5.1). The assumption that is made now extends the validity of the obtained sign pattern to the interiors of the regimes. This is not a strong assumption.

ASSUMPTION As 13. *In the interiors of the regimes the signs of the derivatives of the excess demand functions are given by Table* 5.1.

5.3.3. Inflation equilibria

First, the existence of an Inflation equilibrium of system (4.30) is investigated. Let $w^M(m)$ be implicitly defined by $M[m,w^M(m)] = 0$ and $w^W(m)$ by $W[m,w^W(m)] = 0$. If real savings are positive in the origin, then there can only exist an Inflation equilibrium if the slope of w^M exceeds the slope of w^W (see Figure 5.6). The opposite is necessary if real savings are negative in the origin (see Figure 5.7). In the case of zero savings in the origin the set $\mathcal{SWE}$ is nonempty and consists of the origin. Then there may exist an Inflation equilibrium of system (4.30) as well. In none of the situations mentioned above, it is excluded that there exist two or more (Inflation or other) equilibria.

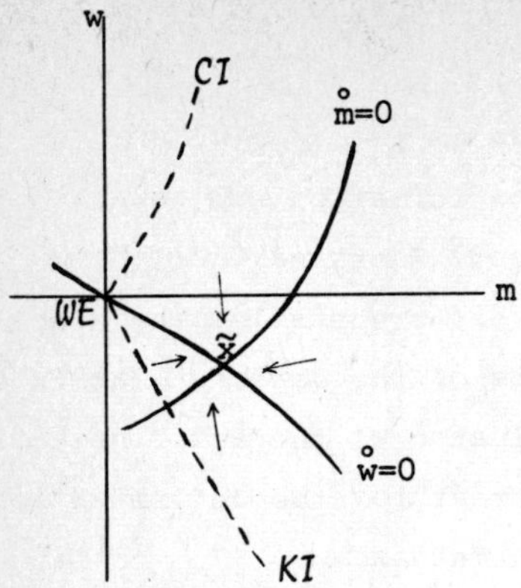

Figure 5.6.
Stable equilibrium S(0) > 0.

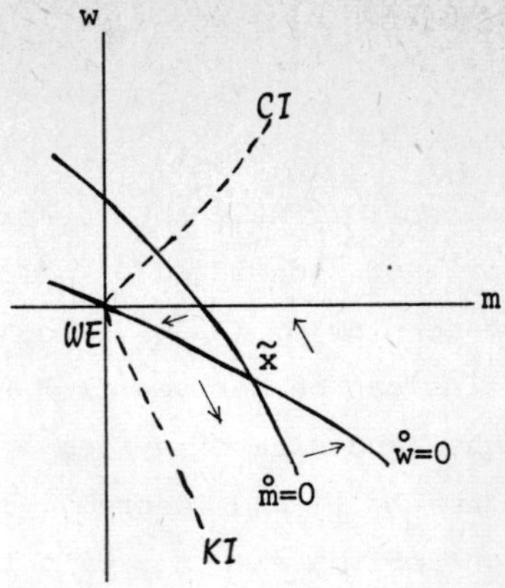

Figure 5.7.
Unstable equilibrium S(0) < 0.

An Inflation equilibrium is determined by

$$(5.27) \qquad S(x) \,/\, (m+m^*) = k^{rC}\, E^{rC}(x) = k^{\ell P}\, E^{\ell P}(x) \;,$$

where S is the real savings function and E^{rC} and $E^{\ell P}$ are excess demand functions (see Section 4.2). Let $\tilde{x} = (\tilde{m},\tilde{w}) \in I$ satisfy the above equations. The location of $\tilde{x}$ depends on the values of the weight factors k^{rC} and k^{P}. The first equality of (5.27) determines the set $\{x \in I \mid M(x) = 0\}$ of points with a constant real money stock m. It can be noticed that the location of the set $\{x \in I \mid M(x) = 0\}$ is independent of $k^{\ell P}$ (see Figure 5.9). If the value of the weight factor k^{rC} changes, the values of m and w for which this equality holds, change. The effects of such a change depend on the derivatives of the real savings function S to the variables m and w. The direction of the shift of the set $\{x \in I \mid M(x) = 0\}$ for varying k^{rC} is determined by the signs of the terms

$$S_m(\tilde{x}) - S(\tilde{x}) \,/\, (\tilde{m}+m^*) \quad \text{and} \quad S_w(\tilde{x}) \;.$$

Let, for instance, $S_m(\tilde{x}) - S(\tilde{x}) \,/\, (\tilde{m}+m^*) < 0$. If k^{rC} is increased, solutions of the first equation of (5.27) must have lower m-components; the set $\{x \in I \mid M(x) = 0\}$ is shifted leftward (see Figure 5.8). In a similar way, the latter set is shifted upward if $S_w(x) > 0$ and downward if $S_w(x) < 0$. The intersection of the sets $\{x \in I \mid M(x) = 0\}$ and $KI \cup WE \cup KC$ is the same for all values of k^{rC}.

The set $\{x \in I \mid W(x) = 0\}$ of points with a constant real wage rate is determined by the second equation of (5.27). This set is shifted downward when k^{rC} is increased or $k^{\ell P}$ is decreased. For every value of the weight factors k^{rC} and $k^{\ell P}$ the latter set contains the origin. Of course the mentioned effects should be considered simultaneously.

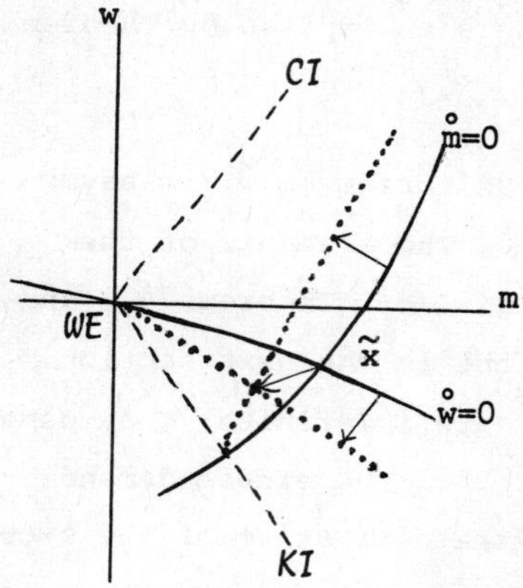

Figure 5.8.
Possible shift at an increase of k^{rC} if $\tilde{S}_m - \tilde{S} / (\tilde{m} + m^*) < 0$.

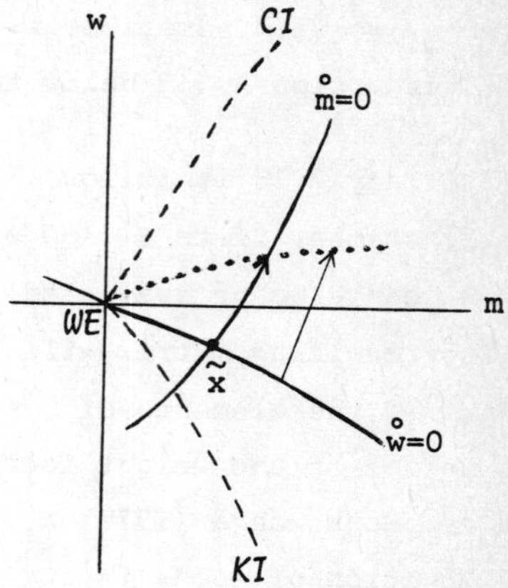

Figure 5.9.
Shift at an increase of $k^{\ell P}$.

Following Honkapohja (1979), we can take a linear approximation around the equilibrium (cf. Theorem 2.16 and Remark 2.24). The right-hand side of system (4.30) is continuously differentiable in a neighbourhood of the equilibrium x. For any function $f: \mathbb{R}^2 \to \mathbb{R}$ we will denote $f(\tilde{x})$ by $\tilde{f}$. The Jacobian matrix of the right-hand side of system (4.30) evaluated at $\tilde{x}$ is

$$\tilde{B}^I = \begin{pmatrix} \tilde{M}^I_m & \tilde{M}^I_w \\ \tilde{W}^I_m & \tilde{W}^I_w \end{pmatrix}$$

where

$$\tilde{M}^I_m = \underset{+}{\tilde{S}_m} - (\tilde{m} + m^*)k^{rC} \underset{+}{\tilde{E}^{rC}_m} - k^{rC} \underset{+}{\tilde{E}^{rC}} ,$$

$$\tilde{M}^I_w = \tilde{S}_w - (\tilde{m} + m^*)k^{rC} \tilde{E}^{rC}_w ,$$

$$\tilde{W}^I_m = (\tilde{w}+w^*)[k^{\ell P} \underset{+}{\tilde{E}^{\ell P}_m} - k^{rC} \underset{+}{\tilde{E}^{rC}_m}] ,$$

$$\tilde{W}^I_w = (\tilde{w}+w^*)[k^{\ell P} \underset{-}{\tilde{E}^{\ell P}_w} - k^{rC} \tilde{E}^{rC}_w]$$

(cf. (4.22)), where E^{rC} etc. are the excess demand functions. Henceforth, we will sometimes write the signs as implied by Theorem 4.3 and Assumption As 13 below the terms.

From Corollary 2.18 it follows that the equilibrium $(\tilde{m},\tilde{w})$ is asymptotically stable, if tr $\tilde{B}^I < 0$ and $|\tilde{B}^I| > 0$. The elements of the matrix $\tilde{B}^I$ can also be evaluated at the origin (cf. Theorems 4.3 and 4.5). The resulting matrix will be worked out in the next section. The signs of the elements of the matrix $\tilde{B}^I$ are indefinite. They depend on the values of the weight factors k^{rC} etc. of the excess demand functions. Honkapohja (1979) assumes that the derivative of the excess demand function of goods is sufficiently large compared to the one of labour. A consequence is that (in a neighbourhood of the origin) the inequality $\tilde{W}^I_m < 0$ holds. The sign of Honkapohja's $\tilde{W}^I_w$ is indefinite.

Changes in the weight factors are very inportant for stability. For sufficiently large values of the weight factors k^{rC} and $k^{\ell P}$ we might have

$$\tilde{S}_m - (\tilde{m}+m^*)k^{rC} \tilde{E}^{rC}_m - k^{rC} \tilde{E}^{rC} + (\tilde{w}+w^*)[k^{\ell P} \tilde{E}^{\ell P}_w - k^{rC} \tilde{E}^{rC}_w] < 0$$

so that tr $\tilde{B}^I$ is negative.

For high values of real savings S(0) in the Walras Equilibrium, phase diagrams indicate stability of the Inflation equilibrium, at least if it is unique (see Figure 5.6). The opposite is true for low values (see Figure 5.7). However, the slope of w^M, defined by $M[m,w^M(m)] = 0$, in Figure 5.7 seems to be less usual than the one in Figure 4.5.

For an investigation of the dependence of stability of Inflation equilibria on the weight factors, it is important to notice that if the weight factors k^{rC} and $k^{\ell P}$ change, then the evaluation point of the linear approximation matrix $\tilde{B}^I$ changes. This feature complicates a thorough investigation. If the effects of a movement of the equilibrium are large, the effects of an increase of the weight factors on the terms $\tilde{S}_m$, $\tilde{E}^{rC}_m$, $\tilde{E}^{\ell P}_w$, $\tilde{E}^{rC}_w$ and especially $\tilde{E}^{rC}$ might be unfavourable for stability. On the other hand, if these effects are small (if the terms $\tilde{S}_m - \tilde{S} / (\tilde{m} + m^*)$ and $\tilde{S}_w$ are approximately zero) an increase in the weight factors k^{rC} and $k^{\ell P}$ might be in favour of stability. It is also possible that the effects of a movement of the equilibrium are favourable for stability, for instance, if the term $\tilde{E}^{rC}$ increases.

5.3.4. Keynesian equilibria

With respect to the conditions for the existence of a Keynesian equilibrium of system (4.30) we can refer to the preceding subsection. Only the signs of the real savings at the origin must be reversed (see Figures 5.10 and 5.11).

The locations of the sets $\{x \in K \mid M(x) = 0\}$ and $\{x \in K \mid W(x) = 0\}$ once again depend on the terms $S_m(\tilde{x}) - S(\tilde{x}) / (\tilde{m} + m^*)$ and $S_w(\tilde{x})$. Possible shifts are depicted in Figures 5.10-5.13.
The Jacobian matrix in an equilibrium $\tilde{x} \in K$ of system (4.30) is

$$\tilde{B}^K := \begin{pmatrix} \tilde{M}^K_m & \tilde{M}^K_w \\ \tilde{W}^K_m & \tilde{W}^K_w \end{pmatrix}$$

where

$$\tilde{M}^K_m = \underset{-}{\tilde{S}_m} + (\tilde{m} + m^*) k^{rP} \underset{-}{\tilde{E}^{rP}_m} + k^{rP} \underset{+}{\tilde{E}^{rP}} ,$$

$$\tilde{M}^K_w = \tilde{S}_w + (\tilde{m} + m^*) k^{rP} \underset{-}{\tilde{E}^{rP}_w} ,$$

$$\tilde{W}^K_m = (\tilde{w} + w^*) [- k^{\ell C} \underset{-}{\tilde{E}^{\ell C}_m} + k^{rP} \underset{-}{\tilde{E}^{rP}_m}] ,$$

$$\tilde{W}^K_w = (\tilde{w} + w^*) [- k^{\ell C} \tilde{E}^{\ell C}_w + k^{rP} \underset{-}{\tilde{E}^{rP}_w}]$$

(cf. (4.24)), where $\tilde{S} = S(\tilde{x})$, etc.
The matrix $\tilde{B}^K$, evaluated at the Walras Equilibrium, is worked out in Section 5.2.
If the weight factor $k^{\ell P}$ is sufficiently large compared with $k^{\ell C}$, then the derivative $\tilde{W}^K_w$ is negative. Sufficiently close to the Walras Equilibrium the constraint of the production sector on the goods market

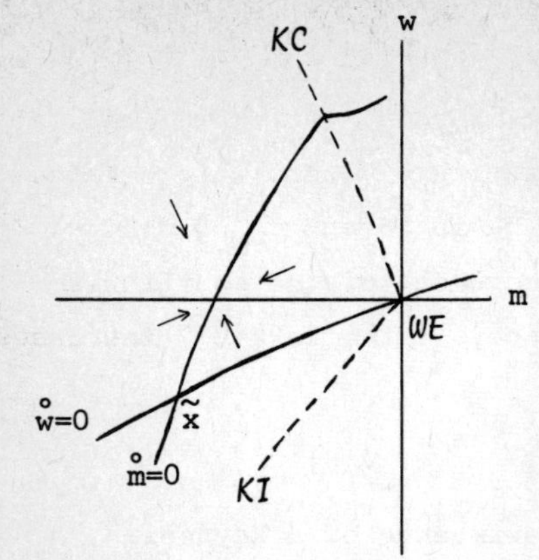

Figure 5.10.

Stable equilibrium S(0) < 0.

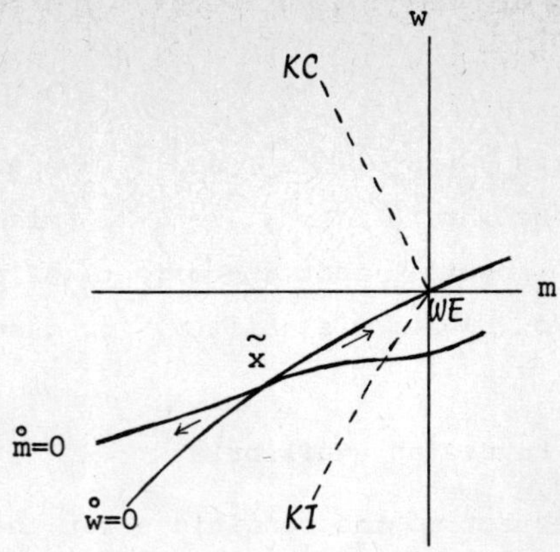

Figure 5.11.

Unstable equilibrium S(0) > 0

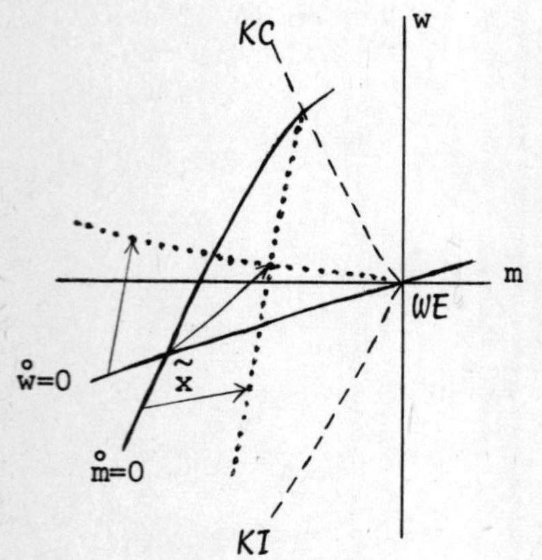

Figure 5.12.

Possible shift at an increase of k^{rP} if $\tilde{S}_m - \tilde{S}/(\tilde{m}+\hat{m}) < 0$.

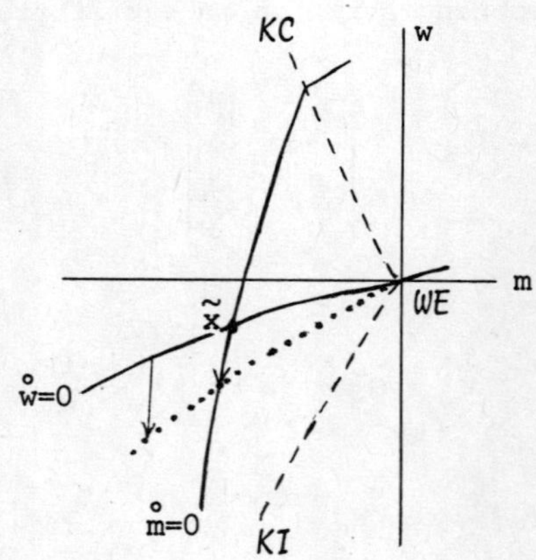

Figure 5.13.

Shift at an increase of $k^{\ell C}$.

(related with the term $\tilde{E}^{rP}$) is so small that the derivative $\tilde{M}_m^K$ is negative. Hence, close to a Walras Equilibrium tr $\tilde{B}^K < 0$, if the price flexibility in case of a rationed production sector is sufficiently large compared with the wage flexibility in case of a rationed consumption sector.

The derivative $\tilde{M}_w^K$ is positive, if the sensitivity of real savings for the real wage rate $\tilde{S}_w$ is sufficiently large. The sign of $\tilde{W}_m^K$ is indefinite.

Similar to $\tilde{W}_m^I$, Honkapohja concludes that the derivative $\tilde{W}_m^K$ is negative. Once more, the underlying assumption of Honkapohja is, that the derivative of the excess demand function of goods is sufficiently large compared to the one of labour. The signs of the elements of the Jacobian matrix $\tilde{B}^K$ lead Honkapohja to the conclusion that a Keynesian equilibrium (in a neighbourhood of the origin) is asymptotically stable. Under our assumptions, however, stability is not guaranteed.

Figures 5.10 and 5.11 indicate, that a stable Keynesian equilibrium is more likely for small values of the real savings function S(0) in the origin. For stability in relation with the weight factors the same conclusions can be obtained as for an Inflation equilibrium: For most cases an increase in the weight factors is positive for stability, but the effect of an increase may be spoiled by the fact that the location of the equilibrium is influenced as a result of a change in the weight factors.

A movement of the equilibrium may again have positive as well as negative effects on stability.

Summarizing this section we can say that the location of Inflation and Keynesian equilibria of system (4.30) depends on the magnitude of the weight factors of the excess demand functions, relative to the real savings. Furthermore, these weight factors influence stability of an equilibrium. Unfortunately, unequivocal stability results cannot be given. The stability depends on too many factors.

In the next section it will appear that we can say more about the matrices $\tilde{B}^I$ and $\tilde{B}^K$ if these matrices are evaluated at the Walras Equilibrium.

5.4. Walras Equilibria in $\mathbb{R}^3$

5.4.1. Introduction

After the analysis of the BGM-model in the preceding sections, the original model with the possibility of an inventory in the production sector will be considered. This section is devoted to the stability analysis of a Stationary Walras Equilibrium in system (4.20), the system with three variables. The origin is assumed to be a Stationary Walras Equilibrium of system (4.20), i.e., savings and inventory adjustments are equal to zero in the origin. Similar to Section 5.2 linearizations of the regimes and the right-hand sides are determined. Next, the discontinuity of the right-hand side of (4.20) will be dealt with. This discontinuity is important for the existence of solutions of system (4.20). In Subsection 5.4.4 a description is given of the mathematical problems that are involved. Subsequently, the stability of the subsystems and of the total system will be investigated in Subsections 5.4.5 and 5.4.6. We end this section with a heuristic approach of the stability problem. In the last four subsections the analysis is confined to linearized versions of system (4.20).

5.4.2. Linearization of regimes and right-hand sides

The set $\mathcal{C}$ in the model with the variables real money stock m, real wage rate w and inventory y can be represented as follows:

$$\mathcal{C} = \{x \in X \mid E^{\ell C}(x) > 0 \wedge E^{rC}(x) > 0\} .$$

The sets $\mathcal{I}$, $\mathcal{U}$ and $\mathcal{K}$ can be expressed in a similar way.
The boundary $\mathcal{CI}$ is determined by the equalities

$$E^{\ell C\mathcal{C}}(x) = E^{\ell P\mathcal{I}}(x) = 0$$

that are satisfied if

$$\ell^{P*}(x) - L^{C}[r^{P*}(x);x] = 0 ,$$

where $(\ell^{P*}(x), r^{P*}(x))$ is the notional solution of the production sector and L^C is the effective labour supply function. The gradient $a^{\mathcal{CI}}$ of the left-hand side of the latter equality evaluated at the origin is given by

$$(5.28) \qquad a^{CI} := -(L^C_m, L^C_w + r^{P*}_w L^C_r - \ell^{P*}_w, L^C_r),$$

where the derivatives of L^C are evaluated at the Walras Equilibrium. The vector a^{CI} is the analogue of the gradient b^{CI} in Section 5.2. The gradients a^{IU}, a^{UK} and a^{KC} are given similarly by

$$(5.29) \qquad a^{IU} := (\ell^{C*}_m R^P_\ell - r^{C*}_m, \ell^{C*}_w R^P_\ell - r^{C*}_w, 1),$$

$$(5.30) \qquad a^{UK} := (\ell^{C*}_m - r^{C*}_m L^P_r, \ell^{C*}_w - r^{C*}_w L^P_r, L^P_r),$$

$$(5.31) \qquad a^{KC} := (R^C_m, R^C_w + \ell^{P*}_w R^C_\ell - r^{P*}_w, -1).$$

In order to arrange these vectors conveniently the matrix $\hat{Z}$ below is introduced:

$$(5.32) \qquad \hat{Z} := \begin{pmatrix} r^{C*}_m - r^{P*}_m & r^{C*}_w - r^{P*}_w & r^{C*}_y - r^{P*}_y \\ \ell^{C*}_m - \ell^{P*}_m & \ell^{C*}_w - \ell^{P*}_w & \ell^{C*}_y - \ell^{P*}_y \end{pmatrix}.$$

It can be observed that, under our assumptions, $r^{P*}_m = \ell^{P*}_m = r^{C*}_y = \ell^{C*}_y = \ell^{P*}_y = 0$ and $r^{P*}_y = 1$ (see Theorem 3.21). Furthermore,

$$\hat{Z} = (Z, -e_1),$$

where the matrix Z is given by (5.5) and $e_1 = (1,0)'$.
The row vector a^{CI} is also the gradient of the functions $E^{\ell CC}$ and $E^{\ell PI}$ evaluated at the origin. Similar relations hold for a^{IU}, a^{UK} and a^{KC}.

The analogue of Proposition 5.1 is the following.

PROPOSITION 5.8. *Under Assumptions* As 1-10 *and* As 12, *the signs of the derivatives evaluated at the Walras Equilibrium are given by Table* 5.2.

TABLE 5.2. The sign pattern of the derivatives of the excess demand functions evaluated at the Walras Equilibrium.

	$E^{\ell C}$	m	w	y	E^{rC}	m	w	y
third upper index	$\mathcal{C}$	-	+	+	$\mathcal{C}$	+	+	-
	$\mathcal{K}$	-		+	$\mathcal{I}$	+		-

	$E^{\ell P}$	m	w	y	E^{rP}	m	w	y
third upper index	$\mathcal{I}$	+	-	-	$\mathcal{U}$	-		+
	$\mathcal{U}$	+		-	$\mathcal{K}$	-	-	+

The signs of $E_w^{\ell C\mathcal{K}}$ and $E_w^{rC\mathcal{I}}$ are indefinite again. Furthermore, the signs of $E_w^{\ell P\mathcal{U}}$ and $E_w^{rP\mathcal{U}}$ are indefinite. Under the assumptions of Proposition 5.8, instead of (5.7) the following equalities hold.

$$\text{(5.33)} \qquad \operatorname{sgn} E_w^{\ell P\mathcal{U}} = -\operatorname{sgn} E_w^{\ell C\mathcal{K}} = \operatorname{sgn} \ell_w^{P*} - \ell_w^{C*} + L_r^P(r_w^{C*} - r_w^{P*}) \quad ,$$

$$\text{(5.34)} \qquad \operatorname{sgn} E_w^{rP\mathcal{U}} = -\operatorname{sgn} E_w^{rC\mathcal{I}} = \operatorname{sgn}(w\ell_w^{C*} - r_w^{C*}) \ .$$

In (5.33) the derivative L_r^P is evaluated at $(r^{P*}(x);x)$.
The analogues of the matrices $\underline{B}^{\mathcal{C}}$, $\underline{B}^{\mathcal{I}}$ and $\underline{B}^{\mathcal{K}}$ defined in (5.9) are the following matrices:

$$\text{(5.35)} \qquad \underline{A}^{\mathcal{C}} := \begin{pmatrix} a^{\mathcal{KC}} \\ -a^{\mathcal{CI}} \end{pmatrix} , \quad \underline{A}^{\mathcal{I}} := \begin{pmatrix} -a^{\mathcal{IU}} \\ a^{\mathcal{CI}} \end{pmatrix} , \quad \underline{A}^{\mathcal{U}} := \begin{pmatrix} a^{\mathcal{IU}} \\ -a^{\mathcal{UK}} \end{pmatrix} , \quad \underline{A}^{\mathcal{K}} := \begin{pmatrix} -a^{\mathcal{KC}} \\ a^{\mathcal{UK}} \end{pmatrix} .$$

The tangent cones of the regimes of system (4.20) are given by

$$\mathrm{Co}(\mathcal{C}) = \{x \in \mathbb{R}^3 \mid \underline{A}^{\mathcal{C}} x \geq 0\} ,$$

etc. It follows from (5.28)-(5.32) and (5.35) that

$$\underline{A}^{\mathcal{C}} = \begin{pmatrix} 1 & -R_\ell^C \\ -L_r^C & 1 \end{pmatrix} \hat{z} , \quad \underline{A}^{\mathcal{I}} = \begin{pmatrix} 1 & -R_\ell^P \\ L_r^C & -1 \end{pmatrix} \hat{z} ,$$

$$\underline{A}^{U} = \begin{pmatrix} -1 & R_{\ell}^{P} \\ L_{r}^{P} & -1 \end{pmatrix} \hat{z} \ , \quad \underline{A}^{K} = \begin{pmatrix} -1 & R_{\ell}^{C} \\ -L_{r}^{P} & 1 \end{pmatrix} \hat{z} \ .$$

The Jacobian matrices of the subsystems of system (4.20) evaluated at the Walras Equilibrium are denoted by A^{C}, A^{I}, A^{U} and A^{K}, respectively. They are defined similar to the matrices B^{C}, B^{I} and B^{K} in Section 5.4. We will derive a convenient expression for the former matrices.

First, the third rows of the Jacobian matrices are analyzed. These rows are gradients of the inventory adjustment function Y (see Definition 4.1) evaluated at the origin. We denote these vectors by d^{C}, d^{I}, d^{U} and d^{K}, respectively. The application of Theorems 3.21, 3.22 and 4.3 yields the following relations:

(5.36) $\quad d^{C} = d^{I} = (0,0,-1)$,

(5.37) $\quad \zeta_1 \, a^{UK} = d^{U} - d^{K} \qquad (\zeta_1 > 0)$,

(5.38) $\quad a^{IU} = d^{U} - d^{I}$,

(5.39) $\quad \zeta_2 \, a^{KC} = d^{C} - d^{K} \qquad (\zeta_2 > 0)$,

where ζ_1 and ζ_2 are certain positive scalars.

With Theorem 4.3 and (5.36)-(5.39) it can be found that if the matrix Π is defined by

$$\Pi := \begin{pmatrix} 0 & \ell^{*} & -1 \\ 0 & 0 & 0 \\ 0 & 0 & -1 \end{pmatrix} ,$$

the Jacobian matrices of system (4.20) can be expressed as follows (cf. (5.10)-(5.12)):

(5.40) $$A^{C} = \Pi - \begin{pmatrix} \alpha_1 & 0 \\ \alpha_2 & \alpha_3 \\ 0 & 0 \end{pmatrix} \underline{A}^{C} ,$$

(5.41) $$A^{I} = \Pi - \begin{pmatrix} \alpha_4 & 0 \\ \alpha_5 & -\alpha_6 \\ 0 & 0 \end{pmatrix} \underline{A}^{I} ,$$

$$(5.42) \qquad A^{U} = \Pi + \begin{pmatrix} \alpha_7 & 0 \\ \alpha_8 & \alpha_9 \\ 1 & 0 \end{pmatrix} \underline{A}^{U} ,$$

$$(5.43) \qquad A^{K} = \Pi + \begin{pmatrix} \alpha_{10} & 0 \\ \alpha_{11} & -\alpha_{12} \\ \zeta_2 & 0 \end{pmatrix} \underline{A}^{K} ,$$

where α_i, $i = 1,\ldots,12$, are certain positive scalars and ζ_2 is the same as in (5.39).

Thus it comes out that the Jacobian matrices of the subsystems of (4.20) and (4.30) can be decomposed in a matrix corresponding with the stock adjustments and a matrix product corresponding with the price adjustments. The "stock adjustment matrix" has a simple structure. In (5.13)-(5.15) the only nonzero element of the relevant matrix is ℓ^*, the Walrasian labour input level. The matrix Π has two elements that are equal to -1. These elements correspond with the derivatives of savings function S and inventory adjustment function Y with respect to the inventory variable y.
Clearly, the matrices $\underline{A}^{C}$, $\underline{A}^{I}$, $\underline{A}^{U}$ and $\underline{A}^{K}$ rule the "price adjustment part" of the Jacobian matrices in (5.40)-(5.43). The premultiplication matrices correspond with the weight factors of the excess demand matrices. A large value of α_i is related to a large value of one of the weight factors. It is obvious that according as the weight factors are larger the relative role of the price adjustments is more important.

Next, we address ourselves with the linearized regimes of system (4.20). The set of Walras Equilibria $\mathcal{WE}$ is determined by

$$\{x \in X \mid \ell^{C*}(x) = \ell^{P*}(x) \wedge r^{C*}(x) = r^{P*}(x)\} .$$

Therefore, the line $\mathrm{Co}(\mathcal{WE})$ is the intersection of the planes with the normals, respectively, $(\ell_m^{C*}, \ell_w^{C*} - \ell_w^{P*}, 0)'$ and $(r_m^{C*}, r_w^{C*} - r_w^{P*}, -1)'$ that are the rows of the matrix $\hat{Z}$. This line is generated by the following vector $q^{\mathcal{WE}}$ with positive components:

$$q^{WE} := \begin{pmatrix} \ell_w^{C*} - \ell_w^{P*} \\ -\ell_m^{C*} \\ |Z| \end{pmatrix}$$

where the matrix Z is defined by (5.5). Clearly, the vector q^{WE} is the normal of the plane generated by (transposes of) the rows of the matrix $\hat{Z}$ and each of the gradients a^{CI}, etc., is perpendicular to the vector q^{WE}. Hence, the quadruple

$$(\mathrm{Co}(C), \mathrm{Co}(I), \mathrm{Co}(U), \mathrm{Co}(K))$$

is a common line partition of $\mathbb{R}^3$ (see Definition 2.39 and Figure 2.4).

Another consequence of the fact that the gradients a^{CI} etc., are perpendicular to the vector q^{WE} is that the tangent cones

$$\mathrm{Co}(\{x \in I \mid W(x) = 0\}) ,$$

$$\mathrm{Co}(\{x \in K \mid W(x) = 0\})$$

both contain the line $\mathrm{Co}(WE)$ generated by the vector q^{WE}. This property is the "linearized" version of the zero wage rate adjustment in Walras Equilibria.

5.4.3. Discontinuity of the right-hand sides

As mentioned already in Section 4.2 the right-hand side of system (4.20) may be discontinuous. In this subsection the case of discontinuity is examined further.

In the right-hand side of (4.20) three functions appear: the real money stock adjustment function M (see (4.18)), the real wage rate adjustment function W (see (4.19)) and the inventory adjustment function Y (see Definition 4.1). The latter function is continuous by Theorem 4.3. The function M is built up of a function S which is continuous (see Theorem 4.3) and a price adjustment part. The function W is the difference of nominal wage rate and price adjustments. The nominal wage rate and price adjustments (see (4.8)-(4.9)) in their turn are built up from excess demand functions. The latter may cause discontinuities.

It can be checked that on the set $KC \cup WE \cup IU$, where the price of goods p is constant, the function M is equal to the real savings function S, and therefore continuous. Consequently, on this set discontinuity only comes out via the real c.q. nominal wage rate adjustment. On the set $UK \cup WE \cup CI$ the nominal wage rate is constant. Hence, the discontinuity is caused by the price adjustment and so both functions M and W can be discontinuous. It can also be concluded that in a Walras Equilibrium (in the set WE) where there are no price and wage rate adjustments, the right-hand side of (4.20) is continuous even if the excess demand functions are not continuous everywhere.
The question can be raised if the continuity properties for the linearized system are similar. It can be checked that the equalities (5.36)-(5.39) ensure the continuity of the linearizations of the (continuous) function Y. For instance, on the plane given by $a^{UK}x = 0$, the equality

$$d^{U} x = d^{K} x$$

holds.
If the adjustment functions M of real money stock and W of real wage rate are discontinuous, it can not be expected that the linearizations of these functions are continuous on the tangent cones of the regimes. Finally, the continuity of the linearized right-hand side of (4.20) on the linearized set of Walras Equilibria will be shown in the next subsection.

5.4.4. Mathematical description of the linearized system

In this subsection we will have a closer look at the linearized version of system (4.20) and summarize the results of the preceding subsections.
It has been shown in Subsection 5.4.2 that the quadruple (Co(C),Co(I), Co(U),Co(K)) is a common line partition of $\mathbb{R}^3$ and the vector q^{WE} is the vector q in Definition 2.39. The linearized version of (4.20) can be based on this common line partition. The definition of the right-hand side on the boundaries of the cones is not very essential. For this reason we only consider the interiors of the tangent cones of the regimes. The linearized system can be represented as follows

$$(5.44) \qquad \overset{\circ}{x} = A^{A} x \quad \text{for } x \in \text{int Co}(\mathcal{Z}), \quad \mathcal{Z} = \mathcal{C},\mathcal{I},\mathcal{U},\mathcal{K}.$$

An important result from Subsection 5.4.2 is that the cones $\text{Co}(\mathcal{Z})$ as well as the matrices $A^{\mathcal{Z}}$ can be written in terms of "price adjustment matrices" $\underline{A}^{\mathcal{Z}}$ defined by (5.35). For $\mathcal{Z} = \mathcal{C},\mathcal{I},\mathcal{U},\mathcal{K}$,

$$\text{Co}(\mathcal{Z}) = \{x \in \mathbb{R}^3 \mid \underline{A}^{\mathcal{Z}} x \geq 0\},$$

$$A^{\mathcal{Z}} = \Pi + N^{\mathcal{Z}} \underline{A}^{\mathcal{Z}},$$

where

$$N^{\mathcal{C}} = \begin{pmatrix} \alpha_1 & 0 \\ \alpha_2 & \alpha_3 \\ 0 & 0 \end{pmatrix},$$

etc.

Next it can be shown that the continuity of the right-hand side of (4.20) in the set of Walras Equilibria is preserved when the system is linearized. Since for $\mathcal{Z} = \mathcal{C},\mathcal{I},\mathcal{U},\mathcal{K}$

$$\underline{A}^{A} q^{\mathcal{WE}} = 0$$

if $x = \lambda q^{\mathcal{WE}}$ $(\lambda \in \mathbb{R})$, then

$$A^{\mathcal{Z}} x = \lambda \Pi q^{\mathcal{WE}}$$

which implies continuity of the right-hand side of (5.44) in the points of the ray generated by the vector $q^{\mathcal{WE}}$ even if there are discontinuities in the excess demand functions elsewhere. On this ray the motion of the trajectory is ruled by the matrix Π.

The discontinuity pattern of system (5.44) on the four separating half planes is similar to the one of the original system (4.20) described in the previous subsection: on the half planes $\text{Co}(\mathcal{KC})$ and $\text{Co}(\mathcal{IU})$ the possible discontinuity is exhibited on the second component, while on the half planes $\text{Co}(\mathcal{UK})$ and $\text{Co}(\mathcal{CI})$ discontinuity at most involves the first and the second component. Thus, for instance, consider a vector $x \in \text{Co}(\mathcal{KC})$, so that the equality $a^{\mathcal{KC}} x = 0$ holds. It can be checked that only the second component of the vector $(A^{\mathcal{K}} - A^{\mathcal{C}})x$, hence of

$$(N^{\mathcal{K}} \underline{A}^{\mathcal{K}} - N^{\mathcal{C}} \underline{A}^{\mathcal{C}})x$$

is possibly unequal to zero.

With respect to the existence of solutions of system (5.44) let us first consider the case in which excess demand functions and hence system (5.44) are continuous. Since the functions in the right-hand side of system (5.44) are continuously differentiable on the (closures of the) regimes, continuity here implies Lipschitz continuity of the right-hand side of (5.44) (see Definition 2.11 and Theorem 2.12). Therefore, the existence of solutions is warranted on a compact neighbourhood of the origin.

If the excess demand functions are discontinuous, Theorem 2.34 can be applied. The following conditions are sufficient for the existence of solutions of system (5.44) in a neighbourhood of the equilibrium (cf. condition (2) of Theorem 5.4):

$$\forall\, x \in \mathrm{Co}(\mathcal{CI}):\ a^{\mathcal{CI}} A^{\mathcal{C}} x \cdot a^{\mathcal{CI}} A^{\mathcal{I}} x > 0$$

$$\forall\, x \in \mathrm{Co}(\mathcal{IU}):\ a^{\mathcal{IU}} A^{\mathcal{I}} x \cdot a^{\mathcal{IU}} A^{\mathcal{U}} x > 0$$

$$\forall\, x \in \mathrm{Co}(\mathcal{UK}):\ a^{\mathcal{UK}} A^{\mathcal{U}} x \cdot a^{\mathcal{UK}} A^{\mathcal{K}} x > 0$$

$$\forall\, x \in \mathrm{Co}(\mathcal{KC}):\ a^{\mathcal{KC}} A^{\mathcal{K}} x \cdot a^{\mathcal{KC}} A^{\mathcal{C}} x > 0\ .$$

With respect to the linearized set of Walras Equilibria $\mathrm{Co}(\mathcal{WE})$ we take a closer look at the above inequalities. Existence problems can arise if the vector $\Pi q^{\mathcal{WE}}$ points into one of the separating planes. It can be checked that in this case the above inequalities are not satisfied.

5.4.5. Stability of the subsystems

The Jacobian matrices $A^{\mathcal{C}}$, $A^{\mathcal{I}}$, $A^{\mathcal{U}}$ and $A^{\mathcal{K}}$ can be analyzed further with the aid of Theorem 2.20. For that purpose it is necessary that each of the traces of these four matrices is negative. Recall that under our assumptions tr $B^{\mathcal{C}}$ is negative and tr $B^{\mathcal{I}}$ and tr $B^{\mathcal{K}}$ are negative for sufficiently large values of the weight factors $k^{\ell P}$ and k^{rP} relative to, respectively k^{rC} and $k^{\ell C}$ (see Section 5.2).

By Theorem 4.3 the following equalities hold:

$$Y_m^{\mathcal{C}} = Y_w^{\mathcal{C}} = Y_m^{\mathcal{I}} = Y_w^{\mathcal{I}} = 0\ ,$$

$$Y_Y^{\mathcal{C}} = Y_Y^{\mathcal{I}} = -1\ .$$

It can be concluded from Theorem 2.20 that the origin is an asymptotically stable equilibrium of the system $\overset{\circ}{x} = A^{\mathcal{C}} x$, if and only if the origin (in $\mathbb{R}^2$) is an asymptotically stable equilibrium of the system $\overset{\circ}{\underline{x}} = B^{\mathcal{C}} \underline{x}$ $(\underline{x} \in \mathbb{R}^2)$. There exists a similar relation between the systems $\overset{\circ}{x} = A^{\mathcal{I}} x$ $(x \in \mathbb{R}^3)$ and $\overset{\circ}{\underline{x}} = B^{\mathcal{I}} \underline{x}$ $(\underline{x} \in \mathbb{R}^2)$.

The case of Underconsumption is absent in system (4.30). We define

$$B^{\mathcal{U}} := \begin{pmatrix} M_m^{\mathcal{U}} & M_w^{\mathcal{U}} \\ W_m^{\mathcal{U}} & W_w^{\mathcal{U}} \end{pmatrix}, \quad q^{\mathcal{U}} := (Y_m^{\mathcal{U}}, Y_w^{\mathcal{U}}) \quad \text{and} \quad c^{\mathcal{U}} := \begin{pmatrix} M_Y^{\mathcal{U}} \\ W_Y^{\mathcal{U}} \end{pmatrix}.$$

First, we consider the trace of the matrix $B^{\mathcal{U}}$:

$$\operatorname{tr} B^{\mathcal{U}} = S^{\mathcal{U}}_{m_-} + m\, k^{rP} E^{rP\mathcal{U}}_{m_-} + w^* k^{\ell P} E^{\ell P\mathcal{U}}_{w_?} + w^* k^{rP} E^{rP\mathcal{U}}_{w_?} .$$

The latter two terms in the right-hand side of the above equality depend on the specifications of the objective functions (cf. (5.7). Clearly, $\operatorname{tr} B^{\mathcal{U}} < 0$ for small values of the weight factors k^{rP} and $k^{\ell P}$. However, it is not a necessary condition that these factors are small. Furthermore, we concluded in Section 5.2 that *large* values of these factors are favourable for stability of the subsystems of system (4.30)! Let us assume $\operatorname{tr} B^{\mathcal{U}} < 0$. With the definitions of $B^{\mathcal{U}}$, $q^{\mathcal{U}}$ and $c^{\mathcal{U}}$ given above, Theorem 2.20 can be applied once again. Since $Y_Y^{\mathcal{U}} = 0$ by Theorem 4.3, the origin is an asymptotically stable equilibrium of the system $\overset{\circ}{x} = A^{\mathcal{U}} x$, if and only if the following inequalities hold:

$$-(\operatorname{tr} B^{\mathcal{U}}) \cdot |B^{\mathcal{U}}| + (q^{\mathcal{U}})' B^{\mathcal{U}} c^{\mathcal{U}} > 0 ,$$

$$(q^{\mathcal{U}})' P (B^{\mathcal{U}})' P c^{\mathcal{U}} < 0 .$$

It can be proved with Theorems 3.21–3.23, Assumption As 8 and Lemma 3.29 that the second inequality is satisfied. With respect to the first inequality, we regard the highest powers in the weight factors, $(k^{\ell P})^2 k^{rP}$ and $k^{\ell P} (k^{rP})^2$. It can be proved again with Theorems 3.21–3.23, Assumption As 8 and Lemma 3.29 that the coefficients of these terms are positive. Hence, the origin is an asymptotically stable equilibrium of the subsystem $\overset{\circ}{x} = A^{\mathcal{U}} x$, if the weight factors $k^{\ell P}$ and k^{rP} are sufficiently large and for those values of the weight factors still tr A^{U} is negative. A similar conclusion holds for the subsystem $\overset{\circ}{x} = A^{K}x$.

Thus, in most cases an increase of the weight factors of the excess demand functions is favourable for stability of the subsystems.

This result is not so elegant as Theorem 5.3. The fact that the signs of $E_{w}^{\ell pU}$ and E_{w}^{rpU} are unknown spoils the extension of this Theorem. For the two terms mentioned above more data are necessary with respect to the objective functions.

It can be observed that for a zero value of the weight factors, the matrices A^{C}, A^{I}, A^{U} and A^{K} have eigenvalues that are equal to zero, so that the origin is not an asymptotically stable equilibrium of the subsystems of system (4.20).

5.4.6. Stability of the total system

In Subsections 5.4.2, 5.4.4 and 5.4.5 we have analyzed the linearized version (5.44) of system (4.20). Existence conditions for solutions have been derived (see Subsection 5.4.4). It is investigated in Subsection 5.4.3 when the Stationary Walras Equilibrium is an asymptotically stable equilibrium of the subsystems of (5.44).

The overall stability of the original system (4.20) still has not been solved. The main problem is that Laroque's Theorem 2.26 cannot be generalized to higher dimensions.

For the rest it has not been proved that if the linear system (5.44) has the origin as an asymptotically stable equilibrium the origin is also an asymptotically stable solution of the original system (4.20) (cf. Theorem 2.32 for $\mathbb{R}^{2}$).

The overall stability of (5.44) will be tackled in the next subsection in a heuristic way.

5.4.7. A heuristic approach

In this subsection system (5.44) is considered.

The method which will be followed is a generalization of condition (3) in Theorem 5.4.

We start with Assumptions As 1-12 and (5.26), so that the following inequalities hold:

(5.45) $\quad M^I_m, M^K_m, W^I_w, W^K_w < 0$.

In addition, we restrict by assuming

(5.46) $\quad M^I_y = M^K_y = 0 \wedge M^I_w, M^K_w > 0 \wedge W^I_m, W^K_m < 0$.

Since the second row of A in (5.41) is perpendicular to the vector q^{WE} which has positive components, it follows from $W^I_m < 0$ and $W^I_w < 0$ that W^I_y is positive. Similarly, W^K_y is positive,

(5.47) $\quad W^I_y, W^K_y > 0$.

It is also assumed that in the $y = 0$ - plane the situation of Figure 5.2 holds. In this situation the real money stock m and the real wage rate w for the optimal inventory only grow simultaneously in the case of Keynesian unemployment and only decrease simultaneously in the case of Inflation (see also Figure 5.14).
If we define

(5.48) $\quad \psi^I := M^I_w W^I_m / M^I_m W^I_w \quad (M^I_m W^I_w > 0)$,

(5.49) $\quad \psi^K := M^K_w W^K_m / M^K_m W^K_w \quad (M^K_m W^K_w > 0)$,

where the signs are given by (5.45) and (5.46), then condition (3') of Lemma 5.6 is satisfied, if

(5.50) $\quad \psi^I \psi^K < 1$.

Under our assumptions, the terms ψ^I and ψ^K are negative.

The stability conditions will be derived from the construction of a block which has the property that trajectories of system (5.44) point inward on the sides. Such a block is called a "Liapunov block".

DEFINITION 5.7. *A <u>Liapunov block</u> of system* (5.44) *is a block consisting of lower bounds* $\underline{x} \in -\mathbb{R}^3_{++}$ *and upper bounds* $\bar{x} \in \mathbb{R}^3_{++}$ *such that for* $i = 1,2,3$,

1) $\quad x_i = \underline{x}_i \Rightarrow \mathring{x}_i \geq 0 \wedge \mathring{x} \neq 0$,

2) $\quad x_i = \bar{x}_i \Rightarrow \mathring{x}_i \leq 0 \wedge \mathring{x} \neq 0$.

Scalar multiplication of a Liapunov block of system (5.44) yields another Liapunov block. A Liapunov block corresponds with a Liapunov function (see Definition 2.25). The existence of a Liapunov block is sufficient for asymptotic stability of the origin as an equilibrium of system (5.44).

We will construct a block in (m,w,y)-space with the sides $m = \underline{m}$, $w = \underline{w}$, $y = \underline{y}$, $m = \bar{m}$, $w = \bar{w}$ and $y = \bar{y}$, where $\underline{m},\underline{w},\underline{y} < 0$ and $\bar{m},\bar{w},\bar{y} > 0$.
Let $x \in \mathrm{Co}(Z)$ $(Z = \mathcal{C},\mathcal{I},\mathcal{U},\mathcal{K})$ be a vertex of such a block. Then the following conditions have to be satisfied:

$$m = \underline{m} \Rightarrow M^Z_m\, m + M^Z_w\, w + M^Z_y\, y \geq 0 \wedge \mathring{x} \neq 0 ,$$

$$m = \bar{m} \Rightarrow M^Z_m\, m + M^Z_w\, w + M^Z_y\, y \leq 0 \wedge \mathring{x} \neq 0 ,$$

$$w = \underline{w} \Rightarrow W^Z_m\, m + W^Z_w\, w + W^Z_y\, y \geq 0 \wedge \mathring{x} \neq 0 ,$$

etc. We only consider the case in which the four vertices on the side $m = \underline{m}$ are elements of the set $\mathrm{Co}(\mathcal{K})$ and those on the side $m = \bar{m}$ are elements of the set $\mathrm{Co}(\mathcal{I})$ (cf. (5.25)).
There are $8 \times 3 = 24$ conditions of the above kind. The strategy of the construction of a block is to situate its vertices in such a way that only two conditions remain to make the block a Liapunov block. The construction is similar to the construction of the spiral in Lemma 5.4. We start with arbitrary values of the bounds $\bar{w}$, $\bar{y}$ and $\underline{y}$. The other bounds are determined in such a way that as much conditions of Definition 5.7 as possible hold. The two remaining conditions yield an existence problem in the original upper bounds $\bar{w}$, $\bar{y}$ and $\underline{y}$.

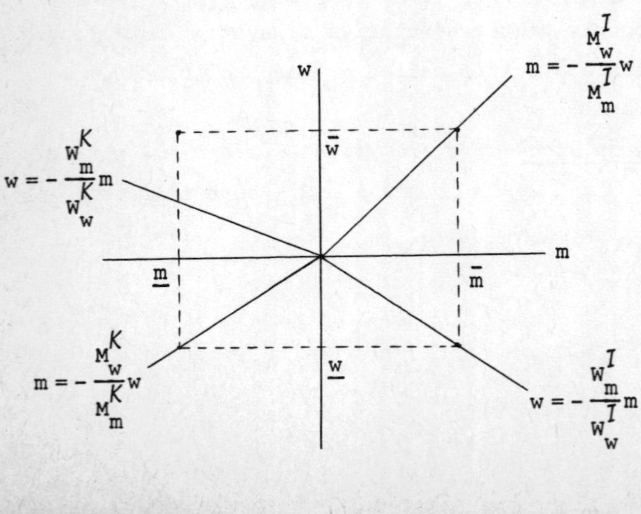

Figure 5.14.
Rectangle in the $y = 0$ - plane.

We construct a rectangle in the $y = 0$-plane with the sides $m = \bar{m}$, $m = \underline{m}$, $w = \bar{w}$, $w = \underline{w}$ (see Figure 5.14), where $\bar{m}, \bar{w} > 0$ and $\underline{m}, \underline{w} < 0$. Let $\bar{w} \in \mathbb{R}_{++}$ be given. Then $\bar{m}$ is defined by

$$(5.51) \qquad \bar{m} := -(M_w^I / M_m^I)\bar{w} \qquad (M_m^I < 0) .$$

Clearly, $\bar{m}$ is positive under our assumptions (cf. (5.45) and (5.46)). The lower bound $\underline{w}$ is given by

$$(5.52) \qquad \underline{w} := -(W_m^I / W_w^I)\bar{m} \qquad (W_w^I < 0) .$$

Then, $\underline{w}$ is negative and

$$(5.53) \qquad \underline{w} = \psi^I \bar{w} .$$

Finally, the side $m = \underline{m}$ is determined by

$$(5.54) \qquad \underline{m} := -(M_w^K / M_m^K)\underline{w} \qquad (M_m^K < 0) .$$

The term $\underline{m}$ is negative.

With respect to the inventory variable y an important remark can be made. The half space of negative y values is included in the set in which y increases. Formally,

$$y < 0 \Rightarrow \mathring{y} > 0 .$$

Furthermore, the inventory y cannot converge to a negative value. It can be concluded that trajectories of system (5.44) cannot stay infinitely long in the half space of negative y values. Consequently, the value of the lower bound $\underline{y}$ can be taken arbitrarily close to 0. Even then, y is increasing on every point of the side $y = \underline{y}$. Therefore, the bound y can be considered to be equal to zero in the inequality conditions. Furthermore, a condition like, for instance, $W_m^K \underline{m} + W_w^K \underline{w} + W_y^K \underline{y} \geq 0$, is automatically satisfied by choosing $\underline{y}$ close to 0.

As a consequence of the fact that the sets $\{x \in Co(I) \mid y = 0\}$ and $\{x \in Co(I) \mid \mathring{y} = 0\}$ coincide, the elements of the set $Co(I)$ satisfy the conditions with respect to the inventory change. Since $(Y_m^K, Y_w^K, Y_y^K)'$ is a vector with negative components, we only have to check the sign of the inventory change in the vertex $(\underline{m}, \underline{w}, \bar{y})'$.

It can be checked that for $\underline{y}$ close to 0, due to the signs of the components of the vectors $(W_m^I, W_w^I, W_y^I)'$ and $(W_m^K, W_w^K, W_y^K)'$ all the points on the side $w = \underline{w}$ satisfy the condition that the real wage rate is nondecreasing.

Sufficient conditions for the block determined by $\bar{w}$, etc., to be a Liapunov block are given by the following inequalities:

$$W_m^K \underline{m} + W_w^K \bar{w} + W_w^K \bar{y} < 0 , \tag{5.55}$$

$$Y_m^K \underline{m} + Y_w^K \underline{w} + Y_y^K \bar{y} < 0 . \tag{5.56}$$

Under our assumptions, all the other inequality conditions are satisfied if (5.55) and (5.56) hold.

Substitution of $\bar{m}$, $\underline{m}$ and $\underline{w}$ into (5.55) and (5.56) with the help of (5.51)-(5.54) yields a system of two linear inequalities in the upper bounds $\bar{w}$ and $\bar{y}$:

$$W_w^K(\psi^I\psi^K - 1)\bar{w} - W_y^K \bar{y} > 0 , \tag{5.57}$$

$$\psi^I(M_m^K Y_w^K - M_w^K Y_m^K)\bar{w} + M_m^K Y_y^K \bar{y} > 0 . \tag{5.58}$$

Inequality (5.50) is a necessary condition for (5.57).

Under (5.50), there exists a pair $(\bar{w},\bar{y}) \in \mathbb{R}^2_{++}$, which satisfies (5.57) and (5.58), if and only if

$$\begin{vmatrix} M_m^K & M_w^K & 0 \\ W_m^K & W_w^K/\psi^I & W_y^K \\ Y_m^K & Y_w^K & Y_y^K \end{vmatrix} > 0 . \tag{5.59}$$

Hence, if (5.59) holds, then under our assumptions, the origin is an asymptotically stable equilibrium of system (5.44).

We have investigated only one of many possible cases. Nevertheless, a method has been followed which can be applied in other situations as well. For instance, (5.46) is certainly not essential.

Moreover, it should be emphasized, that it is not proved that asymptotic stability of the origin as an equilibrium of the linearized system (5.44) implies asymptotic stability of the original system (4.20).

Unfortunately, the conclusions with respect to system (4.20) are less pronounced than those with respect to system (4.30) (see Section 5.2). The results are less general. The reason of this is that we were not able to extend Theorems 2.32 and 2.38 to higher dimensions. More data concerning specifications of objective and excess demand functions are necessary to verify the conditions of this subsection.

5.5. *Stability of other equilibria in* $\mathbb{R}^3$

5.5.1. Introduction

Finally, we have to deal with Inflation and Keynesian equilibria of system (4.20). Before doing so in Subsections 5.5.3 and 5.5.4 the analogue of Assumption As 13 for the three-dimensional model is formulated.

5.5.2. An assumption concerning the signs of the derivatives of the excess demand functions

Similar to Assumption As 13, it will be assumed for system (4.20) that the signs of the derivatives of the excess demand functions evaluated at a point in the interiors of the regimes are the same as those evaluated at the Walras Equilibrium (cf. Proposition 5.8).

ASSUMPTION As 14. *In the interiors of the regimes the signs of the derivatives of the excess demand functions are given by Table* 5.2.

5.5.3. Inflation equilibria

In Section 4.2, it was stated that trajectories in the set I tend to the $y=0$ -plane (related to the $y=y^*$ -plane in the original coordinate system). Let $\tilde{x} = (\tilde{m},\tilde{w},\tilde{y})' \in I$ be an equilibrium of system (4.20). The application of Theorem 2.20, in which $\alpha = Y_y(\tilde{x})$ and $q' = (0,0)$ can be substituted, leads to the conclusion that the equilibrium x is asymptotically stable, if and only if the corresponding equilibrium $(\tilde{m},\tilde{w})'$ of system (4.30) is asymptotically stable. Therefore, we can refer to the stability analysis of Subsection 5.3.3 and conclude that the addition of the inventory variable does not affect stability.

5.5.4. Keynesian equilibria

Let $\tilde{x} = (\tilde{m},\tilde{w},\tilde{y})' \in K$ be an equilibrium of system (4.20) and let the Jacobian matrix in this equilibrium be

$$\tilde{A}^K := \begin{pmatrix} \tilde{M}^K_m & \tilde{M}^K_w & \tilde{M}^K_y \\ \tilde{W}^K_m & \tilde{W}^K_w & \tilde{W}^K_y \\ \tilde{Y}^K_m & \tilde{Y}^K_w & \tilde{Y}^K_y \end{pmatrix}$$

where $\tilde{M}^K_m$, $\tilde{M}^K_w$, $\tilde{W}^K_m$ and $\tilde{W}^K_w$ are similar to Subsection 5.2.3 and

$$\tilde{M}^K_y := \tilde{S}_y + (\tilde{m}+m^*)k^{rP}\,\tilde{E}^{rP}_{+y} ,$$

$$\tilde{W}^K_y := (\tilde{w}+w^*)\,[-k^{\ell C}\,\tilde{E}^{\ell C}_{+y} + k^{rP}\,\tilde{E}^{rP}_{+y}] ,$$

$$\tilde{Y}^K_m := F_\ell[\hat{\ell}(\tilde{x})]\hat{\ell}_m(\tilde{x}) - \hat{f}_m(\tilde{x}) < 0 ,$$

$$\tilde{Y}^K_w := F_\ell[\hat{\ell}(\tilde{x})]\hat{\ell}_w(\tilde{x}) - \hat{f}_w(\tilde{x}) < 0 ,$$

$$\tilde{Y}^K_y := F_\ell[\hat{\ell}(\tilde{x})]\hat{\ell}_y(\tilde{x}) - \hat{f}_y(\tilde{x}) < 0 .$$

The signs of $\tilde{Y}^K_m$, $\tilde{Y}^K_w$ and $\tilde{Y}^K_y$ follow from Theorem 4.3.

We are especially interested in the way the variable y, related with the inventory in the production sector, affects the stability analysis of Subsection 5.3.4. Again Theorem 2.20 will be useful.

Let $(\tilde{m},\tilde{w})'$ be an asymptotically stable equilibrium of the corresponding system (4.30). Since $\tilde{Y}^K_y < 0$, then also $\operatorname{tr}\tilde{A}^K < 0$ holds. Hence, Theorem 2.20 and Remark 2.24 imply that $\tilde{x}$ is an asymptotically stable equilibrium of the system (4.20), if the following expressions are positive:

$$(5.60)\qquad -(\operatorname{tr}B)(\alpha^2 + \alpha\operatorname{tr}B + |B|) + q'(\alpha I + B)c ,$$

$$(5.61)\qquad -|B|\,\alpha - q'PB'Pc ,$$

where

$$B = \begin{pmatrix} \tilde{M}^K_m & \tilde{M}^K_w \\ \tilde{W}^K_m & \tilde{W}^K_w \end{pmatrix} , \quad \text{with tr } B < 0 \text{ and } |B| > 0 ,$$

$$\alpha = \tilde{Y}^K_y < 0 ,$$

$$q' = (\tilde{Y}^K_m, \tilde{Y}^K_w) < (0,0) ,$$

$$c = (\tilde{M}^K_y, \tilde{W}^K_y)' .$$

The coefficients of α^2 in (5.60) and $-\alpha$ in (5.61) are positive. Hence, (5.60) and (5.61) are positive, if the derivative $\tilde{Y}^K_y$ is sufficiently low. The same conclusion prevails, of course, if the elements of the vectors q and c are small in absolute value. Changes of the weight factors do not yield unequivocal changes in (5.60) and (5.61). Also movements of the equilibrium have to be considered (cf. Subsection 5.3.4).

If the pair $(\tilde{m},\tilde{w})'$ is an unstable equilibrium of the corresponding system (4.30), the triple $(\tilde{m},\tilde{w},\tilde{y})'$ can still be an asymptotically stable equilibrium of system (4.20). In particular, this is the case for low values of $\tilde{Y}^K_y$ and high values of $\tilde{Y}^K_m$ and $\tilde{Y}^K_w$, such that the inequality tr $\tilde{A}^K < 0$ holds and expressions (5.60) and (5.61) are positive.

6. CONCLUSIONS

6.1. General concluding remarks

In the models introduced in this thesis Non-Walrasian Equilibria appear. The conditions for Non-Walrasian Equilibria can be summarized as "*optimality*", "*voluntariness*" and "*rationing on the long side only*" (see Subsection 1.4.2). We have investigated the Non-Walrasian Equilibria of the Barro and Grossman/Malinvaud model (see Barro and Grossman (1971) and Malinvaud (1977)) extended with the possibility of an inventory change in the production sector.
This inventory is introduced in a rather simple way via a valuation function of stock. The objective function of the production sector is the sum of the real cash flow and the valuation function of stock.
The "voluntariness" condition leads to the introduction of "*voluntary trades*". A trade is called voluntary for a sector, if there exists a pair of upper bounds such that the trade is the solution of the maximization problem. The graphs of the effective demand/supply functions, that give the demand/supply for given constraints on the other market, are boundaries of the "sets of voluntary trades".
A "Non-Walrasian Equilibrium (NWE-) state" is introduced as a sequence of a parameter vector, a "transaction" and two pairs of upper bounds. The transaction is the *optimal* solution for both sectors simultaneously under the given upper bounds. For the two pairs of upper bounds the condition "*rationing on the long side only*" holds. Under Assumption As 9 the transaction is unique for given parameters. Under this assumption the transaction is the *voluntary* trade which is *optimal* for both sectors.
Assumption As 9 implies that the parameter space can be divided into disjoint sets, that correspond with Walras Equilibrium, Classical Unemployment, Repressed Inflation, Underconsumption and Keynesian Unemployment NWE-states. The names of the market states are given following Malinvaud (1977) and Muellbauer and Portes (1978). The locations of the above sets are investigated.

We have studied a dynamic version of the Barro and Grossman/Malinvaud model. In this model the price of the consumption good and the wage rate are adjusted following "excess demand functions". Assumptions As 12-14 have been made with respect to the differentiability and signs of derivatives of the excess demand functions. Stock relations for the dynamic model have been formulated. The dynamic model can be described by a differential system with a piecewise differentiable right-hand side. This right-hand side may be discontinuous, which causes existence problems with respect to solutions of the system. A set on which the right-hand side is differentiable is called a "regime".

The stability properties of equilibria of two systems have been investigated. The first system is based on the Barro and Grossman/ Malinvaud model extended with price adjustments and an adjustment of money holdings (cf. Honkapohja, 1979). In the second system, additionally a variable stock of goods in the production sector is incorporated.
Under the "Law of demand and supply", these systems can have Walrasian, Inflation and Keynesian equilibria. In each of these three kinds of equilibria the transaction is constant. The nominal money stock, the price of goods and the nominal wage rate grow at the same rate, which is, respectively, zero, positive and negative in Walrasian, Inflation and Keynesian equilibria.

The first system mentioned above has two variables and the second has three. The transition from the two-variable into the three-variable model leads to difficulties. The results from the two-variable model cannot be generalized. Fortunately, the regimes of the three-variable model have a pleasant structure, which is called a "common line partition". This structure enables us at least to solve existence problems of solutions.
The main conclusions with respect to stability can be found in Section 6.2.

6.2. Conclusions concerning stability

6.2.1. Some general stability results

In this section some stability conclusions are given. They are presented, in particular, in comparison with the results of Arrow, Block and Hurwicz (1959), Veendorp (1975) and Honkapohja (1979). Similar to the tâtonnement process in Arrow, Block and Hurwicz and the adjustment process of Veendorp, the price adjustments are based on the "Law of demand and supply". The great difference is that the tâtonnement process starts with "notional" excess demands, while Veendorp considers "effective" excess demands. The latter are based on the "dual decision hypothesis" (see Subsection 1.4.2) and can be called (neo-) keynesian concepts. We also consider price adjustments based on excess demands and, additionally, we consider adjustments of both money stock and inventory. One of the crucial assumptions of both Arrow, Block and Hurwicz and Veendorp is "gross substitutability" (see Section 1.5). Instead of "gross substitutability" we have made Assumptions As 8, As 13 and As 14. These assumptions are not expressed in derivatives to prices only, but in derivatives with respect to the real money stock, the real wage rate and the inventory of goods in the production sector. The Assumptions As 13 and As 14 seem to be reasonable, especially under Assumption As 8.

Other important assumptions made by Arrow, Block and Hurwicz are "Walras' Law" and "homogeneity" (see Section 1.5).

Walras' Law does not hold for effective excess demands! A homogeneity assumption is implicit. We have normalized the price of money.

The differential systems describing the models of Arrow, Block and Hurwicz and of Veendorp have only one type of equilibrium. This is the Walras Equilibrium, which has been proved to be asymptotically stable in both systems.

In systems (4.20) and (4.30) equilibria can be Walrasian as well as Inflationary and Keynesian. These equilibria are not necessarily stable. Stability depends on the excess demand functions and on their weight factors.

The values of the functions χ_I and χ_K defined in Lemma 3.29 are also important. For high values of these functions the derivatives in Theorem 3.30 are small in absolute value. For small (positive) values

of χ_I and χ_K the transaction is sensitive for changes in the real money stock, real wage rate and the inventory.
Inflation and Keynesian equilibria of system (4.30) have been investigated in Honkapohja (1979). Honkapohja's conclusion is that Keynesian equilibria and most of the Inflation equilibria are asymptotically stable. However, he assumes that the nominal wage rate is more sticky than the price, which is not assumed by us.

The obvious way to compare our results concerning Stationary Walras Equilibria with the results of Arrow, Block and Hurwicz and of Veendorp is to analyze the Jacobian matrices of the subsystems.
Let us denote the matrix corresponding with regime i by A_i. Then the matrix A_i can be worked out as follows:

$$A_i = \Pi + N_i \underline{A}_i .$$

The matrix Π can be called the "stock adjustment matrix". Its first row contains derivatives of the real savings function. Its third row contains derivatives of the inventory adjustment function. The matrix $\underline{A}_i$ can be called the "excess demand matrix". The rows of this matrix are the gradients of the excess demand functions relevant for regime i and evaluated at the Walras Equilibrium. These rows are dependent with the boundaries of the tangent cone of regime i. The matrix N_i can be called the "weight factor matrix".
If the matrix Π is absent, then the Stationary Walras Equilibrium is an asymptotically stable equilibrium of the systems $\overset{\circ}{x} = A_i x$, $i = 1,..,4$, irrespective the weight factors in the matrix N_i (under "gross substitutability").

The "linearized" differential systems in Veendorp (1975) can be represented by $\overset{\circ}{x} = \underline{A}_i x$, $i = 1,..,4$, where the matrices $\underline{A}_i$ are "excess demand matrices". Veendorp's systems are particular cases of our systems and for each of the regimes the origin is an asymptotically stable equilibrium of the corresponding subsystem.
In Arrow, Block and Hurwicz (1959) there is only one regime. The differential system on this regime can be expressed in terms of an excess demand matrix. Under "gross substitutability", this matrix can be multiplied by a diagonal weight factor matrix without affecting the stability of the equilibrium.

The conclusions with respect to stability depend on many factors. For stronger results, however, we need stronger assumptions and our assumptions are strong already. Especially Assumption As 8 is very important for the stability results. We have to admit that this assumption is rather arbitrary and restrictive. Assumptions As 13 and As 14 are important for the stability of Inflation and Keynesian equilibria. For Stationary Walras Equilibria the signs of the derivatives of excess demand functions are implied by the foregoing assumptions. The signs that follow in this way are compatible with Assumptions As 13 and As 14. Assumption As 9, which implies the unicity of an NWE-state for given parameters is also relevant for the stability results.

6.2.2. The weight factors

The weight factors k^{rC} etc., of the excess demand functions can be interpreted as the propensity to change the price of a commodity for which a sector is rationed. For instance, if the consumption sector is rationed on the goods market and is is prepared to pay a much higher price, then the value of k^{rC} is large.
Arrow, Block and Hurwicz (1959) assert that under gross substitutability the weight factors, that they call "speeds of adjustment", are immaterial for the stability of a Walras Equilibrium in the tâtonnement process. They choose the units of measurement in such a way that the values of the weight factors are unity.
We consider the value of a weight factor to be the relative value with regard to the weight factors of the stock adjustments (see Subsection 4.2.1). A proportional change of both weight factors and stock adjustment factors does not influence stability. Hence, a change in the period length does not affect stability.

In our models the weight factors of the excess demand functions are really important. It has been shown that due to stock adjustments they play a role in the location of Inflation and Keynesian equilibria of systems (4.20) and (4.30) and in the stability properties of equilibria of these systems. Furthermore, values of the weight factors are important for the existence of solutions of systems (4.20) and (4.30). Not only the size but also the mutual proportions may be important. It has been shown that it is favourable for stability if especially the weight factors are large in the cases the producers are rationed. Following Theorem 5.7 higher levels of the weight factors make asymptotic stability of a Walras Equilibrium of system (4.30) ("Stationary Walras Equilibrium") more likely. The same conclusion holds for a Stationary Walras Equilibrium of system (4.20). It is obvious that an increase of the weight factors weakens the relative importance of the stock adjustment matrix Π in the preceding subsection. Hence, such an increase enlarges the resemblance between the systems (4.30) and (4.20) on the one hand and the system of Veendorp on the other.

6.2.3. Consequences of the addition of an inventory

From a comparison of Sections 5.2, 5.3 with Sections 5.4, 5.5 the consequences of the addition of a variable inventory of goods in the production sector to the Barro and Grossman/Malinvaud model appear. For Inflation equilibria this variable does not play an important role since in an Inflation NWE-state the production sector is unconstrained on the goods market. In a Keynesian NWE-state, on the other hand, inventory increases may appear. The variable inventory may be favourable or unfavourable for stability of a Keynesian equilibrium.

6.2.4. Specifications of excess demand functions

The price adjustments can be based on neoclassical and on monopolistic excess demand functions specifications (see Subsection 1.5.2). We have only investigated the former, although the latter are very worthwhile studying. The neoclassical price adjustments presume competitive behaviour of a great number of agents. Hence the consumption and production sector in our models are built up of a large group of individual agents. If the aggregate groups acted as units, then a monopolistic specification would be a better choice. The actual functioning of market mechanisms in practice will be somewhere between neoclassical and neokeynesian, depending on the sort of commodity.

The excess demand functions can be either continuous or discontinuous. The continuous specifications are not very attractive for two reasons: they are unrealistic and unfavourable for stability of a Stationary Walras Equilibrium. Continuous specifications are unrealistic since a rationing of the production sector on both markets is not or hardly expressed (see Section 4.6). Assumption As 13 does not hold for these specifications. The set in which the real wage rate is nondecreasing degenerates to (a neighbourhood of) the set in which the production sector is constrained. A Stationary Walras Equilibrium is unstable in most of these cases.

Discontinuous price adjustment functions, on the other hand, lead to existence problems with respect to solutions of systems (4.20) and (4.30). In Sections 5.2 and 5.4 sufficient conditions are given to warrant the existence. These conditions do not seem to be very restrictive. It is shown by Laroque (1981b), that existence of solutions is not a problem in the model of Veendorp (1975). Nevertheless, in our models cases can be constructed in which the given sufficient conditions are violated.

6.3. *Epilogue*

Some simplifications in this thesis need to be mentioned.

The specifications of the utility function and valuation function of stock presuppose that expectations concerning prices and constraints are implicit. In this respect Assumption As 10, the stationarity assumption, is hardly satisfactory.

A complete long term analysis has to include investments, capital accumulation and a thorough treatment of money flows. The incorporation of these topics could be the subject of further research.

LIST OF SYMBOLS

SUBJECT INDEX

LIST OF ASSUMPTIONS

As 1: The consumption set Δ is given by $\Delta = \{(\ell,r,z) \in \mathbb{R}_+^3 \mid \ell \le \ell_{max}\}$.

As 2: The utility function of the consumption sector $U: \Delta \to \mathbb{R}_+$ satisfies

1) $U \mid \text{int}\,\Delta \in C^2(\text{int}\,\Delta \to \mathbb{R}_+)$ and $U \in C(\Delta \to \mathbb{R}_+)$,

2) U has a negative definite bordered Hessian for all $(\ell,r,z) \in \text{int}\,\Delta$,

3) U is monotonously increasing in r and z and decreasing in ℓ.

As 3: The production function of the production sector $F: \mathbb{R}_+ \to \mathbb{R}$ satisfies

1) $F \in C(\mathbb{R}_+ \to \mathbb{R})$, $F \mid \mathbb{R}_{++} \in C^2(\mathbb{R}_{++})$,

2) $F(0) \le 0$,

3) F is strictly concave,

4) F is increasing,

5) $\lim_{\ell\to\infty} F(\ell) = \infty$,

6) $\lim_{\ell\to\infty} F_\ell(\ell) = 0$.

As 4: The valuation function of stock of the production sector $Q: \mathbb{R}_+ \to \mathbb{R}_+$ has the following properties:

1) $Q \in C(\mathbb{R}_+ \to \mathbb{R}_+)$, $Q \mid \mathbb{R}_{++} \in C^2(\mathbb{R}_{++} \to \mathbb{R}_+)$,

2) $Q(0) = 0$,

3) Q is strictly concave,

4) Q is increasing.

5) $\lim_{q\downarrow 0} Q_q(q) > 1$.

As 5: The objective function of the production sector $V: \mathbb{R}_+^3 \times \mathbb{R}_{++} \to \mathbb{R}$ satisfies the equality $V(\ell,r,q;w) = -w\ell + r + Q(q)$, for all $(\ell,r,q;w) \in \mathbb{R}_+^3 \times \mathbb{R}_{++}$.

As 6: The production correspondence $D^P: \mathbb{R}_{++}^3 \rightrightarrows \mathbb{R}_+^2$ satisfies
$D^P(x) = \{(\ell,r) \in \mathbb{R}_+^2 \mid F(\ell) \geq 0,\ y + F(\ell) - r \geq 0\}$.

As 7: For every $x \in X^C$ and $\bar{r} \in (0, r^{C*}(x)]$: $\tilde{U}_{\ell r}[L^C(\bar{r};x),\bar{r};x] > 0$.
For every $x \in X^C$ and $\bar{\ell} \in (0,\ell^{C*}(x)]$: $U_{r\ell}[\bar{\ell},R^C(\bar{\ell};x);x] > 0$.

As 8: For every $x \in X^C$: $\ell_m^{C*} < 0$, $\ell_w^{C*} > 0$, $r_m^{C*} > 0$, $r_w^{C*} > 0$.
For every $(r;x)$ with $x \in X^C$ and $r \in (0,r^{C*}(x)$: $L_m^C < 0$, $L_w^C > 0$.
For every $(\ell;x)$ with $x \in X^C$ and $\ell \in (0,\ell^{C*}(x)]$: $R_m^C > 0$, $R_w^C > 0$.

As 9: For all $x \in X$ and $\bar{\ell} \in (0,\ell^{P*}(x)]$: $-\tilde{U}_{r\ell}/\tilde{U}_{rr} < F_\ell(\bar{\ell})$, where the derivatives of $\tilde{U}$ are evaluated at $(\bar{\ell},R^C(\bar{\ell};x);x)$. For all $x \in X$ and $\bar{r} \in (0,r^{P*}(x)]$: $\tilde{U}_{\ell r}/\tilde{U}_{\ell\ell} > \tilde{V}_{\ell r}/\tilde{V}_{\ell\ell}$, where the derivatives of $\tilde{U}$ are evaluated at $(L^C(\bar{r};x),\bar{r};x)$ and those of $\tilde{V}$ at $(L^P(\bar{r};x),\bar{r};x)$.

As 10: The utility function U, the production function F and the valuation function of stock Q are constant over time.

As 11: $k_m = k_y = 1$.

As 12: $E^{rCC} \in C'(X \cap \mathrm{cl}\ C)$, $E^{rCI} \in C'(X \cap \mathrm{cl}\ I)$,
$E^{\ell CC} \in C'(X \cap \mathrm{cl}\ C)$, $E^{\ell CK} \in C'(X \cap \mathrm{cl}\ K)$,
$E^{\ell PI} \in C'(X \cap \mathrm{cl}\ I)$, $E^{\ell PU} \in C'(X \cap \mathrm{cl}\ U)$,
$E^{rPK} \in C'(X \cap \mathrm{cl}\ K)$, $E^{rPU} \in C'(X \cap \mathrm{cl}\ U)$.

As 13: In the interiors of the regimes the signs of the derivatives of the excess demand functions are given by Table 5.1 (p. 110).

As 14: Idem by Table 5.2 (p. 136).

REFERENCES

AOKI, M. (1976), Optimal control and system theory in dynamic economic analysis, Chapter 7, North-Holland Publ. Company: American Elsevier.

ARROW, K.J., H.D. BLOCK and L. HURWICZ (1959), On the stability of the competitive equilibrium II, Econometrica 27, No. 1.

ARROW, K.J. and G. DEBREU (1954), Existence of an equilibrium for a competitive economy, Econometrica 22, No. 4.

ARROW, K.J. and A.C. ENTHOVEN (1961), Quasi-concave programming, Econometrica 29, No. 5.

ARROW, K.J. and F.H. HAHN (1971), General competitive analysis, Holden Day, San Francisco.

BARRO, R.J. and H.I. GROSSMAN (1971), A general disequilibrium model of income and employment, American Economic Review 61, p. 82-93.

BARRO, R.J. and H.I. GROSSMAN (1976), Money, employment and inflation, Cambridge University Press, Cambridge.

BELLMAN, R. (1953), Stability theory of differential equations, McGraw-Hill.

BENASSY, J.-P. (1975), Neo-Keynesian disequilibrium theory in a monetary economy, Review of Economic Studies 42, p. 503-523.

BENASSY, J.-P. (1976), The disequilibrium approach to monopolistic price setting and general monopolistic equilibrium, Review of Economic Studies 43, p. 69-81.

BÖHM, V. (1978), Disequilibrium dynamics in a simple macroeconomic model, Journal of Economic Theory 17, p. 179-199.

BÖHM, V. (1980), Preise. Löhne und Beschäftigung, Tübingen.

BRUIJN, N.G. de (1961), Methods of asymptotic analysis, North-Holland Publishing Company.

CARATHEODORY, C. (1948), Vorlesungen über reelle Funktionen, Leipzig 1927, reprinted: New York 1948.

CLOWER, R.W. (1965), The Keynesian counterrevolution: A theoretical appraisal, in F.H. HAHN and F.P.R. BRECHLING (eds.): The theory of interest rates, Macmillan.

CODDINGTON, E.A. and N. LEVINSON (1955), Theory of ordinary differential equations, McGraw-Hill Book Company, Inc.

DEBREU, G. (1959), Theory of value, Wiley, New York.

DEHEZ, P. and J. JASKOLD GABSZEWICZ (1977), On the convergence of sequences of disequilibria, CORE Discussion Paper, Nr. 7701.

DRAZEN, A. (1980), Recent developments in macroeconomic disequilibrium theory, Econometrica 48, No. 2, p. 283-306.

DRÈZE, J.H. (1975), Existence of an exchange equilibrium under price rigidities, International Economic Review 16, No. 2, p. 301-320.

ECKALBAR, J.C. (1980), The stability of non-Walrasian processes: Two examples, Econometrica 48, No. 2, p. 371-386.

FISHER, F.M. (1978), Quantity constraints, spillovers and the Hahn process, Review of Economic Studies 45, p. 21-31.

GANTMACHER, F.R. (1959), The theory of matrices, Vol. II, New York, Chelsea Publ. Comp. (Transl. from Russian).

GEPTS, S.J. (1977), An aggregate model of rationing, CORE Discussion Paper, Nr. 7704.

GRANDMONT, J.-M. (1977a), Temporary general equilibrium theory, Econometrica 45, No. 3, p. 535-572.

GRANDMONT, J.-M. (1977b), The logic of the fix-price method, Scandinavian Journal of Economics, p. 169-186.

GRANDMONT, J.-M. and G. LAROQUE (1976), On temporary Keynesian equilibria, Review of Economic Studies 43, p. 53-67.

HAHN, F.H. (1962), On the stability of a pure exchange economy, International Economic Review 3.

HAHN, F.H. (1978), On non-Walrasian equilibria, Review of Economic Studies 45, p. 1-17.

HAHN, F.H. and T. NEGISHI (1962), A theorem of non-tâtonnement stability, Econometrica 30, No. 4.

HAUTUS, M.L.J. (1970), Optimal control of differential systems with discontinuous right-hand side, Ph.D. Thesis, Technological University Eindhoven.

HENRY, C. (1972), Differential equations with discontinuous right-hand side for planning procedure, Journal of Economic Theory 4, p. 545-551.

HICKS, J.R. (1946), Value and capital, 2nd ed., Clarendon Press, Oxford.

HILDENBRAND, K. and W. HILDENBRAND (1978), On Keynesian equilibria with unemployment and quantity rationing, Journal of Economic Theory 18, p. 255-277.

HILLE, E. (1969), Lectures on ordinary differential equations, Addison-Wesley Publ. Comp.

HONKAPOHJA, S. (1979), On the dynamics of disequilibria in a macro model with flexible wages and prices, in: M. AOKI and A. MARZOLLO, eds.: New trends in dynamic system theory and economics (Part III, Disequilibrium analysis), Academic Press, New York, San Francisco, London.

HONKAPOHJA, S. and T. ITO (1982), Stability with regime switching, Journal of Economic Theory, forthcoming.

HUREWICZ, W. (1958), Lectures on ordinary differential equations, M.I.T. Press, Cambridge, Massachusetts.

ITO, T. (1980), Disequilibrium growth theory, Journal of Economic Theory 23. no. 3, p. 380-409.

KEYNES, J.M. (1936), The general theory of money, interest and employment, Harcourt Brace, New York.

LAROQUE, G. (1978). The fixed price equilibria: some results in local comparative statics, Econometrica 46, No. 5, p. 1127-1154.

LAROQUE, G. (1981a), On the local uniqueness of the fixed price equilibria, Review of Economic Studies 48. p. 113-129.

LAROQUE, G. (1981b), A comment on "Stable spillovers among substitutes" Review of Economic Studies 48, n0. 2.

LAROQUE, G. and H. POLEMARCHAKIS (1978), On the structure of the set of fixed price equilibria, Journal of Mathematical Economics 5, p. 53-69.

LA SALLE, J. and S. LEFSCHETZ (1961), Stability by Liapunov's direct method, Academic Press.

LEYONHUFVUD, A. (1968), On Keynesian economics and the economics of Keynes, Oxford University Press.

MALINVAUD, E. (1977), The theory of unemployment reconsidered, Basil-Blackwell, Oxford.

MALINVAUD, E. (1980), Profitability and unemployment, Cambridge University Press.

McKENZIE, L.W. (1954), On equilibrium in Graham's model of world trade and other competitive systems, Econometrica 22.

MOISSEEV, N.D. (1936), Über den unwesentlichen Charakter einer der Beschränkungen, welche den topografischen Systemen in der Liapounoffschen Stabilitätstheorie auferlegt werden, C.R. (Doklady) Acad. Sci. URSS 1936 I, p. 165-166.

MUELLBAUER, J. and R. PORTES (1978), Macroeconomic models with quantity rationing, The Economic Journal 88, p. 788-821.

NIKAIDO, H. (1968), Convex structures and economic theory, New York, Academic Press.

PATINKIN, D. (1956), Money, interest and prices, New York, Harper and Row.

PICARD, P. (1979), Dynamics of temporary equilibria in a macroeconomic model, Université Paris I.

RUDIN, W. (1976), Principles of mathematical analysis, third edition, McGraw-Hill-Kogakusha.

RUYS, P.H.M. (1981), Disequilibrium characterized by implicit prices in terms of effort, in: J. PLASMANS, ed. (1981): Econometric Modelling in Theory and Practice, M. Nijhoff.

SCHITTKO, U.K. (1981), Zur mikroökonomischen Fundierung der makroökonomischen Theorie. Ein temporäres Aussenhandelsgleichgewichtmodell mit Mengenrationierung, Jahrbuch für Sozialwissenschaft 32, no. 3.

SCHITTKO, U.K. and B. ECKWERT (1981), The role of uncertainty in a simple temporary equilibrium model of international trade with quantity rationing under fixed and flexible exchange rates, Institut für Statistik und Mathematische Wirtschaftstheorie, Universität Augsburg, Heft 51/1981.

SVENSSON, L. (1977), Effective demand and stochastic rationing, Seminar Paper, no. 76, Institute for international economic studies, University of Stockholm.

TAKAYAMA, A. (1974), Mathematical economics, Dryden Press, Hinsdale, Illinois.

UZAWA, H. (1962), On the stability of Edgeworth's barter process, International Economic Review 3.

VARIAN, H.R. (1977), Non-Walrasian equilibria, Econometrica 45, No. 3, p. 573-590.

VEENDORP, E. (1975), Stable spillovers among substitutes, Review of Economic Studies 42, No. 3.

WEDDEPOHL, H.N. (1982), Equilibria with rationing in an economy with increasing returns, Journal of Economic Theory 26, no. 1.

WILSON, H.K. (1971), Ordinary differential equations, Addison-Wesley Publishing Company.

Vol. 101: W. M. Wonham, Linear Multivariable Control. A Geometric Approach. X, 344 pages. 1974.

Vol. 102: Analyse Convexe et Ses Applications. Comptes Rendus, Janvier 1974. Edited by J.-P. Aubin. IV, 244 pages. 1974.

Vol. 103: D. E. Boyce, A. Farhi, R. Weischedel, Optimal Subset Selection. Multiple Regression, Interdependence and Optimal Network Algorithms. XIII, 187 pages. 1974.

Vol. 104: S. Fujino, A Neo-Keynesian Theory of Inflation and Economic Growth. V, 96 pages. 1974.

Vol. 105: Optimal Control Theory and its Applications. Part I. Proceedings 1973. Edited by B. J. Kirby. VI, 425 pages. 1974.

Vol. 106: Optimal Control Theory and its Applications. Part II. Proceedings 1973. Edited by B. J. Kirby. VI, 403 pages. 1974.

Vol. 107: Control Theory, Numerical Methods and Computer Systems Modeling. International Symposium, Rocquencourt, June 17–21, 1974. Edited by A. Bensoussan and J. L. Lions. VIII, 757 pages. 1975.

Vol. 108: F. Bauer et al., Supercritical Wing Sections II. A Handbook. V, 296 pages. 1975.

Vol. 109: R. von Randow, Introduction to the Theory of Matroids. IX, 102 pages. 1975.

Vol. 110: C. Striebel, Optimal Control of Discrete Time Stochastic Systems. III. 208 pages. 1975.

Vol. 111: Variable Structure Systems with Application to Economics and Biology. Proceedings 1974. Edited by A. Ruberti and R. R. Mohler. VI, 321 pages. 1975.

Vol. 112: J. Wilhelm, Objectives and Multi-Objective Decision Making Under Uncertainty. IV, 111 pages. 1975.

Vol. 113: G. A. Aschinger, Stabilitätsaussagen über Klassen von Matrizen mit verschwindenden Zeilensummen. V, 102 Seiten. 1975.

Vol. 114: G. Uebe, Produktionstheorie. XVII, 301 Seiten. 1976.

Vol. 115: Anderson et al., Foundations of System Theory: Finitary and Infinitary Conditions. VII, 93 pages. 1976

Vol. 116: K. Miyazawa, Input-Output Analysis and the Structure of Income Distribution. IX, 135 pages. 1976.

Vol. 117: Optimization and Operations Research. Proceedings 1975. Edited by W. Oettli and K. Ritter. IV, 316 pages. 1976.

Vol. 118: Traffic Equilibrium Methods, Proceedings 1974. Edited by M. A. Florian. XXIII, 432 pages. 1976.

Vol. 119: Inflation in Small Countries. Proceedings 1974. Edited by H. Frisch. VI, 356 pages. 1976.

Vol. 120: G. Hasenkamp, Specification and Estimation of Multiple-Output Production Functions. VII, 151 pages. 1976.

Vol. 121: J. W. Cohen, On Regenerative Processes in Queueing Theory. IX, 93 pages. 1976.

Vol. 122: M. S. Bazaraa, and C. M. Shetty,Foundations of Optimization VI. 193 pages. 1976

Vol. 123: Multiple Criteria Decision Making. Kyoto 1975. Edited by M. Zeleny. XXVII, 345 pages. 1976.

Vol. 124: M. J. Todd. The Computation of Fixed Points and Applications. VII, 129 pages. 1976.

Vol. 125: Karl C. Mosler. Optimale Transportnetze. Zur Bestimmung ihres kostengünstigsten Standorts bei gegebener Nachfrage. VI, 142 Seiten. 1976.

Vol. 126: Energy, Regional Science and Public Policy. Energy and Environment I. Proceedings 1975. Edited by M. Chatterji and P. Van Rompuy. VIII, 316 pages. 1976.

Vol. 127: Environment, Regional Science and Interregional Modeling. Energy and Environment II. Proceedings 1975. Edited by M. Chatterji and P. Van Rompuy. IX, 211 pages. 1976.

Vol. 128: Integer Programming and Related Areas. A Classified Bibliography. Edited by C. Kastning. XII, 495 pages. 1976.

Vol. 129: H.-J. Lüthi, Komplementaritäts- und Fixpunktalgorithmen in der mathematischen Programmierung. Spieltheorie und Ökonomie. VII, 145 Seiten. 1976.

Vol. 130: Multiple Criteria Decision Making, Jouy-en-Josas, France. Proceedings 1975. Edited by H. Thiriez and S. Zionts. VI, 409 pages. 1976.

Vol. 131: Mathematical Systems Theory. Proceedings 1975. Edited by G. Marchesini and S. K. Mitter. X, 408 pages. 1976.

Vol. 132: U. H. Funke, Mathematical Models in Marketing. A Collection of Abstracts. XX, 514 pages. 1976.

Vol. 133: Warsaw Fall Seminars in Mathematical Economics 1975. Edited by M. W. Loś, J. Loś, and A. Wieczorek. V. 159 pages. 1976.

Vol. 134: Computing Methods in Applied Sciences and Engineering. Proceedings 1975. VIII, 390 pages. 1976.

Vol. 135: H. Haga, A Disequilibrium – Equilibrium Model with Money and Bonds. A Keynesian – Walrasian Synthesis. VI, 119 pages. 1976.

Vol. 136: E. Kofler und G. Menges, Entscheidungen bei unvollständiger Information. XII, 357 Seiten. 1976.

Vol. 137: R. Wets, Grundlagen Konvexer Optimierung. VI, 146 Seiten. 1976.

Vol. 138: K. Okuguchi, Expectations and Stability in Oligopoly Models. VI, 103 pages. 1976.

Vol. 139: Production Theory and Its Applications. Proceedings. Edited by H. Albach and G. Bergendahl. VIII, 193 pages. 1977.

Vol. 140: W. Eichhorn and J. Voeller, Theory of the Price Index. Fisher's Test Approach and Generalizations. VII, 95 pages. 1976.

Vol. 141: Mathematical Economics and Game Theory. Essays in Honor of Oskar Morgenstern. Edited by R. Henn and O. Moeschlin. XIV, 703 pages. 1977.

Vol. 142: J. S. Lane, On Optimal Population Paths. V, 123 pages. 1977.

Vol. 143: B. Näslund, An Analysis of Economic Size Distributions. XV, 100 pages. 1977.

Vol. 144: Convex Analysis and Its Applications. Proceedings 1976. Edited by A. Auslender. VI, 219 pages. 1977.

Vol. 145: J. Rosenmüller, Extreme Games and Their Solutions. IV, 126 pages. 1977.

Vol. 146: In Search of Economic Indicators. Edited by W. H. Strigel. XVI, 198 pages. 1977.

Vol. 147: Resource Allocation and Division of Space. Proceedings. Edited by T. Fujii and R. Sato. VIII, 184 pages. 1977.

Vol. 148: C. E. Mandl, Simulationstechnik und Simulationsmodelle in den Sozial- und Wirtschaftswissenschaften. IX, 173 Seiten. 1977.

Vol. 149: Stationäre und schrumpfende Bevölkerungen: Demographisches Null- und Negativwachstum in Österreich. Herausgegeben von G. Feichtinger. VI, 262 Seiten. 1977.

Vol. 150: Bauer et al., Supercritical Wing Sections III. VI, 179 pages. 1977.

Vol. 151: C. A. Schneeweiß, Inventory-Production Theory. VI, 116 pages. 1977.

Vol. 152: Kirsch et al., Notwendige Optimalitätsbedingungen und ihre Anwendung. VI, 157 Seiten. 1978.

Vol. 153: Kombinatorische Entscheidungsprobleme: Methoden und Anwendungen. Herausgegeben von T. M. Liebling und M. Rössler. VIII, 206 Seiten. 1978.

Vol. 154: Problems and Instruments of Business Cycle Analysis. Proceedings 1977. Edited by W. H. Strigel. VI, 442 pages. 1978.

Vol. 155: Multiple Criteria Problem Solving. Proceedings 1977. Edited by S. Zionts. VIII, 567 pages. 1978.

Vol. 156: B. Näslund and B. Sellstedt, Neo-Ricardian Theory. With Applications to Some Current Economic Problems. VI, 165 pages. 1978.

Vol. 157: Optimization and Operations Research. Proceedings 1977. Edited by R. Henn, B. Korte, and W. Oettli. VI, 270 pages. 1978.

Vol. 158: L. J. Cherene, Set Valued Dynamical Systems and Economic Flow. VIII, 83 pages. 1978.

Vol. 159: Some Aspects of the Foundations of General Equilibrium Theory: The Posthumous Papers of Peter J. Kalman. Edited by J. Green. VI, 167 pages. 1978.

Vol. 160: Integer Programming and Related Areas. A Classified Bibliography. Edited by D. Hausmann. XIV, 314 pages. 1978.

Vol. 161: M. J. Beckmann, Rank in Organizations. VIII, 164 pages. 1978.

Vol. 162: Recent Developments in Variable Structure Systems, Economics and Biology. Proceedings 1977. Edited by R. R. Mohler and A. Ruberti. VI, 326 pages. 1978.

Vol. 163: G. Fandel, Optimale Entscheidungen in Organisationen. VI, 143 Seiten. 1979.

Vol. 164: C. L. Hwang and A. S. M. Masud, Multiple Objective Decision Making – Methods and Applications. A State-of-the-Art Survey. XII, 351 pages. 1979.

Vol. 165: A. Maravall, Identification in Dynamic Shock-Error Models. VIII, 158 pages. 1979.

Vol. 166: R. Cuninghame-Green, Minimax Algebra. XI, 258 pages. 1979.

Vol. 167: M. Faber, Introduction to Modern Austrian Capital Theory. X, 196 pages. 1979.

Vol. 168: Convex Analysis and Mathematical Economics. Proceedings 1978. Edited by J. Kriens. V, 136 pages. 1979.

Vol. 169: A. Rapoport et al., Coalition Formation by Sophisticated Players. VII, 170 pages. 1979.

Vol. 170: A. E. Roth, Axiomatic Models of Bargaining. V, 121 pages. 1979.

Vol. 171: G. F. Newell, Approximate Behavior of Tandem Queues. XI, 410 pages. 1979.

Vol. 172: K. Neumann and U. Steinhardt, GERT Networks and the Time-Oriented Evaluation of Projects. 268 pages. 1979.

Vol. 173: S. Erlander, Optimal Spatial Interaction and the Gravity Model. VII, 107 pages. 1980.

Vol. 174: Extremal Methods and Systems Analysis. Edited by A. V. Fiacco and K. O. Kortanek. XI, 545 pages. 1980.

Vol. 175: S. K. Srinivasan and R. Subramanian, Probabilistic Analysis of Redundant Systems. VII, 356 pages. 1980.

Vol. 176: R. Färe, Laws of Diminishing Returns. VIII, 97 pages. 1980.

Vol. 177: Multiple Criteria Decision Making-Theory and Application. Proceedings, 1979. Edited by G. Fandel and T. Gal. XVI, 570 pages. 1980.

Vol. 178: M. N. Bhattacharyya, Comparison of Box-Jenkins and Bonn Monetary Model Prediction Performance. VII, 146 pages. 1980.

Vol. 179: Recent Results in Stochastic Programming. Proceedings, 1979. Edited by P. Kall and A. Prékopa. IX, 237 pages. 1980.

Vol. 180: J. F. Brotchie, J. W. Dickey and R. Sharpe, TOPAZ – General Planning Technique and its Applications at the Regional, Urban, and Facility Planning Levels. VII, 356 pages. 1980.

Vol. 181: H. D. Sherali and C. M. Shetty, Optimization with Disjunctive Constraints. VIII, 156 pages. 1980.

Vol. 182: J. Wolters, Stochastic Dynamic Properties of Linear Econometric Models. VIII, 154 pages. 1980.

Vol. 183: K. Schittkowski, Nonlinear Programming Codes. VIII, 242 pages. 1980.

Vol. 184: R. E. Burkard and U. Derigs, Assignment and Matching Problems: Solution Methods with FORTRAN-Programs. VIII, 148 pages. 1980.

Vol. 185: C. C. von Weizsäcker, Barriers to Entry. VI, 220 pages. 1980.

Vol. 186: Ch.-L. Hwang and K. Yoon, Multiple Attribute Decision Making – Methods and Applications. A State-of-the-Art-Survey. XI, 259 pages. 1981.

Vol. 187: W. Hock, K. Schittkowski, Test Examples for Nonlinear Programming Codes. V. 178 pages. 1981.

Vol. 188: D. Bös, Economic Theory of Public Enterprise. VII, 142 pages. 1981.

Vol. 189: A. P. Lüthi, Messung wirtschaftlicher Ungleichheit. IX, 287 pages. 1981.

Vol. 190: J. N. Morse, Organizations: Multiple Agents with Multiple Criteria. Proceedings, 1980. VI, 509 pages. 1981.

Vol. 191: H. R. Sneessens, Theory and Estimation of Macroeconomic Rationing Models. VII, 138 pages. 1981.

Vol. 192: H. J. Bierens: Robust Methods and Asymptotic Theory in Nonlinear Econometrics. IX, 198 pages. 1981.

Vol. 193: J. K. Sengupta, Optimal Decisions under Uncertainty. VII, 156 pages. 1981.

Vol. 194: R. W. Shephard, Cost and Production Functions. XI, 104 pages. 1981.

Vol. 195: H. W. Ursprung, Die elementare Katastrophentheorie. Eine Darstellung aus der Sicht der Ökonomie. VII, 332 pages. 1982.

Vol. 196: M. Nermuth, Information Structures in Economics. VIII, 236 pages. 1982.

Vol. 197: Integer Programming and Related Areas. A Classified Bibliography. 1978 – 1981. Edited by R. von Randow. XIV, 338 pages. 1982.

Vol. 198: P. Zweifel, Ein ökonomisches Modell des Arztverhaltens. XIX, 392 Seiten. 1982.

Vol. 199: Evaluating Mathematical Programming Techniques. Proceedings, 1981. Edited by J.M. Mulvey. XI, 379 pages. 1982.

Vol. 201: P. M. C. de Boer, Price Effects in Input-Output-Relations: A Theoretical and Empirical Study for the Netherlands 1949–1967. X, 140 pages. 1982.

Vol. 202: U. Witt, J. Perske, SMS – A Program Package for Simulation and Gaming of Stochastic Market Processes and Learning Behavior. VII, 266 pages. 1982.

Vol. 203: Compilation of Input-Output Tables. Proceedings, 1981. Edited by J. V. Skolka. VII, 307 pages. 1982.

Vol. 204: K.C. Mosler, Entscheidungsregeln bei Risiko: Multivariate stochastische Dominanz. VII, 172 Seiten. 1982.

Vol. 205: R. Ramanathan, Introduction to the Theory of Economic Growth. IX, 347 pages. 1982.

Vol. 206: M.H. Karwan, V. Lotfi, J. Telgen, and S. Zionts, Redundancy in Mathematical Programming. VII, 286 pages. 1982.

Vol. 207: Y. Fujimori, Modern Analysis of Value Theory. X, 165 pages. 1982.

Vol. 208: Econometric Decision Models. Proceedings, 1981. Edited by J. Gruber. VI, 364 pages. 1983.

Vol. 209: Essays and Surveys on Multiple Criteria Decision Making. Proceedings, 1982. Edited by P. Hansen. VII, 441 pages. 1983.

Vol. 211: P. van den Heuvel, The Stability of a Macroeconomic System with Quantity Constraints. VII, 169 pages. 1983.

B